# daddy dates

# daddy dates

FOUR DAUGHTERS, ONE CLUELESS DAD,
AND HIS QUEST TO WIN THEIR HEARTS

Greg Wright

THOMAS NELSON
*Since 1798*

NASHVILLE   DALLAS   MEXICO CITY   RIO DE JANEIRO

Published in Nashville, Tennessee, by Thomas Nelson. Thomas Nelson is a registered trademark of Thomas Nelson, Inc.

Represented by David Hale Smith, DHS Literary, Inc.

Thomas Nelson, Inc., titles may be purchased in bulk for educational, business, fund-raising, or sales promotional use. For information, please e-mail SpecialMarkets@ThomasNelson.com.

Library of Congress Cataloging-in-Publication Data

Wright, Greg, 1970–
 Daddy dates : four daughters, one clueless dad, and his quest to win their hearts / Greg Wright.
    p. cm.
 Includes bibliographical references and index.
 ISBN 978-1-59555-320-1 (alk. paper)
  1. Fathers and daughters. 2. Fatherhood. 3. Wright, Greg, 1970– I. Title.
 HQ755.85.W725 2011
 306.874'2—dc22

2010045900

Printed in the United States of America
11 12 13 14 15 QGF 6 5 4 3 2 1

# Contents

*Prologue* . . . . . . . . . . . . . . . . . . . . . . . . . . . . . . . . vii

1 The Tree and Me . . . . . . . . . . . . . . . . . . . . . . 1
2 What Do I Know? . . . . . . . . . . . . . . . . . . . . 9
3 The Pursuit of Happiness . . . . . . . . . . . . . 15
4 My Date with Destiny . . . . . . . . . . . . . . . . . 21
5 The Wright Way of Thinking . . . . . . . . . . 31
6 A Walk in the Park . . . . . . . . . . . . . . . . . . . 37
7 Getting It . . . . . . . . . . . . . . . . . . . . . . . . . . 43
8 Daughter Decoding . . . . . . . . . . . . . . . . . . 51
9 Good to Go . . . . . . . . . . . . . . . . . . . . . . . . . 61
10 How to Talk to a Girl . . . . . . . . . . . . . . . . 69
11 Totin' the Load . . . . . . . . . . . . . . . . . . . . . 79
12 Friendship Rocks . . . . . . . . . . . . . . . . . . . 87
13 The River and the Whirlpool . . . . . . . . . 95
14 Bumpy Roads . . . . . . . . . . . . . . . . . . . . . . 103
15 When Daddy Doesn't Live There . . . . . . 113
16 Mommy Dates . . . . . . . . . . . . . . . . . . . . . 121
17 The Dao of Dating . . . . . . . . . . . . . . . . . . 129
18 Whatever Works . . . . . . . . . . . . . . . . . . . . 139
19 Princess Play-Doh . . . . . . . . . . . . . . . . . . 145
20 Tweening . . . . . . . . . . . . . . . . . . . . . . . . . . 151

contents

21  Lucky Number 13 . . . . . . . . . . . . . . . . . . . .159

22  The Apples Grow the Tree . . . . . . . . . . . .169

23  Almost a Woman . . . . . . . . . . . . . . . . . . . .175

24  College Girl . . . . . . . . . . . . . . . . . . . . . . . .185

25  Sliding into Love. . . . . . . . . . . . . . . . . . . .193


*Afterword*. . . . . . . . . . . . . . . . . . . . . . . . . . . . . .199

*Daddy Dates Pop Quiz*. . . . . . . . . . . . . . . . . . 200

*Top 15 Daddy Dates* . . . . . . . . . . . . . . . . . . . . 205

*Acknowledgments* . . . . . . . . . . . . . . . . . . . . . . 211

*About the Author* . . . . . . . . . . . . . . . . . . . . . . 214

# Prologue

et's be honest. I am completely unqualified to write
an advice book. I'm just a guy in Austin, Texas, who
woke up one day at age twenty-nine and realized *four*
girls call me Daddy, and all I could think was, how did *that*
happen?

And a nanosecond later, it hit me: *Whatever you do, don't
screw this up, dude.*

Well, I can tell you *why* it happened. When I was about
seventeen, I made a really, really, really strong wish for my
life: *Please, God, no matter what, I want to be surrounded by
beautiful women.*

Today I am. Their names are Victoria, Whitney, Hailee,
and Madison, and they are 17, 16, 15, and 13 respectively. I share

life with these beauties every day. Although the man of the house messes up on a regular basis, at least my parent passport has four stamps on it and the girls keep letting me into their amazing countries.

How that miracle happened is what this book is about. I'm hardly Mr. Perfect TV Dad. I guess part of it was getting lucky in the gene pool lottery, but there is one strategy I've stumbled upon that I've shared with other dads, and it seems to be working for all of us.

A few years ago I had a paternal *ah-ha!* moment that changed our lives forever in ways that can been seen now— we have a fantastic relationship, and they're all doing well in their teen worlds—but hopefully even more later, when *they're* parents. (If that's what any or all of them choose to do, of course.)

Right now my girls are doing a great job being good human beings. I'm just incredibly lucky that I get a front row seat. Teachers and neighbors always use words like well-mannered, appreciative, creative, and happy, and so far, nobody's got a terminal case of metal face (yet). My hope is that my girls will, at the very least, turn out to be confident and productive adults who have reasonably good taste in partners, perhaps due (in part) to the way they were raised. Of course, the jury's still out on the long-term result, but giving the world four sane, loving women is what Dad is trying his best to contribute to the planet.

Not long ago a couple of friends said, "You need to write a book!" Yeah, right. Like I'm qualified. But then I conducted a limited focus group at my house, and the girls said, "Our friends wish their fathers would do this too. Go for it, Daddy."

And whenever I mention my strategy to other fathers during one of my seminars or while watching a ballgame or at church, it's not uncommon for them to ask, "How does it work, Greg—I mean, what do I have to do in order to have the same result?" And I thought, *I don't think this is quantum physics, but if you need help with a roadmap, sure. I'm in.*

And that's when I realized that *maybe* it's my destiny to share a little idea that came to me as an inspiration one day in the woods . . . I'm pretty sure it was put in my head while He was having a gut laugh remembering my hormonal teen fantasy about how I wanted to live in the company of the lovely opposite sex.

# The Tree and Me

don't come from a family of girls. I have a couple of brothers and a sister, and then all of a sudden there's a wife and four daughters, and I'm not even thirty yet.

Heck, even the dog is female.

I never thought I was the type of guy to have kids, and honestly I probably wasn't the type of guy to get married either. My dad is a country boy at heart, and my mom had a passion for city life, so it came as no big surprise when things didn't work out.

As a young man I was very self-centered and more than a little arrogant. It was all about me, man. If they were giving out awards for being selfish, Big Tex would've had a hard time pinning a blue ribbon on my puffed up chest at the state fair, it was so big. Definitely.

But then I met my wife, fell in love, and we tied the knot on Valentine's Day 1992. I was twenty-one years old. We were only a few months into marriage when my bride gave me a Hallmark card with little booties on it. You'd think that would trigger my comprehension of the big news, but nooooo. What an idiot. When I finally realized she was pregnant, I remember feeling this tiny bit of excitement buried under a mountain of *yikes, now what*?

Then came three more precious baby girls—*bing, bang, boom.* They're about as close together as you can get without having quadruplets.

That much estrogen was too much for me to reasonably understand, and I knew that I was in way over my head. When our littlest entered kindergarten, I had a very dramatic feeling that I was in danger of becoming a complete loser in the dad-of-big-girls department.

Frankly, that thought scared me to death because I knew that when it came to parenting, I was just shooting from the hip every day, and I wanted a solution. I wanted a plan. *Now.*

So I did what any reasonable male would do: I bailed. Not on my wife and kids, but to a mountaintop in Colorado. I thought some manly alone time would help me figure out how in the world I was going to handle my responsibilities. I was petrified that I was going to mess up the most important job I'd ever have.

That's when I found "The Tree."

I plopped myself down under a big ole pine tree and decided to take a business approach to this problem of dad-being and girl-raising. I took a notepad out of my backpack and clicked the pen a few dozen times, as if revving the engines on the paternal horsepower ready to leap onto the page.

The truth was anything but. What was I going to do with these four female dependents who depend on me to be the Great Wise One? What do I know about women—of any age?

That was a nonstarter. I stuck the end of the pen in my mouth and tapped my teeth.

*Okay, relax. I can figure this out. First, I need to set some goals. Yeah, that's it. But wait, I'm missing real goals in my own life, my own career, and my own marriage. And maybe I ought to get my life together first, because that's what mature, responsible men do, right? No, forget about all of that, I just need to get more on track with my wife. Or maybe, I should probably create a solid ten-year plan for my business first so I can top off that college fund. And what about retirement, buddy, you haven't even thought about* that …

Somewhere in this vast jumble of rhetorical nonsense, I realized I just needed to *stop* and focus on my goals for being a dad. Wasn't that my excuse for being here in nature?

So I clicked the Bic to the "on" position and wrote down each child's name.

Good start.

Next I'll make a list of what I really know about them for sure.

And here's what I came up with: *not much.* It wasn't the first time I had that realization. A couple of weeks earlier, I accidentally overheard (okay, eavesdropped) the girls yakking at the table over homework and was struck dumb by my complete and profound ignorance about my own offsprings' desires and opinions.

Clearly, I didn't have a single clue—not even a clue of a clue—what my girls really thought about the world and what's important about it. I knew what my *experiences* of them were, but I couldn't say that I knew *them*. I didn't know what motivated them. I couldn't answer even the simplest question. How do they see me? How do they see their roles in life? What makes their hearts sing? Is the world good and friendly, or evil and hostile? Is their favorite color pink or purple? Crest or Colgate? Who knew?

Not Dad, that's for sure.

And then it struck me that when I met my wife, I didn't know anything about her either, but I was lovestruck and did what a guy does when he thinks she's "the one." I made it my mission to find out what she liked so I could be her hero. (Or at least have a shot at being one.) I decided to discover who she really was and what she loved and feared and wanted in life. I pursued knowing her with gusto and wound up with the woman who gave me the greatest gifts of my life.

That's the moment I became really curious about the four adorable strangers in my house. I realized I needed a better strategy to understand what makes them tick so I could have a shot at connecting with them in a profound way too.

So I decided to write a focused Purpose and Mission statement about this dad thing. Why am I here, what's the point, what do I have to contribute as a father? Well, money, love, wisdom, and that kind of thing. The other X chromosome, of course. What else?

Okay, forget *purpose*. Too murky. We'll circle back around to that later. Let's go with *mission*. Good word. A real guy word if there ever was one. I can do that. So, what is my mission for being a good dad? If I'm here for a particular reason, and none of my children were cosmic accidents, and I'm intended to be Wise Father Wright ... well, then what? What's the next step? Or is that purpose?

I know that to complete a successful mission, you can't just park yourself and accomplish it. You have to have a game plan. Everybody knows that. So I spent an exorbitant amount of time trying to construct Greg's Grand Soliloquy on my fatherly mission and purpose, or purposeful mission, or whatever. I entertained myself and wasted hours trying to come up with that nonsense, only to find out that it was total garbage—meaningless platitudes, dog doodles on the page.

My tail hurt and I was hungry, but I wasn't giving up.

Yet I had to admit I was stuck. Apparently this dad-mission thing is pretty tricky too. I just couldn't get away from thinking of being a dad as if it was like being anything else, like the head of a company or a team leader or a professional coach—because that's *easy*. I know how to do that. What's my purpose? To help other people reach career goals and achieve their ambitions. Get through to the next level. Yada yada to some, but I believed I was pretty good at it. My clients were doing well and my seminar business was too. There was *proof*.

It took me a while to realize that parenting isn't a business, though, and after I drafted pages and pages of lofty language, I finally drilled my Dad Mission Statement down to three simple words.

*Don't screw up.*

Yeah, that works.

**2**

# What Do I Know?

O f course, *don't screw* up is totally fear driven. But at least it sounded right. It was *honest.*

Okay, check. Mission statement accomplished. But how, exactly, was I going to do it? I started looking at each one of my girls, and I realized I needed to know more about what I didn't know. That required research. *Then* an action plan. And I wasn't sure how I was going to do that; I just knew it was a goal.

Now we're getting somewhere.

So like most guys, I fell back on what I already knew. I wandered in my head back to my high school days. I definitely made a ton of mistakes back then, and I'm certainly not proud of some of the more idiotic choices I made as a teenager, but there was one thing I was proud of: I knew how to date. I wasn't a good boyfriend, but I knew how to date. I knew what that looked like.

Actually, I was very creative in my teenage dating life, and even a little competitive. I thought things through, I would plan out the whole scenario, and it would usually be something pretty cool and specially designed to please a particular girl.

Sometimes the date would go awry, but most of the time it worked out and the current object of my desire would say yes when or if I asked her out again. She would also talk to me a lot during the evening, and I knew she meant it when she said, "I had a nice time," because she told her girlfriends, "Hey, that Greg is a fun date." I earned a bit of a reputation in my circle at school for this minor social skill.

I liked that.

For example, in Dallas they have Shakespeare in the Park, and while most of my buddies were dinner and movie guys (at the most), I liked the finesse of something more creative. When I announced that I was taking my dates to Shakespeare, they would look at me like a calf at a new gate. I remember thinking, *You can think* Hamlet *is uncool, but I'm the one getting the girls to say yes to going out with me.*

I learned pretty quickly that I was good at this dating thing, and I dug that.

So here I am a dad now, and why can't I apply some of that same mojo to this situation? With a completely different purpose, of course: one pure of heart, with a new trajectory.

Although I'm ignorant when it comes to many issues about women, there's one thing I do get about our interaction and the nature of our inherent roles: *I believe it's the job of every husband and father to understand that his job—perhaps his most important job—is to be the pursuer.*

Not just at the beginning, but all the way through. I am convinced that to be successful in our relationships with the fairer sex, our role in life is to pursue the understanding of the women who are important to us, until we're no longer breathing.

That's pretty much it. That's why this chapter is super short. In my opinion, any man who gets this concept also "gets" women, including his daughters, wife, sisters, mothers, and female friends. Doesn't matter their age. Girls want us to discover their specialness, praise it, and treasure it.

Gentlemen, we have lift-off.

# 3

# The Pursuit of Happiness

'm not exactly a bejeweled kind of guy. Yet I wear this woven thing around my wrist. My eldest daughter made it about a year ago, and when she gave it to me, I thought, *Oh, that's sweet, but nothing too unusual*–Tori's a thoughtful girl, and we have that kind of relationship.

But as it turns out, this wasn't any ole object d'art she created. I guess you could say it was a form of show-and-tell for high school that's still telling. It was part of an oral report assignment, which was to write an essay about the meaning of a best friend, and she said I was the only one in her life who fit all of the criteria. When she told me what it represented, I was moved to tears.

"*Really?*" Wow.

Yep, this true blue Southern boy wears a bracelet. Whenever I wonder if I'm on the right dad-track, it's right there for inspiration and encouragement. That bracelet will have to rot off of me.

The details are hazy about that conversation, but I clearly remember saying to my daughter at the time, "Gee, you have a million friends. Why did you pick me?" Tori looked at me like I was just plain silly. "Daddy, of *course* You're my best friend. I can talk to you about *anything*."

That just blew me away, and I now realize that this is a core concept for me as a father. Knowing a daughter–really knowing her–won't happen just by going to her soccer practice, no matter how many high-fives and "good jobs" you give her. Pursuing a relationship with your daughter is a conscious choice, and it takes energy and imagination, and (there's no way around this) the willingness to deal with messy emotions and questionable logic.

It doesn't mean you'll always want to do it or that it will be easy. But it *is* achievable, and you can learn how to observe the ups and downs in the relationship without getting seasick. And more than that, it's totally worth it.

Pursuing a daughter with the goal of getting to know what's in her heart and mind is how you will bond with her, build her confidence, and find happiness . . . for both of you.

My payoff is that I have the kind of relationship with my teenage daughters that other dads envy. I have a blast with my girls, and we're super close, but trust me, I'm no pushover. (Well, not always.) Do they mess up? Sure. Do I mess up? *All* the time. But I have their love and respect, and our teens are eager participants in family life. They're not perfect (and neither am I), but we're connected. Like superglue.

Now, by "pursuit" I'm not talking about chasing your little princess, spoiling her, or giving in to endless wishes and whims. I'm talking about making the effort to understand your kid, because that way, as she evolves and navigates the teen years, you will be able to follow where she's going mentally and keep her grounded so she'll be self-confident and less susceptible to losers, scammers, and avoidable disasters when she's out on her own.

She'll turn to *you* when she needs a strong shoulder until she gets married, and she'll actually want to be around the old man later on.

That's what we all want for our girls, right?

Let's get something straight, though. When you intentionally pursue how a girl thinks about things, it usually means how she *feels*. That's where it's a little different from being with a son, when you can sit there with a hot dog, watch a ballgame, yell at strangers, say little to each other, and still have a bonding experience. (Or so I'm told. What do I know about raising boys?) Girls? Nope. If Dad wants to get close and know how his daughter feels about a movie, a sport, a teacher, a trip, the big cosmic question "to diet or not to diet," or—heaven forbid—a boy, then there's only one way to accomplish that. You have to talk. And listen.

That one insight—that I wanted to pursue knowing my daughters—was the lightning bolt ah-ha moment. And then I came up with a strategy: dust off the old dating skills and put them back into action, but this time for a better purpose.

*Pursue daughter-knowing by dating them.* Yeah, that's the ticket.

**4**

# My Date
# with Destiny

Sixteen years ago, my birth-buddy assignment was to be my wife's coach, supporter, and videographer, the last of which I definitely stunk at. (I closed the camera shutter by accident and the first several minutes of the home movie about a major life event has sound but no pictures—a mistake I've never lived down.)

It was an astonishing, life-altering experience, but I didn't have an immediate connection with this newborn child in the delivery room, and I started to wonder if there was something wrong with me for not having a gushier reaction.

Then it was time for my still-slimy daughter to be taken somewhere else by the nurses. I tagged along behind the women in white—I don't know why. It was very quiet when they started cleaning up the infant and doing all those things that I'm sure they do to all babies, but when Nurse Ratched pricked little Victoria's heel and drew a blob of blood, I never wanted to punch a lady more in my life.

The moment that pin-dagger touched the tiny foot, my fist closed hard as a handball, but at the exact same moment my heart opened so wide so fast that I almost passed out from the onslaught of emotion. I suddenly had a feeling of compassion and protection so overwhelming for this brand-spanking-new little person that I literally couldn't breathe.

And that please-God-let-me-throw-myself-on-a-hand-grenade-before-harm-comes-to-my-child feeling has never let up for a second.

Fast forward a few weeks later. We're home, and I can't take my eyes off this kid. I can't even think straight. I can't find the words to describe this feeling I have for baby Victoria. I want another one as soon as possible, which is *nuts* because I didn't think I wanted the first one, and now I want *another* baby? *What's wrong with me?*

God got a good, hearty laugh when he played my heart-strings on March 29, 1993, because before that day I thought I knew all about life and love. Three more babies and years later, the hormones in my house are now thick enough to choke a mule. I'm trying to guide them safely into woman-hood by teaching all of them the right way to date and to treasure their specialness as much as I do.

On Mount Ah-ha, I realized that I didn't want my girls thinking that some ying-yang taking them to the 7-Eleven for a Slurpee makes the cut for a good date. I wanted them to expect better from life and men, by learning clues for how a sincere man behaves when he's interested in a girl as a person, and truly cares about her well-being. Who better to teach that than the guy who would give his life for their happiness? I wanted them to know the difference between genuine interest and selfish male indifference. I wanted to help them develop good dating habits and learn how to be friends with the opposite sex before making any big leap into intimacy.

So when I came home from Colorado, I sat the oldest three down as a group and told them my idea. No over-the-top speech, just something like, "I want to start going on Daddy dates with you. I'm going to call you on the phone and ask you out. You can say yes or you can say no. It's totally your choice. (But if you say no, you're grounded . . . just kidding.)

"If you say yes, then I will tell you what to expect, where we're going, and what we're doing, so you'll know what to wear. Then I'll pick you up, and you'll be ready on time. I won't sit in the car and honk. I will come to the door and you'll open it and smile when you see me, and I will smile when I see you, then we'll go and have a really nice time together. Sound good?"

I thought they might resist or think it was cheesy or roll their eyes, but they got totally excited instead. Now we have a library of vivid experiences and treasured moments, all because these girls said yes in a big way to their dad.

So that's how it started, and one of the more memorable first dates was with my second daughter, Whitney, because of how it ended.

Like I said, I've always been a pretty good date planner. Here's the big secret, which is completely logical: notice what she likes in life, and then plan the outing accordingly.

Whitney's came in a snap. I knew she loved shrimp. She thought shrimp was the coolest food on the face of the earth. It beat Snickers hands down. I mean she'd rather have shrimp than drink Yoo-hoo—and that says a lot. Running a close second is Barnes & Noble, her favorite place in the whole wide world. Whitney Wright is a *big* reader.

I decided to invite my "date" to go to a seafood restaurant and then to the bookstore.

So from my office, I called her up on the phone. I guess it probably seemed a little silly, because she knew to expect the call, but she decided to fake surprise. (To hear her tell it now is really funny.)

"Hi, Whitney. It's Daddy. I hope you're not too busy, but I'm calling to see if you'd like to go on a date with me tonight."

"Ummmm, yes, Daddy, I think I would."

"Great! I will pick you up at six o'clock, and we're going to have a really nice shrimp dinner and then go to Barnes & Noble. Now may I please speak to your mom?"

I told my wife that I'd like Whitney to dress up, and my busy wife did a great job of helping our child get ready. (Back then I always wore a suit for our dates, and the girls took a long time fixing their hair, picking out clothes, and all that. Fancy still happens sometimes, but now we're more relaxed in the apparel department.)

At 6:00 p.m. I knocked on my own front door—admittedly a little weird—and I handed flowers to my date.

"These are for you, beautiful."

"Um, do I bring them on our date, Daddy?"

"It's probably best to put them in the kitchen in a vase." And we did that.

Then I walked Whitney around to the passenger side of the car, and as I opened her door, I explained that I was doing it because I wanted to start teaching her what to expect. I told her a man who knows how to treat a woman will open her door. And that if he's not making that little extra effort, then he's thinking of someone else—like himself. If the guy opens the door, it's one way to show that he's thinking of her.

"Oh, okay, Daddy, cool."

Whitney stood there and let me open the door for her, and after making sure she was buckled in, I walked around to my side. That's when I thought, *This is the first time I've consciously opened the door for my daughter like she's a special young lady.* It was true. I wasn't thinking about work or anything else. I was totally focused on my date.

Who was nine years old.

Dinner went great. I asked her questions about her friends, and I learned more about Whitney's world in that little dinner conversation than I had being her daddy for her entire life. I mean, I couldn't get her to stop chattering, and it wasn't aimless conversation. It was meaningful. She talked about how she felt about people, about a boy who liked her but who she thought was icky. I thought it so strange that I had never heard of this guy. I knew the names of Whitney's basic circle of girlfriends, but clearly not much else.

But I got to know them all that night, as well as my daughter. I was amazed to discover how this child made decisions, which were based on criteria in her little mind about what's good and bad—things I knew nothing about a few hours before. And I was blown away by that discovery because so many of her insights were right on.

Then we left the restaurant and went to Barnes & Noble and sat in the children's section and read books side by side. When we finished, we went over to the café inside the store. Whitney had a hot chocolate and I had a cup of coffee and we talked some more, like any two people would do on a date.

Pretty soon I remembered she had a curfew and that her mom would kill me if I brought my date home late on a school night.

And as I was walking her to the car under the moonlight, I couldn't believe how much was inside that little girl and how smart she was and how much she had shared with me that evening.

We hopped in, I threw it in reverse, and as I put my hand on the back of the passenger seat to look over my shoulder, I caught a glimpse of my daughter's face.

Whitney was weeping. Living with five females I thought, *What the heck did I say now? What did I do?*

I hit the brake.

"Uh oh, what's the matter, honey?"

She looked up at me, her eyelashes wet and shiny and tears streaming down her face.

"Nothing." (Oh right, she's a girl.)

"Honey, you're *crying.* Did I say something to hurt your feelings?"

"No, Daddy, nothing's wrong. It's just that I've never felt this special before."

We both boo-hooed all the way home.

I thought about the impact of a simple evening—a

midweek one, at that—when all I did was carve out special time for this one girl and made a real effort to get to know her in a relaxed, enjoyable environment that suited her unique personality. The result was pure magic and a memory of a lifetime.

I thought, *Hey, maybe I'm not gonna screw up, after all. Maybe I can pursue getting to know my girls and win.*

And from that day on, I haven't questioned Daddy Dates for one single moment.

5

# The Wright Way
# of Thinking

'm not a shrink or a college professor or even a dad whose kids are grown up enough to prove that Daddy Dating is all it's cracked up to be. My theory about this parental strategy is just that—an idea that I am testing in real life.

There are other concepts about parenting that underpin Daddy Dating. Like trust. Each one of my girls and I have a unique, individual relationship that ebbs and flows like any other. Trust is a beautiful dance with my daughters, but it changes all the time as decisions are made, rules are enforced, kids mess up, and they move through stages of insecurity and maturity.

Sometimes I have to be the tough guy and things get a little rocky. But while it's part of my job description to be unpopular when necessary, they also know that I truly, deeply care, and the bumpy bits don't last too long because our relationship is strong.

Here's what I have come to believe about parenting. For me, there are three equations that describe the balance between rules and relationships and yield predictable results:

1. Rules – Relationship = Rebellion
2. Relationship – Rules = Destruction
3. Relationship + Rules = Connection

It's like hanging on to a bar of wet soap in a shower. If you hold the bar too loosely, it will fall; if you grip too tightly, it pops out the top.

Parenting with all rules and no relationship is a strategy based on fear, and it doesn't work. You grip so hard that you actually lose control. It results in teenage blowback and worse, tune-out of all of the positive messages you want to share. The child thinks you don't understand or respect her—or you're just plain scared of her—and she's right.

It's equally ineffective to be loosey–goosey, more of a permissive pal than a productive parent. It will tear the relationship apart and put a kid in real danger.

In my opinion, there is one simple equation that probably dominates all human relationships, and it's never proved truer than in my experience as a father.

Talk + Action + Time = Trust

Trust is a paycheck. You work hard for it so that you can leverage it. Let's say I'm talking to a daughter about a family policy, rule, or proposed activity and there's a difference of opinion. She doesn't think this or that is fair, or she just doesn't want to follow my lead. I don't shoot down her opinion willy-nilly. She gets to say what she wants, as long as there's an element of respect in the discussion. I get to say what I want, without being condescending or mulish.

There are times when there's flexibility, and then there are the moments I have to say, "Sorry, I understand your point of view, but this is what we are going to do." That would produce a rebellious response if we didn't have a connection or if we hadn't already built a trusting bond. Spending the time and effort to get to know my daughter and building a relationship with her has earned the currency to make that decision. And for her to respect it.

Well, *most* of the time, anyway.

When Dad said ixnay to MySpace, man, did *that* cause uproar and upset. But to me, it's a stumble down Bourbon Street with cyber creeps lurking around every corner and scary alley, and it's not where I want my girls to hang out.

So when I discovered that both Whitney and Hailee had secretly set up MySpace pages, I felt betrayed and hurt and I couldn't sleep a wink. It really knocked me for a loop. When the dust settled and I calmed down, I decided to listen to their points of view: "Daddy, your rules are too strict!" And we talked and talked and talked some more until we hit a real communication flow and they understood why this was an important ban. Now they all have Facebook pages but still no MySpace, and they're (sort of) cool with that.

It's not enough to say, "Trust me, I know better about this or any other topic." Daddy Dating gives me relational leverage, because I have earned the right to be heard—and in the end, trusted—by my children about something incredibly important to their safety and security.

There is no false illusion here. Each one of my girls and I have an individual relationship, and some are a little more smooth than others. They flub, I flub. Toes get stepped on, but they follow me as best they can, and they know I'll always catch them when they fall.

**6**

# A Walk in the Park

The other day, Victoria announced that she had an idea for her seventeenth birthday and she thought it sounded pretty cool.

Okay–*gulp*–I figured that a pretty pricey Daddy Date could be on one end of that spectrum, because, after all, it's an important one. (Aren't they *all* for the ladies?) Our former newborn-with-the-blob-o-blood is going off to college next year.

I didn't expect that she was thinking about going *camping*. What? *Really*? Cool. Dirt cheap, fun, and we can fish.

"Uh, Dad, can I bring some friends?" Turns out the old man is only peripherally involved, since it will be a bunch of high school girls "camping" by the lake near town. I'll be the guy in a lawn chair outside the tent with a Dr. Pepper who will try not to act embarrassed when teen shrieks escape from inside that tent.

On the flip side, Tori has mentioned that few of her friends have fathers they can really talk to, and the girls kind of like the fact that I'll be there in the morning. (Clearly they don't have a mental picture of what I look like before coffee.)

I don't know what we'll end up doing, but here's my point. First of all, trust me, there's nothing all that special about me that the other dads don't have. This dating thing is not about being clever or whipping out the plastic.

It is, however, about connecting. If you put in the time and listen to what's in your daughter's heart, it is a walk in the park—literally and figuratively. The daughter-dating thing doesn't have to be elaborate. Or expensive. Actually it can be free, and should always be free of angst and drama. (Although spending a little dough once in a while and dressing up is worth it.)

○ ○ ○ ○

One time a Daddy Date was simply a long leisurely lah-de-dah stroll, which ranks as one of the more entertaining and productive walks of my life. It was with daughter number three, Hailee, because she loves the outdoors and I wanted to have plenty of time to visit with her. That girl could crack up a statue in the courthouse square.

Hailee is Wright comic relief. She's hilarious, really the funny bone of the family, and she loves a practical joke. (One time she swiped my phone, used it to text her sister Whitney, and pretended to be me scolding her.) She's bright and insightful beyond her years, but she's also the one who has a tendency to have relationship issues. That's what we talked about that day.

I listened to the way she thinks about life and was really

impressed by how she sizes up situations and people—way above her pay grade.

I remember hearing how she viewed one particular friendship and a behavioral pattern she recognized that wasn't working for her. It was enlightening for both of us and gave me an opportunity to help her examine the pros and cons of changing tactics and to help take the sting out of a touchy situation.

Let's call this friend Gwen.

"I think Gwen was just trying to get me to do what she wanted. She tried to bully me, then she wanted me to feel sorry for her. Then she blew me off but a few days later wanted to come back and be nice again. That doesn't make me feel good. I don't think I want to be friends anymore. Is that okay, Daddy?"

That's pretty deep for a kid, and since she asked, I had a chance to make a few observations while dodging squirrels and pinecones, but I still wanted Hailee to come to her own conclusion.

"Yeah, sure, if it doesn't work for you, then you don't have to spend a lot of time with Gwen. But you don't want to turn it into a big dramatic breakup either. Just be straightforward about how her behavior makes you feel and what you are—and aren't—willing to do to stay close, and the rest is up to her. Maybe she'll want to do something different. Maybe not. Ball's in her court after that, and you have lots of other friends if she chooses to back off."

On the opposite end of "meaningful life lesson" is a date with our baby girl, Madison. Sometimes it's just about flying on the mental kiddie plane and being scrunched up in the middle seat with the coke and peanuts.

I think our first date was when she was about six, and for our inaugural outing I took her to dinner, then to the mall. That kid *loves* to shop. Now some people might think taking a child that young shopping on a date is pretty lame and materialistic, but I decided this was a specific destination that would please both of us. Or so I thought.

I took her to a children's jewelry store to let her pick out "a little something." That was Big Daddy's idea, anyway. And lo and behold, the kid wanted to buy like a hundred dollars worth of stuff. Suddenly it was more bumpy than smooth, but at the same time I got to witness who she was and what she did and didn't know about life and money at that age. Why did I expect her to have self-control, anyway? She had only graduated from *kindergarten*.

I thought, *Hey, I'm molding clay here, this is great! I can teach her to be sensible.*

Yeah, right. I stuck to my guns and only purchased the trinket, but as for a "teaching moment"? Well, maybe someday Madison Larae Wright will be a personal shopper—or, she'll *have* one.

It just won't be me.

7

# Getting It

Life isn't a cover band.

We're all originals marching to our own beat, and it doesn't really work out too well if we're tuned out to our relationships.

One time I had a coaching client, "Bud," who was a muckety muck for a major lifestyle brand. He was the kind of guy who emotionally lives in a tree. You know the type. We met in his office and I knew right away that, somewhere along the line, this guy had drunk about fifty gallons of apathy and it was slopping over into his business and personal life, which was at a dead halt.

Of course, Bud didn't know he was the donkey. It took about five minutes to learn he needed help to drop forty pounds of flab and pick up where he left off in his marriage the day after she said "I do."

I felt bad for him and really wanted to help, but our interview was the funniest thing because I couldn't get much of anything but "uh, I dunno" out of this otherwise successful executive.

The only thing he knew for sure was that he didn't like

where he was in life, and worse, didn't know how he got there.

"When was the last time you took your wife on a date?" Softball, slow and easy.

"What do you mean by 'date'?"

*Seriously?*

This guy so didn't get it. And by "it" I mean life.

I realized immediately that I had a choice here. I could get this first session over with, shake hands, and ride that pony into the sunset, or I could drop my attitude stick and pull the man out of the ditch with my free hand.

I talked to him about how men are wired to pursue, not to watch passively—unless he's in a deer blind, of course. As the weeks went by, I started giving Bud some ideas about dating Miz Bud, because he really was the most boring date in the whole world. (Or so I thought at the time. Now I know that there are a *lot* of us who are stalled out in this department.)

First I challenged him with two rules: Numero uno, *no dinner.* You would have thought I had yanked the rug out from under him. He was just stunned. Number two, *no movies.* He stared at me, bug-eyed. He'd always thought the world was a nail but by golly he had a hammer, and now I had taken his favorite tool away.

"You need to do something romantic that doesn't involve eating or staring at something other than her. And you need to have a conversation that doesn't involve money or kids."

Bud sat in that chair and looked as if I had asked him the square root of 9008. He had lost the English language.

Okay, new approach.

"I want you to go to the grocery store and I want you to buy a loaf of bread. There is an area down by the lake where there are ducks. Choose bread she likes, and if you don't know what kind of bread she likes, look in the kitchen. Or ask her, white or wheat? Then I want you to go home and get a blanket and grab your wife's favorite beverage. And don't forget Martha. She is going to feed the ducks. You are going to feed the ducks. Then you are going to sit on the blanket, and you are going to ask her three nice questions that can't be answered with yes or no and listen until she's completely done. Do you think you can do that?"

"Uh, maybe."

"Okay. Tell ya what. I'll make you some little cue cards, and you can memorize them to help with dialogue."

"That would be great."

Disconnection. It starts as a layer of skin, but if you're not careful it becomes a scab, then a callous, then pretty soon you just feel numb and dumb.

Here's the deal regarding your daughter. Daddy Dates are about breaking away from the household rut and getting real with your kid—away from school, sports, and family. There's no such thing as a total flameout. You're already in love with your date and she loves you, and no matter what you do, *it's better than not doing it at all.*

And you don't need cue cards; although not to worry, there are handy conversation tips throughout this book if you're the strong, silent type. Sleepwalkers can do this. Look,

I've had a lot of guys ask me about risks and percentage of failures and outright rejection, and nobody—not one single dad—has ever regretted actively pursuing a relationship with his daughter or couldn't figure out something to talk about. If you remember the risk of asking your wife out the first time, it's *nothing* like that. You don't have to worry about getting dumped if you look like an idiot or say something stupid. To teens, Dad always looks like an idiot and says stupid things.

The difference is, she'll like you anyway. Or at least say yes the next time you call for a date, for sure. And she will always love you even if the food stinks.

I think most men are relationship challenged. No one teaches us how to be married. (You can learn to be a doctor.) And truth be told, until a problem smacks us upside the head, we're pretty dense. I definitely fit into that category. Back when I wasn't all that connected to my kids, I sure didn't know it. I thought I was doing okay. I mean, I knew the job description for little girls and I tickled them and tucked them in and said prayers and even made up some of the bedtime stories. I didn't really worry about *then what* until I was going full throttle into teen territory completely blind and knew that nobody was going to hand out the map to this mystifying maze.

The "then" and the "what" is that sure, you can still feed the ducks with girls of any age, but *then* you have to sit on the plaid blanket and talk—if you want to get to know a female, that is. Even if your daughter is tatted up or tuned out or, heck, she's a mom herself now, it's not too late to reconnect.

It's never too late to show your love by being curious about who she is—and then listening.

If you don't do it, good luck, chief. You're about to crash on Irrelevant Road.

The first step to successful change is the awareness that even if you don't know what you don't know, you have a grasp on the most important thing. You want to bond with your daughter on a more profound level, so now your natural male ability to pursue can kick into gear. You already learned how to court a female, because at some point you sealed the deal with her mom, right? But if you think there is a "destination" in your pursuit of a relationship with a daughter, nope, no way. This is a lifetime assignment. It's never done, and that's a good thing.

I guess I'm lucky that this thought occurred to me in time and that I was given the idea I didn't know everything and that was okay, because dang it, I was capable of figuring it out. The payoff is that it will keep you feeling vital and alive for the rest of your life and someday you'll be the favorite grandpa.

I'll bet you're wondering what happened to Bud and Martha. When I first met Martha, she looked just as annoyed as Bud did with life in general. Then Bud actually did it! He got back in the game. At my last session, he wore his fat pants all cinched up from major weight loss and an amazing thing happened. He brought the trousers *and* his bride. Martha wanted to meet the man who sprinkled fairy dust on her husband, and she wanted some too. She had morphed into a lady with a twinkle in her eye, and they were cutting up with each other in my office. It was like aliens had invaded their bodies.

We were also applauding the promotion he had secretly coveted and had recently received. Bud woke up at the office too, much to the delight of staff and management, and it paid off in more ways than one.

Funny how it works that way.

# 8

# Daughter Decoding

S neaking behind the lines of girl culture took a little . . . tradecraft.

When this average Joe decided to ferret out the truth
of their hearts and minds, I felt a little James Bondish, but my
covert mission wasn't to whack bad guys or spy. (Okay, maybe
not James, but at least his good ole cousin Jimmy with a bit
of a gut who prefers blue jeans and open collars to the fancy
pants and dinner jacket.)

It was to find my kids' best God-given qualities and
nurture them. And to help them develop their own inner
compass, since Daddy's job is not to live their lives for them.

What I discovered has been worth all of the effort, and
the rest of this book is simply one father's compass, map, and
not-so-secret guidebook. It is written in Manglish, because
sometimes what you hear from the opposite sex sounds like
a foreign language.

While I stumbled my way through the first years of
Daddy Dating, I landed on a more logical place to start by
the time I got to daughter number three. A relationship
expert I admire, Dr. Gary Smalley, worked for years with

Dr. John Trent. In their book, *The Two Sides of Love*, Dr. Trent created a quiz that I have used in my Wright Track seminars to help people understand each other at work, as well as their clients, customers, and family. (You'll find a version of Dr. Trent's quiz at the back of this book, shared with his permission—"Daddy Dates Pop Quiz.") Basically, this short assessment uses four animals that make it easy and fun to help your daughter (or spouse) understand how valuable she is, and how to better get along with others.

By knowing if you're a Lion, if the boss is an Otter, or your client (or daughter) is a Golden Retriever—or some such combo—this personality snapshot really helps reduce conflict and boost productivity. I figured it couldn't hurt to give this a rip at home.

I had the girls take the same type quiz, and then combined the results with the "what she likes" lists and *voila!* I had a cheat sheet that helped me plan successful dates with my daughters. I found a way to use my personal experience and put Dr. Trent's work and my experience to practical use.

I've discovered that most women *love* personality tests, yet guys have little experience with them. I mean, you put a "What's Your Love IQ?" on a magazine cover, and they'll grab that sucker in the checkout line and take it lickety split. I don't know why guys cop an attitude about quizzes and think they're silly, as if *Field & Stream* did a "Find Your Inner Bass" test. I'm telling you, personality profiles are the cheat sheet for planning dates that rock with the females in your house.

Chances are you don't really know all you need to know about the females under your roof, and just asking doesn't deliver the information you need. There's a Daddy Dates Pop Quiz at the back of the book that you'll both take. It's based on personality and interests and will give you the intel you need to succeed.

Each category (Lion, Otter, Golden Retriever, Beaver) has word clues and triggers that can give insights into what will move us both in the right direction, which includes an understanding of her preferences *and* fears, as well as my own.

For example, if a kid is an Otter she is *expressive* and values *activity*. That means by nature she's social and chatty and will probably be talking and texting in the bathroom. Most of all, she really cares what people think of her and is eager to please.

An Expressive daughter enjoys being out and about in public, but she also needs to feel "heard," with plenty of verbal pats on the back. Interrupting an Otter will backfire every time. She has a deep-seated need to talk and talk—until she runs out of steam—before anyone can chip in effectively. Fortunately, a lot of the time an Expressive is highly entertaining and often funny. An Otter is outgoing as all get out and connects with the world through communication and shared experience.

At the opposite end of the spectrum is a Beaver. This daughter is an *analytical* type whose go-to word is *information* and thrives—in fact, insists—on having data before coming to conclusions. She doesn't want 97.5 percent of the facts; she wants to know *all* about the banana before committing to the split. (The cherry on top is another story.) What percentage of ripeness is the fruit? What is its country of origin? How much is the combined amount of gas used in all modes of transport for every part of the desired dessert—including the fudge, the dish, and the car of the kid scooping the ice cream?

An Analytical's mind is her playground, but she is pretty picky about who she lets in to play. The way to connect with her is through learning and discovering things together, because she doesn't get her information from reading people face-to-face and she doesn't rely on social interaction for amusement. Beaver/Analyticals aren't particularly people-smart and don't really understand feelings very well, and this girl will be a better listener than talker. (If the whole world blew up and just her PC and her were left? *Cool.*)

Therefore, getting your daughter out and about and exposed to new ideas is a really good Daddy Date tactic. And if you're *both* Beavers? I guess you can just put the desktop on a cart and push it around the neighborhood for some real fun. Just kidding—sort of.

By the way, Analyticals are touchy about the one thing they're most afraid of: criticism. It's their biggest fear, so if you have a girl like this, it's important to avoid any hint of disapproval of your daughter's speech, dress, or opinions. You can win the argument, but you'll lose the opportunity to deepen your relationship with your girl.

In between is the Golden Retriever, who has an *amiable* personality whose trigger word is *family*. She craves security, enjoys her privacy, and resists change; yet she may also be your social but quiet one. These kids are measured, kind, and endearing, but they are not very direct and will avoid risk, even in conversation. She evaluates everything through two personal filters in her head: *How does this affect me?* and *How does this make me feel?*

So while anything Dad suggests for a date will get an "oh, that sounds nice" response, I can tell you from personal experience with Amiables: don't mistake no resistance for no opinion. She can act like the picnic you planned is great, but in reality she's allergic to mosquitoes and is seething because you forgot. It's okay. You'll get another chance. It may take a bit of trial-and-error to discover what she truly enjoys, but it's crucial to figure it out.

The other thing to remember as an overall theme is that change is difficult and an Amiable needs turn signals and reassurance. That's where a dad can make a positive difference, by walking her through steps about why a new situation can be a good one—and safe. She will definitely want to know the date plan in advance, so she'll know what to wear.

The strongest—and sometimes most combative—category is the Lion, who has a *driver* personality and is all about *achievement*. She is a future leader—fearless, independent, and skeptical. A Lion lives in the now and isn't too worried about the future, and she is likely to say exactly what's on her mind—tact isn't in this kid's toolbox. A Driver daughter is a black-and-white, give-it-to-me-straight young lady who is endlessly multitasking, enjoys snappy chat, and usually thinks everybody else is a little dense. She will want to be someplace where everything happens efficiently, including conversation.

Of course, daughters are female, and nobody's just one thing in the personality category. Whitney, for example, is an amazing Otter/Lion combo with a smidge of Beaver for privacy and organization. She's an analytical list maker who has zero problems standing up for her own convictions, but she's also very friendly and artistic. Recently the girls and I were visiting with friends at the burrito shop, munching on chips and salsa, while Whitney was, of course, organizing costumes for the dance team and not missing a beat in the conversation.

And thank goodness, Whit's also a reader. So guess where we end up a lot of the time on a date? Yep, at the bookstore, where she can play to her own interests, be in control, but also share her choices with me over a beverage in the coffee place on the other side of the store. I learn something interesting about her, every time.

There's one thing to remember, though: people change over time. While most people are a mix (just to keep things interesting), there's usually a dominant feature. My wife is getting more Lioness, when for years she was a Golden Retriever. My third child, Hailee, has added Otter to her Retriever personality over the years, and those two qualities race to the finish line for control every single day. (She used to be very reserved in her relationships, but now she's more open and entertaining and is definitely operating in the world as an Otter with tons of friends.)

Now that I think about it, there's not a true Beaver type in the bunch. When I was younger and more ego-driven and running a company, I was more of a Driver personality Lion, but as a business coach and dad I'm generally a mellower guy—in other words, I'm over myself and the fun-loving Otter is swimming to the surface.

Here's how to do it.

Take the test for your daughter, based on your observations and assumptions about her. Then have her take the test for herself, without sharing your conclusion. Finally, take the test for yourself to get a bead on your personality. *And then compare notes on the first date.* You will be surprised at how different her answers will be, and now you have relevant conversation she'll love. Better yet, this will help plan more dates because you won't have to guess or mess around. You'll have *data*.

The next step is to start compiling a list called "What She Likes." The point is to find out what she actually likes, as opposed to what she thinks you want her to like. Or what you think she likes, but doesn't actually and she's just been humoring the old man all this time. Are sports, music, or books a big deal to her, really? What do her five closest friends enjoy? Does she truly like that burger shack you take her to (because the volume-to-price ratio is high), or is it time to pony up and have that heart-to-heart in a swankier setting because she longs for a special experience?

Much of this will be revealed over a period of time, but if you want to find out faster, you can ask your daughter if she'll take an additional quiz to help you out, which can be found online at www.daddydatesthebook.com.

But don't get me wrong. Creature typing isn't the top dog in discovering your daughter's inner life, and you still have to put in the sweat equity to know how she thinks, what moves her and motivates her as a human being.

Think of it this way. Her basic personality traits are in the backseat of her car, and she takes them along for the ride wherever she goes. The real action happens in the front seat, through conversation. And it's more than a metaphor. The ride to and from a Daddy Date is where Jimmy Bond has the best chance to get the girl *and* the secret code.

**9**

# Good to Go

Recently we all met up with a couple of people curious about whether the Daddy Dates were as meaningful to my teens as they were to me. I looked over at my quietly observant eldest, who was drinking her Frappuccino with extra sprinkles, while her sisters chatted with our guests.

"Victoria, do you remember when I called to ask you to go on a first date with me, and I came home to pick you up?"

"I wore a red dress with roses and we went to Macaroni Grill."

That was eight years ago.

At the other end of the mutual memory scale, it wasn't long ago that I was cruising through our 'hood in the Dad-mobile and discovered that somebody wasn't being totally candid about what she was up to. So I did an end run and asked her out. I wanted to find out where her head was at regarding boys, because that kind of sneaky behavior was so unusual.

I asked some searching questions and listened carefully to her point of view and was prepared with a few facts in case she tried to play me. That's not the path she chose at all, and the date was a real turning point in our relationship. I was able to get to the heart of the matter and let her know that I care enough to pay attention and am 100 percent committed to helping her stay out of major trouble.

There's been a subtle shift in her decision making since then, and I believe that dinner date made a difference. I'm not naïve, though. This dance music will be on repeat a *lot* for the next few years. My girls are not clicking their heels and saluting. They have minds of their own, just like their mother, and that's a good thing.

The magic of the Daddy Date is that I can gauge exactly where my princess is at any given time, which—trust me—is *always* different from where it was a month ago. And while you need to plan topics in advance, the conversation might lead in entirely different directions too. You have to be nimble and flexible.

Like Gumby, man.

First, remember this is a date, not an inquest or a lecture series. Once you turn on the *Dragnet* light, you're toast. (There's a reason Joe Friday was single.)

When some friends asked me the "hows" of Daddy Dating, that sort of stumped me. I never really thought about this as a program. It's just something I do with my own kids. But in thinking about it, I can tell you that it is absolutely essential to do some planning, especially at the beginning, but not to lose sleep over it. Choose something or somewhere she likes, where you can talk easily. *Take your own tastes and desires completely out of the equation.* It's not like you have to get your toenails painted together. If she's not into meat and you like a big mess of ribs, go to the BBQ joint with your pal Fred instead. Or maybe skip the heavy meal and take peanut butter sandwiches on the rowboat you've rented on the lake. It's connection—not digestion—that's important here.

Next, have a few open-ended questions handy. I usually have a general theme I want to explore, but mostly I want to experience what my date's thoughts are like at that exact moment because she's growing up and changing, so everything's in flux. True, I had to learn how not to get dizzy listening to my daughters' flowing streams of thought, but now I am fascinated by how they've evolved since I started this in 2002.

And then there's really only one major "do" on a Daddy Date, and it has nothing to do with hair. *Girls want you to pay attention when they're talking.* Big girls, little girls, your sister, your mother—I think they're pretty much all the same in this regard. That means you have to look at her, speak to her, and listen to her. Do an activity together where you are not distracted and you can really concentrate on her and her interests. She's on a different wavelength, man, and we can't tune in if all our attention is on the pizza box and 52" TV.

Even if you barely understand what she's saying, the jist of where she's at will stick, and *that's golden.* This little nugget will help you be a clued-in dad, rather than a totally clueless one, and you'll be a better parent.

Which leads us to the major "Think Agains":

At the top of the list? It doesn't matter if you're Wall Street Dad, Camo Dad, or Ponytail Dad; it's all the same. *Keep your mitts off the flip phone, iPhone, or BlackBerry.* Turn that sucker *off.* Movies are over and out too. (In our household, we only do movies as a group anyway. Fortunately, I like kiddie flicks.) And for a while, it's not a good idea to go bowling, to a concert, rodeo, ballgame, or whatever, unless you can talk while looking at her during the action—which defeats the point of paying to go there in the first place. (And come on, those choices are usually more about our comfort zone anyway, right?)

This is the golden rule: *the Daddy Date only counts if she's the main event.*

So *do* flop on the beach or throw a line in the water, if she's into fishing too. You can go for a run or a walk or ride a bike. You can cruise the mall or find a scenic spot and sit on the hood or tailgate and eat a Subway. I know one guy who's been dancing with his girls since they were rug rats, and they still like it now that they've graduated from ritzy colleges (go figure). You can ask for a cozy booth in a restaurant or share an ice cream under the stars. Or both.

Or neither.

It really doesn't matter what you choose if you've done your homework and the date suits your baby girl's personality and interests. All you're doing is showing your daughter that you understand her—the location is just a backdrop for connecting anyway.

You'll know when you get it right, because she will light up like Friday night lights at kickoff when you ask her out. (And if you pick a dud? She'll hem and haw, but she'll go anyway.)

What if you have urgent business going on at home or at work? Tell people you're turning your phone off for two or three hours. If there's a real emergency, they can call the restaurant or bookstore or wherever you are. If it's a mission-critical issue and you are likely to get interrupted on the date, reschedule for a day or two later, *but that's it*. Don't put this off. You will never remember what you accomplished at work that week, but she will *always* remember her Daddy Dates— and so will you.

Oh, and here's a Wright trade secret. Keep your eyes on her. Looking at your daughter and not cutting your eyes to what walks by takes a little practice. Sure, you can look up at the server once, but that's it after you order.

So here's the core list. *Do* call her up and formally ask for the date. *Do* hold the door for her. *Do* tell her she looks nice. *Do* have her choose the music in the car. *Do* give her a flower. *Do* talk to her. But more important, *listen* and ask follow-up questions and share some personal—but appropriate— things about yourself.

And snap a few photos once in a while. You don't want to forget how she smiled at her daddy, especially in a pretty red dress with roses on it.

# 10

# How to Talk to a Girl

O kay, you called her up, she said yes, and you're ready to go.

Now what?

If you want to succeed on Daddy Dates, the first step is to learn how to talk. To a girl. It's *different*. I've done a little studying about the mystery of this phenomenon, and I'm still chasing clues myself, but I'd like to take you on a quick road trip to the Man Brain, then to the Woman Brain, and see if there's a shortcut to no-brainer conversation with your female child—as well as others of the opposite sex.

First, open the big, heavy oak door of the Man Brain and you'll see the Container Store. It's got a million separate boxes in it. There's the Work box, the Play box, the Wife box, the Kid box, the Learning box, the Pay-the-Bills box, the Poker box, the Cut-the-Grass box—all the things that make up *men* are compartmentalized in there.

There's only one thing in each box. And it's clearly labeled. And what it says is in the box is actually *in* the box.

Now we go through the lovely French doors with the cute curtains and step inside the Woman Brain. You are now completely and utterly disoriented, because you've just stumbled into the Earth-size space where all of her experiences and knowledge and relationships are bumping into each other. The Friendship piece is connected to the Work piece, which is connected to the Children piece and the Fashion piece and the Education piece and the Emotion piece, and all these things are touching and interconnected and moving around.

It's intimidating enough for a male visitor to make the blood stop flowing and start getting measured for a casket. There's no way a guy can understand this environment, and it explains the auto reach for the remote. *Click*. Sports. *Click*. News. *Click*. Action. *Click, click, click*. Box, box, box. *Sweet*.

So logically, conversation with a female can be a problem, at least as it runs through personal relationships. (At work there are some rules and structure and goals, and somehow it works out better.) Half the time I get woozy in conversation with girl relatives because of a basic processing snafu. I know words are coming out of their mouths, but I can't make sense of the flow, which just won't stay in one place.

That's why we often think they're nuts and they always think we're stupid. What I stub my toe on all the time is that I am trying to hear what my wife or daughter says, but my Man Brain is scrambling to figure out which compartment to stick stuff into, which in itself is nuts *and* stupid.

God gave us two ears and only one mouth for a reason. The key to talking to women is to listen (not that I always take my own advice). But in His infinite wisdom, He didn't give us a handbook or an interpreter. It's been said that we're supposed to hear with our hearts. I'd like to meet the guy who can actually do that. All I know is that it's relatively easy to communicate when they're little but way more problematic as the years march to and through womanhood.

Let's get real about our lame efforts to communicate with women at different ages. The wee ones are simple, because their minds haven't filled up with experiences and sensitivities yet and nobody expects them to even like boys. You're pretty much *it* in the dude department. (Brothers don't count.) And your compartment for "little girl" is defined and if you don't know what to do, you make a funny face, put her on your shoulders, or give her a snack. Done.

But when you go on a Daddy Date with your tween or teen, you need a passport. You're entering foreign territory, and face it—you're unprepared. (There really ought to be a security checkpoint where they look in your car and ask if you're visiting the country for business or pleasure and if you've got any contraband fruit.) You don't speak the language. The rules of engagement are different. The way you conducted yourself in your controlled Man World is not effective at your new destination. You need to leave those rules behind as soon as you bail from work.

The good news is that you love this fascinating foreign land, even if you don't fully understand its customs. You love to go back whenever you can. It's beautiful, you're happy there, and it's always worth the time and money to visit if you can relax and enjoy the view. Who cares if you can't read the menu?

For a successful, happy journey, when you get in your vehicle to pick up your date, stick two things in the trunk before you leave the parking lot, because you won't need them: 1) your compartment catalog, and 2) your Sherlock Holmes hat. It won't do you any good to try to solve the mystery of her life or offer solutions to some problem you don't really understand. Females are wired for context and may seem to talk around something to get to something, but what they're really doing is rounding up all the pertinent parts of the picture hoping that we'll "get it." Which, ironically, pretty much ensures that we won't.

And then we wonder why a teen will ignore us or we get the cold shoulder from the missus when we sigh heavily, glaze over, or say, "Get to the point, will ya?"

Honestly, most women can't—and don't want to—go to a compartment and stay there, so it pays to give up that expectation. You aren't going to change the way they think. When you want to get to know your daughter on a date, act like Matt Lauer (when he's interviewing a celebrity, not a politician). I don't know what it's like to be Matt Lauer, but the reason he has a job is that people feel comfortable talking to him. He's prepared, he's curious, and he's paying attention. He's the front man for the rest of us, and when he asks a question, he's hoping for a glimpse of the "real" Angelina Jolie. Once in a while, he gets that magic answer from his guest and *bingo*! the network pays him another million or so bucks to re-up his contract because he's the rare guy who knows how to engage in productive conversation with just about anybody.

The way I think about Daddy Dates is that I may not be a newsman, but I want to get the front row seat in the theater of my daughter's mind. I've been watching this show a long time, and I'm never bored.

To Matt-etize the conversation, all you have to do is ask open-ended questions about things she is definitely interested in, like "I'm curious, sweetie. Out of all the friends that you have in your life, which ones are your best friends right now?"

Maybe her answer is "Julia." Maybe she'll say, "I don't really have one." Usually it's in between: "Um, Julia and Eliza." Note that you don't ask for one choice. You want to get a bigger picture. This is a really good conversation starter—in my experience, the number one spot to get a girl to open up. Her friends are about 99 percent of her play right now, and you're only peeking into the theater.

Then there's the follow-up.

"Really? What is it about Julia and Eliza that puts them in the 'best friend' category?"

The answer might take ten minutes. Focus, breathe, take a slow—silent, please—sip of your beverage.

(Note: I didn't ask, "Why do you like these girls?" That's too confrontational. I always make sure my tone and posture are inviting. I try not to sound like Dad the Dictator; I dwarf down to be a guy who's interested in getting to know her world on her turf, not mine. There's no throne room with a red carpet and a serf bent over on one knee saying, "Oh, Great King, let me offer you the name of my best friend."

If you want your princess to spill the beans, step down and take off the crown.)

Whatever she says, I'm in, at least while we're talking. A general compliment is good to throw into the mix, no matter what you may think of her answer.

"Oh, okay, that's interesting. She seems like a nice girl." If I think Julia is a bad influence because she got her first tattoo in the fourth grade, I might offer, "Well, who else? Who's the next closest to being your best friend?" Then I pay more attention and ask more about that friend and ignore Tatt Girl. We'll deal with her later.

What I'm trying to figure out is her criteria for a best friend. "Tell me more about Eliza. What do you like about her the most?" Or the opposite. "Everybody has annoying stuff that make us go *ugggghhh*. What's annoying about Eliza?"

For the older girls I might broach the boy topic, but with a touch of velvet in my voice. "Just wondering. What boys do you like these days? I mean, when you're in class and you see a guy and you think, *Oh, he's cool. I kind of like him*, what's he like, usually?"

When I approach a topic on a Daddy Date, I talk maybe 20 percent and she gets 80 percent. When it's something a little touchy or she disagrees with a decision I've made, I don't shut her opinion down and maybe I'll throw in a few words of wisdom—if she wants it, that is. We have a whole, real relationship, and honestly, if I ruled with an iron fist, I'd punch myself with it.

Of course, as the parent I have the right and the

responsibility to set the rules, but I will consider whether I've jumped to a conclusion without having all the facts and circumstances. There are times where I have to say, "This is what we're going to do anyway," and sometimes there's some wiggle room.

The Daddy Date is scheduled sacred time to unveil thoughts and feelings, but I'll admit that I've had to learn patience. This is the time to check your ego in the coatroom and be completely unselfish. Most guys will listen for a while, get antsy, and jump in with a bunch of suggestions for improving or solving an issue to speed things along.

Buddy, don't go there without permission. I know this sounds dumb, but it works. "Can I offer a suggestion, or do you just want to talk about it some more?" Then shut it. Anything else backfires.

And if you start sentences with "That's ridiculous" or "The problem with you is_____," you're just an idiot. *Nobody* listens after that. And unless you're willing to modify that approach, you don't have a chance, because nobody wants to hug a dictator.

Conversation is a two-way street, but her lane is a *lot* wider. She needs plenty of room to maneuver. If you don't want to crash, stick to the speed limit . . . until you've had plenty of practice at the controls.

# 11

# Totin' the Load

Every roadblock to the masculine understanding of femaleness can be explained by one object.

The Purse.

When I go out into the world, I am sufficiently prepared with keys, wallet, and a phone. I know where they are. My hands are free. My mind is on the next destination. Check.

When my girls get in the car, they are prepared to go to a ball, climb Everest, and have snacks when they get there.

And they're lost in What-if-ville. What if you-know-who is wearing the exact same thing? What if oh-my-gosh there's a flood and my makeup gets washed totally off? And worst of all, what if you-know-what starts early and I'm wearing white?

It's mind-boggling. Somebody's always digging for something, and heaven forbid when they discover that the desired tube of goo isn't in that dang thing. Then it's, "Daddy, I *have* to go back home, *please!*?"

I have a whole box in my head labeled "What The–?" These are the moments where nothing makes sense but you just have to accept that girls have mysterious needs and worries and it's pointless to do anything but deal.

But is their thinking really so weird? When I am talking to somebody different from me, I've learned that it pays to understand their goal and work backward. Young ladies think they're supposed to get good grades, be popular, excel in sports, and, no matter what, *always* look cute. (Reason number 2,016 that I thank my stars I have a Y chromosome.)

That's a load to carry in your head, much less in an accessory. They carry luggage every day of their lives. Even so, I'll only do a U-turn for two things. Homework and unmentionables. Okay, maybe their cell (a fairly recent phenomenon).

Now when it comes to the mental baggage, *that's* where the old man tries to have an effect. Life gives us all kinds of things to deal with, and Daddy Dates is where I try to lighten their load a little—before gently handing it back.

It's not like they're worrying about the electric bill. They worry about how their clothes fit, or more specifically about what people *think about* how their clothes fit. They worry about an event or looking stupid or being embarrassed. Most of the time it's a feelings thing, but sometimes it's about something like a quiz. Fear often comes from feeling alone or ill prepared, and that's a pain point where a Daddy Date can help.

Believe it or not, their worries are the greatest gift in conversation. Yes, their dreams are sweet, their ambitions can be cool, their talents sometimes truly awesome—and what dad doesn't love talking about those, right? But worry is the dirty laundry you want to see. That's the gold, but most guys don't want to mine for it because we don't know what to *do* with it.

The answer is (as usual) *nothing*. The one thing I'll never really understand about women is that they can sit around forever and talk about their worries without solving a darn thing—and leave feeling better.

If, after a time, you've proven to her that she's not on thin ice when talking to you and she can share fears without reservation, Dad won't be relegated to the last exit ramp on the freeway of her racing adolescent mind. You know you have traction with a girl when she's sharing her concerns.

I think the easiest way for me to deal with the worry thing is not to see this as anything but normal. It's part of who they are. Fretting over so-called nothing is normal for daughters, and if you embrace it as being as natural for a teen to feel anxious as it is for her to have brown hair, then you can help her manage it. Like pain management. You can't get rid of it, but you can help her reduce it to an acceptable level so she can carry on with life productively.

That said, her worry and anxiety are creative little works of art in progress, and she may or may not want to show them to you. The first thing I usually ask is, "Are you in a place to be able to talk about [fill in the fear]?" If she says yes, then you have Yahtzee. (If she says no, shelve it.)

"So, you're worried about kids making fun of you? What are you most afraid will happen?"

"I don't know, Daddy." Sit with that a few beats.

"Are you afraid of not being liked?"

If she says yes, you can try a *tiny* bit of encouragement and compassion by sharing a bit of your own observations about life. Just make it snappy and get back to the main event.

"What control do you have over what people think of you?"

"I dunno."

"Have you ever done the right thing, but somebody talked about it as if you'd done the wrong thing? Boy, I have. I'll be cruising around when I'm ninety-eight, minding my own business in a wheelchair, and I guarantee you there will be a critic in the rest home talkin' trash about me. Just the way it is, baby. But let's get back to your current situation. If you're afraid they won't like you, which way stands out the most?"

I don't know about other people's daughters, but the Wright sisters usually have an answer. There's nothing you can say that will make her not care what others think, but you can get her to air out specifics, and that helps. For example, if there's a conflict or a fear about conflict, then I ask her to talk about that. She will see it out in the open and start talking and come up with a resolution all by herself, and I will say something lame like, "That sounds good."

The really strange thing? Sometimes she will act out both sides of the conversation, then say, "Thank you, Daddy. That really helped." And I will think, *Good grief, I should be a shrink and collect two hundred bucks for showing up with two ears and the sympathy nod.*

The way women think is way too complicated and what they choose to fuss over is their business. All a father can offer is focus and understanding. They have a whole lot of stuff to lug around, but it's by choice and they're equipped for it by nature, so don't get in a knot about it. This, too, shall pass.

I know in the end, their worries are theirs to carry, and they have both the strength and outfit to match.

# 12

# Friendship Rocks

Every girl deserves to be a child and not get thrust into the grownup world before she's ready. I've never met a woman who thought she was too old when she started dating, but there are plenty who regret being too young and gullible and needy for attention.

That's why I thought long and hard about what I was going to do about my girls dating. I know families that have raised kids successfully, whose daughters got through their teens pretty well and turned out to be great human beings. There was *one* common denominator in how they were parented: *Mom and Dad didn't allow their children to date until they were in college.*

That was a heavy thought, partly because I was a date nut in high school. It sounds unbelievably old school to most people, but no matter how much I turned it over in my head, I arrived at the same conclusion. After talking it over with my wife, we decided that our girls would not be allowed to go out on one-on-one dates until college.

So I sat them down and let them know that these are my

terms: In high school we don't have boyfriends. We don't do ownership. We do friendship, and that's it.

I believe in my gut that the core of any successful relationship is a solid, enjoyable, and fun friendship. People often get to the physical part before they become great friends, and once that happens, the friendship becomes secondary to the romance.

What I am trying to teach my daughters is how to relate to a guy without having to worry about the sex part. I want them to develop all their friendship pieces, and I am motivated to give them something to live toward, not to live down or get past.

All my girls are gorgeous and will have *no* trouble finding guys who want them. I'm not a fool, though. Sure, they'll probably try to sneak around with boys they like, but right now everyone's still pretty much with the program.

What I am really concerned about is helping them avoid getting hooked up and stuck with bad decisions and giving them a few extra years to mature. They need that period between thirteen and eighteen years of age to develop their own personalities, thoughts, and feelings, without it being complicated by romance, heartbreak, and some randy kid's opinion of their looks or personality. A real relationship is a big responsibility, and teenagers are so ill prepared to have that control. There's absolutely zero risk in letting girls be girls before expecting them to be women.

So I tell my kids, "Go, have a great time in a group, but dating? Hey, that's my job and I'm not ready to quit yet."

Now, it's not like I did one big soliloquy and they said, "Okay, Daddy." They're not goody-two-shoes robots. The Wright girls can be stubborn and opinionated, and they question the dating ban *all* the time, which is fine by me. Of course, they have rampant emotions and intense crushes and boys at school wanting to date them. And if they like them back, they want to act on it. Every time that happens it's just another opportunity for me to make my case that they do group dates, not one-on-one, and why they have to tell boys that right away. And it's not like I get off scot-free. I get the what-for back, almost every time.

In fact, it happened just recently. She-who-shall-not-be-named liked a boy in middle school who, I'm sorry, looks like a pterodactyl. Kid can't help it—he's just got that kind of face, but with zits. I didn't get it but she thought he was cute and I know his folks and I thought what the heck. Pterodactyl Boy needs friends, too, and my girls are kind and compassionate. I won't butt in. Yet.

I knew they liked each other and figured there's only so much mischief a girl can get into in school when her sisters are lurking around ready to rat her out. I haven't—and couldn't—put the kibosh on liking or having certain strong feelings. It's normal to dig someone's chili and for them to dig yours back, regardless of species.

"I really like Jason, Daddy. We're not doing anything bad. I just don't understand what's wrong with having a real boyfriend. I'm like the only girl in school who's not allowed to have one!"

"What have you promised, sweetie?"

"Nothing. He knows you've said we can only be friends, but he wants more, and so do I."

Bingo. Instead of getting irritated, I saw this as a chance to connect with my teen and discuss that whole dynamic, and I made sure to ask her out on a date so we could do that. This was an opening to go through the whole shebang and discuss nature's pull of physical attraction and the different ways men and women think about sex. We discuss how a girl can tell when a guy really loves her, and I try to role model that behavior by putting extra effort into the dates. We talk about why the Wright family is making a choice that is admittedly tough and goes against popular culture: It's so the sisters have extra time to develop a solid sense of themselves before passion has an opportunity to overwhelm reason.

In other words, I want each of my girls to know who she is before there's a chance she'll make that first trip to Heartbreak Hill, so she'll know her own value as a person when the romance is over.

People find this surprising, but by the time we circle back to reviewing the boundaries—if that's even necessary—and the reasons behind the decisions, it's like hitting the reset button on "Okay, Daddy, I get it." I don't get a lot of pushback. The "friendship, not ownership" theme is a dog that hunts, because they watch their friends get in a twist over boyfriends, time and again, and mess up in school and change their dreams for the future.

What I love about my relationship with my daughters

is that these girls feel free to talk to me about their whole range of emotions. I am not suggesting that the girls tell me everything or that nobody will ever try to tiptoe around the rules. That would be absurd. There's a lot of asphalt ahead on that one.

I do know, however, that they feel safe enough to share where they're at, because I will just sit there and let them download their feelings without overreacting, spacing out, or, heaven forbid, saying, "Uh-huh, yeah, okay," while I'm texting somebody. They know that I respect their opinions, even if I don't agree with them. Or have the foggiest clue what was just said.

Plus, my hound dog sniffer catches a whiff once in a while, and I'm not above the daddy drive-by. The girls and I have built up a nice cushion in the trust bank account, but there have been some withdrawals. Exerting parental authority isn't an issue for me. I think they know they're likely to get busted if they scam me. It's not really worth it.

Maybe one reason my girls seem to listen and enjoy my company is that I've intentionally built bridges to their world. Not bashing in the gate, just staying reasonably current. I've overheard the girls telling other adults that kids at school think I'm a straitlaced Nazi until they come to our house and Dave Matthews or hip-hop is blasting and they see that I'm not the uncool khaki dad they pictured. (No offense to beige pleated cotton. I'm just more of a denim guy off the clock.)

There are a lot of other ways my wife and I stay on top of where the girls go, who they're with, and what they like.

I'm strategically involved in the youth group at church, so I know most of the potential BFs at their school. I say "hey" at the coffeehouse and we invite kids of both sexes over for barbeque. I've made sure that I've hung out with most of the young guys in some way or another, and apparently they don't think I'm a total dweeb because they show up in droves at our house for group parties. (It's probably the pool and the free food, but I'd like to think it's because I'm so entertaining.)

Of course, outfits, facial hair, or radio preset don't mean a thing in the fathering department. What does count is to man up and put our best effort into protecting a daughter's right to grow into young womanhood with dignity and self-confidence.

And she ain't gonna get that from hanging out with a pterodactyl.

# 13

# The River and the Whirlpool

The Lone Ranger is an idiot. Yes, he's got Tonto, but it's not like they're sitting around the campfire chatting about the meaning of life. The Lone Ranger goes about his hi-ho-ing business as if he doesn't need anything but a mask, a trusty steed, and a yes man.

You know what I think? That's why he's always getting into the same scrapes over and over and over.

Or maybe I'm just not hero material. When I try to go it alone and keep things to myself, I don't do very well. I stumble, I make mistakes, and I get in knots over nothing. I recently went to a conference about how men are, by nature, loners —capable of deception, depression, and questionable deeds if left to our own devices. But we tend to stay out of trouble when we're open and connected to other responsible men who hold us accountable. I made that same observation a while ago, which is why I sought out more seasoned men as advisors—like my friend and neighbor Melvin, who is an emotional gas station where I can fill up and keep going when I've hit a speed bump in life.

When I look back to the times I've been winning, there is one absolute: I am always accountable to somebody. Or multiple somebodies. When I'm accountable, positive things happen. When I'm not, negativity prevails. When left to my own devices, thoughts bounce around in my head and I come to a screeching halt on squares like Discouragement, Insecurity, and Boneheadedness. When I try to be the Lone Ranger and hide behind a fake mask of invulnerability, I lose perspective and get sucked into my own thoughts—not a good thing personally, financially, or spiritually.

This is one of the ways that I try to serve my girls too. On Daddy Dates they have an opportunity to air out their thinking with somebody they can trust, a man who loves and encourages them.

Bob is one of my accountability guys. He's the one I talk to about the good, the bad, and the ugly sides of my finances. Bob's not on a payroll and has nothing to gain from helping me. He's just on a roll as a human being, a brilliant executive who kindly offered to act as an advisor when I hit the financial skids—after years of doing pretty well—and was trying to control the situation by crawling into a mental hole. He is always encouraging while I explore options for cutting spending and creating income.

When we first started talking about the green stuff, I was embarrassed about the whole topic and extremely self-conscious. Coming clean was hard, but as we built trust, the floodgates opened and suddenly I wanted to tell Bob *everything.* I got the words and ideas out, then he would give me a new way of thinking about them, and soon the sifting process filtered the nuggets from the mud. Pretty soon

I regained my footing, the path became clearer, and good things started to happen materially.

As it turned out, I could help Bob get a grip on marketing and sales for a new business he was launching, and we became iron sharpening iron. Today I also have accountability guys like Jeff and Cordel, who help me see things clearly in all parts of life.

*Accountability.* I wish there were a sexier word for combining a boring money term such as *account* with talent or *ability*, because this strategy rocks for me. The difference between accountability and brooding is the difference between a river and a whirlpool. The river has momentum, traction, it's going somewhere, it's fresh, it's got life, energy, and direction. The whirlpool gets all clogged up and traps debris from the riverbanks—sometimes even a rotting carcass. I see my life like that when I'm not accountable to somebody. I am trapped in my own world and I don't have linear vision; it's just circular. I stay the same. But when I take advantage of my accountability guys, I have forward motion. I'm good.

I have been consciously doing this same kind of thing with my daughters for seven years. Now I'm the accountability guy for the girls. During a Daddy Date, my daughter can say the kookiest thing, but it just gives me an opportunity to help her think through her thoughts and feelings. I can't cop an attitude about it, because I remember my first snap-out-of-it moment with accountability. It came in the form of a man named Glen.

There was a time I was getting lots of compliments about a particular topic I was speaking on, and I decided to send my tape to a nationally known speaker to wow him. I was looking for a compliment from a professional I admired. I imagined that he would say, "That was the most incredible thing I've *ever* heard! You're the *man*."

At least Glen was brief.

"I think you're too silly, Greg."

I was stunned.

"You have good content hidden in there. But the way you use humor and sound effects isn't funny or effective. Frankly, it's just plain silly."

*Nobody* else in the sea of people around me had ever said that! All I heard was, "Great job, amazing!" and I'd think, *Okay, it's great and amazing, time to add more of the same stuff.* I took them at their word and, once again, became a little too proud of myself.

Glen wasn't being mean or spiteful. He was playing a vital role and telling me the truth, but he did it with the best of intentions. Accountability is about having people around you who do that, but do it with love. You need somebody who is in the foxhole for the long haul and says, "Okay, you're acting foolishly and that's why things are going wrong for you." We *need* people like that in our lives.

I take these lessons home, slap some pink paint on them, and repurpose them with my kids. It's not about yakking. Personally, I don't like the term "bouncing ideas," because you can play that game all day and get nowhere. We all need somebody who listens to what's coming out of our mouths and can say, "I love you, but that really is a dumb idea."

For example, Hailee's shot out of the blocks lately and is maturing and questioning at lightning speed. Friendship is the cornerstone of her world. All my girls are friendly, but to Hailey it's the oxygen of life. In her circle she's the influencer, but she also has a zany side and can be egged on to do something risky, so it's important for us to be free to talk about what she's tempted to do. I remind her of the age-old question: "If one of your friends dared you to jump off a bridge, would you?"

I can't say that it always changes her thinking, because she did jump off a bridge near our house, but it wasn't very high and she told me about it. Hopefully I can influence her to resist something crazier.

We make up all kinds of excuses for staying alone in our heads in our personal and professional lives, such as, "I'm the only one I can trust" or "He won't respect/love/like me." I've learned that we're all screwballs in some way with the tendency to stay in the whirlpool of secrecy. The truth is, we can learn from other screwballs who are smart in ways we aren't. Accountability is exciting because it provides growth and strength so you're not stuck all by yourself.

I believe I'm a far better dad because of the guidance from these men. I think we all need accountability partners to help us keep a healthy perspective. Maybe Kimosabe doesn't need anybody. All I know is that I do, my girls do, and Tonto could probably use somebody to say about his life with the masked man: "*Really*? Sure you don't want a job where you can talk?"

# 14

# Bumpy Roads

Victoria is a young woman with two names and one very old soul. My seventeen-year-old "Tori" is the caretaker of the family, a quality that's core to her very nature.

Tori and Whitney were born only about a year apart, back when her mother and I were in our early twenties with barely two nickels to rub together in Louisiana. When we brought home our newest infant, she slept in a handmade rocking bassinet given to us by an old Cajun craftsman in our parish in New Orleans.

One day when we thought both children were asleep, we heard this *clunk clunk clunk* from the other room. We ran in to find barely toddling Tori sitting at the base of the cradle, rocking that thing as hard as she could, trying her best to comfort her new baby sister when Whitney awakened and made those little mewling sounds.

Of course, the *clunk* was Whitney's noggin hitting the side of the cradle.

The point is that even with the sweetest of intentions, every dad on the planet is going to make mistakes or say the wrong things, especially during the teen years. You think it's smooth sailing so you do a little innocent teasing, or you say something you think is helpful, like, "Still having a hard time memorizing your lines?" and bam, a thirty-foot wave of emotion comes out of nowhere. What's a guy to do but just throw up his hands out of frustration and stomp out.

Heck, I do that sometimes and have to go to the corner before getting back in the ring. Sometimes walking away is the smart move. But if it really is about hurt feelings—heaven forbid—your basic hug can be the ticket back in.

But then . . . there are those combustible moments when somebody gets wily and forgets the chief coyote. Your teen is testing you, big time. You can't blow it off but you don't want to blow it. That's when I thank my stars for modern gadgets.

There was a time when I dropped one of the kids off, supposedly to watch a chick flick with a girlfriend. Suddenly she got a hankering to see the *Transformers* movie instead and texted the new end time. I smelled a rat, so I went into the theater and peeked in. There were two others sitting next to the girls—and they were not female.

My impulse was to march down the aisle, tap her on the shoulder, and say, "Surprise!" then give her a tongue-lashing. But instead, I took a little time to calm down, then chose the same route that she probably would have chosen for me if things were the other way around.

I texted.

"How's the movie?"

"Great."

"Are you and your friend enjoying it?"

"Yep."

"Is anybody else enjoying the movie?"

"What do you mean?"

"Well, who else is with you in the theatre?"

"Uh . . . whole bunch of people."

"How are the two guys next to y'all enjoying the movie?"

No text back. This is a moment where I bet she needed toilet paper. Lord knows what her little heart was doing. The palpitations from holy-cow-Dad-knows realization must've sounded like drums on a Rush CD.

Moments later that door flies open and she sees me sitting in the lobby area. She's three sheets white and starts begging me to understand. It was a Daddy Don't Kill Me, moment instead of a Daddy Date, but it was a teaching moment too. Yes, she got into *big* trouble, but she got authentic about her real issues and it gave me an opportunity to connect over the idea of trust.

It's not uncommon for a dad to say, "Greg, come on, I'd love to do this, but there's no way my daughter wants to go out with me. Heck, she barely says two words to me—and they're usually ugly words. I think she hates me. We have a bad relationship and there's nothing I can do about it."

"Let me make sure I understand. Her snarky reaction makes you uncomfortable so you don't even want to try? So, this is really about your comfort and the fact that you're quitting on your own kid?"

"She just won't talk to me. I don't know what to do."

"Maybe it's because you haven't created a safe place for conversation. If you'll rearrange the furniture in your brain so it's not all rigid and create an inviting atmosphere instead, which has the really comfy sectional for you both to sit on—if you take that approach, well, maybe Katie will start to open up."

"*Huh?*"

And then we start discussing what that means.

I think almost all women want to talk to us, but sometimes they just plain give up. If a guy is judgmental or dismissive or angry or has to be right all the time or is a big know-it-all, geesh, who'd *want* to talk to you?

Instead, if a father shows that he's excited about getting to know his daughter and shelves the need to control or command, she will most likely come around. But it won't be easy. And clearly you have to change tactics because if she won't talk to you, duh, it ain't workin'. Forget trying to boss her into a relationship. She's a kid, and it doesn't matter if her hair's chartreuse, she's wearing clodhoppers, or she's a mute by choice. Keep knocking. Your little girl is in there somewhere, and she wants and needs your love and approval.

That doesn't mean you drop boundaries. Just walls. If you will do a little checkup from the neck up on yourself first, you might be surprised to find that the solution's really not that hard, and she'll come around—eventually.

Generally speaking, if a guy hits an impasse in his relationship with a female, he's probably been one of three things in his communication with the fairer sex, whether she is seventeen or seventy:

1. Lazy
2. A jerk
3. A clueless lazy jerk

And we have no idea until a door slams or somebody needs a tissue that we are any of these, or what the heck we said wrong. As your daughter grows and changes, she will test you. And she will probably try to tune you out. If so, change the channel.

But you will not achieve success by clicking to Dad TV for endless reruns. Channel changing doesn't mean going to one of the stories from your past and thinking, *Yeah, baby, that's the ticket.* The big mistake guys tend to make is starting a conversation with "Well, when I was a kid . . ." Because in my case that means listening to Milli Vanilli, sporting a *Dog the Bounty Hunter* mullet, and wearing parachute pants, all of which render me completely irrelevant (even to myself).

We see everything through our own experiences, and it pays to put those Ray-Bans down in order to appreciate our kid's point of view. When she says, "Here's what's happening to me," don't rush to your precious mental box labeled "Eighth Grade Memories" for something that worked back in the good old days and try to hand it off to her as a helpful remedy: "This ought to solve your problem right there, little girl."

You might as well put traffic cones around that conversation. We go into problem-solving mode because it's a relationship double whammy: we're fathers *and* fathers of girls. Coming up with solutions is what we *do*. We think they actually want our advice, when all they need is to get it all aired out in the open, with you there for safety as they examine it. She's not really punting her issue to you, because remember you're the wackadoo who wore acid-washed jeans, and she thinks she's super cool, so what do you know anyway?

Dads are also really big on something called *reality*. We always think we know what that looks like and they don't, and we *love* to talk about it as if we have the keys to the inner sanctum and we're giving them a peek through the secret "reality window." Okay, sometimes what we're saying is true, but this kind of lecture is a dud. Instead, I try to let my kids come to their own conclusions about possibilities.

For example, one of my daughters told me during a Daddy Date that she wanted to be a rock star. "Oh, *really*?" I replied noncommittally.

"Yeah, Daddy, I want to stand up in front of people and sing and play the guitar." So when we went home, I taught her some basic chords on my guitar, then took my tape recorder, put it on a shelf, and hit the record button. She sang and we did a playback.

She hasn't mentioned it since. (If she does, who am I to judge? I will have only one word of advice for her. *Lessons*.)

One of the hardest parts of parenting is watching my girls go over the road humps without letting them know how nerve-wracking that is from the passenger side and having confidence that they will learn to take it a little slower next time.

Speaking of... Remember the clunkee in the cradle? Last

week she had a dance recital I was so skeptical about that I "forgot" the video recorder. What a dope. Whitney aces everything she tries. Our super-bright creative list maker survived being almost loved to death from the get-go—like all my kids.

Parents mess up. Kids mess up. Lucky for me, we're family, and even when I'm clueless or say something boneheaded or think I know everything and yet forget the digicam, I get a do-over the next morning with a bunch of girls who pout or snicker on a regular basis but love me anyway.

That's the *real* reality for all the recovering mullethead or otherwise flawed dads—like me.

# 15

# When Daddy Doesn't Live There

Every weekday our family gathers in the kitchen at 7:45 a.m. for a quick pre-work, pre-school prayer time. That's when we share anything out loud that we're concerned about that day and ask for a little assistance. It's a must-do.

Recently, one of the girls said she was worried about having to take a fitness test in front of the whole class. Clearly, since she's in good shape, it wasn't about being able to pass. It was about an imaginary scene in her mind where she flubbed and was somehow humiliated in front of the other kids.

I didn't tell her she was freaked out over nothing. I listened and said, "Hope everything goes okay, honey. I look forward to hearing about it after school."

That took what? Three seconds? Maybe five. She settled down and went off a little happier into her day. Sometimes just sharing a concern is enough to dissipate its power and allows a daughter to move past her mental knot. Just being in that space with her is enough.

So here's how the daddy dynamic works when you wake up without her in the house: it's exactly the same.

Except for the insane logistical hassles and enormous

challenges a noncustodial parent experiences, that is. What I'm trying to say is that being a loving father is not dependent on family structure. It has far more to do with a man's commitment to the parent/child relationship than the state of his adult attachments.

In other words, a divorced dad may have to phone it in, but you still suit up and show up just the same, albeit in different form. This is going to sound strange, after all I've written about family, but deciding to know your daughter and keep tabs on where she is in her head doesn't really have anything to do with whether you are married to her mother.

That's true for *any* dad. There are plenty of fathers still with the original mom who aren't particularly interested in their kids and don't want to make any effort. Creating a strong bond with a daughter is not about physical proximity. Many girls go through life in the same house every day with the guy who contributed chromosomes, but Checked-Out Dad is so disconnected from her that he might as well live in Beijing.

Study after study shows that a girl's relationship with her father often will determine how well she fares in womanhood. A father's role isn't optional. It's crucial, and we can't be replaced. Unless there's an extreme situation, only you can take yourself out of the parenting picture completely.

So there are three possible scenarios:

1. Dad goes away.
2. Dad gets shoved away.
3. Dad is Dad, no matter what.

I haven't walked in the shoes of a divorced father, but I sure know what it's like to be the child of one, and I have friends who are doing an excellent parenting job in spite of a failed marriage, a difficult ex-wife, and the restricted access mandated by a divorce decree. So I'm going to put my two cents in from that point of view, even though it's touchy territory.

On one extreme, it's heartbreaking and mystifying when men completely give up on their children after the kind of split where feelings run red hot on all sides. Fortunately that's rare, and most noncustodial dads try to hang in there no matter what their ex does. But there are some guys who trot out all kinds of excuses why they can't connect to their daughters or conclude there's an insurmountable wall, such as: "I can't because she's so angry." "I can't because she hates my new wife/girlfriend." "I really can't because her mom's crazy and I'm not." "I can't because my ex ripped me off with child support." "I can't because I'm super busy." "I can't because they're super busy." I can't because, because, because . . . If that sounds familiar, sell the drama to your mama. Even if all of that is true and you want to throw in the towel because it's too dang hard, I hope you'll rethink, reboot, and reengage instead. I understand the frustration, but the price of giving up is too high and the teen years are too important to miss.

Assuming that your head, heart (and wallet) are in the game—which they must be if you're reading this—almost everything about Daddy Dating is the same, except that it's way too easy for the part-timer to turn into Disney Dad. Yes, they love it when you buy them stuff and eat out, and you might get a temporary reward with a smile or hug (that will feel especially good when you've gotten the cold shoulder otherwise), but your relationship can slide too far down the slippery slope of Visa cards. Teenagers are a shortsighted, self-involved lot, busy with their friends, school, and activities, and we're not going to buy anything but trouble by whipping out the credit card too often with our girls. (I'm a sucker sometimes too. But still, there's a limit.)

What I'm trying to say is that Daddy Dates are *not* for every occasion. Your daughter needs to maintain her schedule, homework, and activities, and time away from that norm should be special. The Good Dad thing has to do with laying down all your other ambitions, priorities, and feelings to focus attention on your kid, whatever that looks like, even if she pitches a fit when she has to help wash the dishes.

My other suggestions, from the child-of-divorce perspective? If at all possible, live close by. Try to keep a home routine as similar to her mom's as possible—assuming it's a healthy one, of course. Make sure your girl gets enough sleep and eats decent food at your place. When you're not together, use e-mail, scheduled phone time, install free Skype and get a camera on the computer, text (as appropriate), go to her ballgames and recitals and meet her friends—there are many ways to stay connected. She may get sassy or defiant, but in the end she will respect you and you'll keep your natural parental bond. (And really, like she wouldn't be sassy and defiant without the divorce?)

Of course, all I have to do is meet up with them down

the hall, but I have to recommit to the relationships every morning too. Noncustodial dads have it much tougher, but if it means driving fifty miles or hopping on a plane to make it happen, then I hope you will find a way to do it. If it means being respectful about her mother *no matter what the woman says or does*, okay then. It's not fair, but it's essential. If it means not getting remarried because the new sweetie resents the time—or money—you spend on your kids, well, that's a choice that few make, but in my opinion, most should.

There are plenty of divorced men who are devoted dads and continue to provide for their kids, but factors beyond their control impact the amount of time they can spend with their children and their ability to influence their "other" home life. Agreeing with the mother on things like discipline and consequences seems to be the most challenging, and I don't have any good strategy for that. My opinion is (take it for what it's worth), if there's one chance in a thousand that you and bio-mom can elbow past the issues that caused the split and maintain a cordial and effective co-parenting relationship, grab it. (Even if you think your ex is a jerk and her new guy's a creep.) I have seen pre- or post-divorce mediation and counseling work, and maybe the whole thing isn't just or right and she's spiteful and you really are broke . . . but maybe you can back off of a dug-in position for the good of your child, even if her mother doesn't. It's worth a shot anyway.

I also hope that you can off-load the guilt and, instead, put that energy into getting your girl through her teens with her relationship with Dad intact. Remember *The*

*Cosby Show*, where Doctor Dad never had a patient and Lawyer Mom never had a case, and everybody's happy in thirty minutes? No matter what, they ended up in bed snugglin' and smilin' every night. Pure Hollywood fantasy, yet the way I've heard some divorced dads talk, it's as if they think everybody else lives in Marital-bliss-ville, so there's no way they can compete with that or be an effective parent. Nonsense. Your daughter needs to know you care, period.

I guess for most divorced dads, if hard feelings rule the day, just pretend that your ex has gone on a long trip down the Nile and won't be heard from again until she's a grandma. And if your "date" wants to gripe about her mother or step-family, do your best to steer the conversation back to her, where the focus of the date should be.

Or maybe you're the Bonus Dad. Bio-Dad stepped out of the picture for whatever reason and you're doing your darndest to be a father to your wife's children and that's why you're reading this book.

If that's you, you're a *hero*, man.

# 16

# Mommy Dates

There's a place near Amarillo called Palo Duro Canyon. In North America it's second in size only to the Grand Canyon. If you drive down to the base and you look up, you'll see a big space in the side of a cliff. I only do a little climbing, but there's one thing I've observed, no matter where the death-defying wall is. If there's a cave and you see just a little bit of light coming out and it's big enough, by Jove, any normal guy is going in to peek around.

It's the way guys operate. Exploration amps us up. There's this moment when curiosity rules and you get kind of jazzed and you think, *I wonder what's in there, this is so cool!* Maybe you have headgear or maybe just a flashlight, but you're going to figure out how to get around that mysterious place because you're motivated by some instinct for discovery.

The funny thing is, pursuing that experience is never what we expect. There are twists and turns and pools to get around and all kinds of challenges, yet somehow, whether a cave, an ocean, or a road trip, we're propelled forward by some basic male desire to scratch the exploration itch to look at the unknown.

It may be a totally lame analogy, but it seems to me that this is what it's like for a man regarding getting to know a woman's heart and mind, whether you've married her or procreated her. Except she's not a cave—and even if she were, it would be a huge fake-out because every time you step into the darkness, everything is completely different.

Oh, and you've only got a matchbook. The kind they give out free. And it's wet.

She talks to you and she confuses the tar out of you. And she says things that make you go, "What the heck are you even talking about?" And then she changes what she likes. Then she changes the way she thinks about what she likes, and then she changes her career. And then she changes the kinds of shoes she likes now. And then she changes and she's super down on herself, so she changes and she's super proud of herself.

You get the drift.

That's why dating your better half is so important and you should never stop. The apple doesn't fall far from the tree, so if you wanna know the fruit, you better be watering the roots. Change is inevitable, and dates are a great way to keep up with it. Look at the divorce stats. If it's not infidelity, addiction, bankruptcy, or some other major catastrophe, couples will say, "We just drifted apart." Yeah, like on an ice flow and it's almost impossible to get back on land when you've already broken off the continent.

People have asked me if my wife is jealous of how much attention I pay to our girls, or how I can possibly have enough left over for my wife if I'm so focused on dating four young ladies.

As far as how she feels at any given time, I don't speak for her, only for myself. Frankly, I still think she is hot. It's a mystery how she can be so super cute after four kids and putting up with me for eighteen years. I would rather go out with her than anybody, and I will be pursuing that woman until I'm buried, if she'll let me, partly because there will always be a lot to discover about her.

Unfortunately for women, the parenting-girls road often isn't so simple for Mama. I think we have it a *lot* easier than they do when daughters hit the teen years. I don't have sons but assume that the opposite would be true for me if I was captain of Team Guy. It's just the way of things to give our own gender more grief while we're raising them, and for them to give it right back in spades when they're growing up. Most of the time my girls are pretty soft on me and I get points for every thoughtful thing I do, but they can be much tougher on their mom, who takes some lumps when I get a free pass. (I know it can be a different experience for divorced dads.) The point is that for better or worse, when girls get older, Dad needs to understand he has a comparatively smooth ride down parental easy street. All most girls expect from Dad is to show up at their volleyball games and to see each other once in a while at dinner. The demands on their mother are endless, and friction is inevitable.

The best thing you can do for your kids is to stay married, if possible, and the best way to stay happily married is to keep courting your wife and supporting her during this phase. I think it all ties into the reality about what we want from marriage. If you have the typical male-female dynamic and what you crave is significance and what she needs is security, well, the only way to achieve that is to do your best to provide for and pay attention to your main squeeze.

Let me put it this way: Your daughter gets a rose. Your wife gets the bouquet. Literally. I've enjoyed surprising my wife with a fistful of flowers when it's not her birthday, and taking her on more inventive dates than my daughters from time to time. The whole concept behind Daddy Dates is that we have a God-given need to pursue, and if you stop dating your wife, you end up like Bud from an earlier chapter. Bored, weary, out of gas, with a dead marriage and a disconnected life. Mommy was your girl first and will be your girl after your kids leave home and start their own lives, so if you have to choose between an evening with them and one with her, go for Mom. Your marriage is also the dress rehearsal for theirs, and you want them to expect to keep romance alive with their husbands and for their guys to be devoted and engaged partners.

Of course, all that is so much easier said than done. At heart I'm just as lazy as the next guy. Besides, it's not like a 1950s TV show, where there's always one breadwinner (who never seems to actually go to work) and the woman stays home vacuuming in heels and pearls waiting for the king to stroll in the front door and eat the meatloaf at five thirty sharp. Whether she is a stay-at-home mom or earns a paycheck,

American women have other interests and demands for their time, so try to act like you would if you were single and dating her. Call her up and ask her out—with a place, a time, and a renewed commitment to personal hygiene. (Yours, not hers.) And for heaven's sake, open the car door, tell the lady she looks pretty, and give her a *really good* kiss before you walk back into the house.

Sure, sometimes my wife and I just want to chill at the movies, but pencil in that intimate dinner or free outdoor summer concert or a weekend in Vegas if you can swing it—or whatever she thinks is romantic and special. It pays to act more like a boyfriend than a husband on a date. Ask about how she's feeling about things besides the business of life, and don't editorialize or think you have to *do* anything. Don't dismiss what's been going on in her head as insignificant. Sit with it, just like you do with a buddy.

Friends will gripe, "I don't have the time for all these dates, Greg." *Really?* Every time I get all balled up in my head about my schedule, I put down the remote, get off the computer, turn off the phone, and wow, there he is. Father Time gives me a little chump change, and I use it to make one of my girls feel loved. Sometimes a date with your wife is just forty-five minutes at a local coffee joint, but if you are focused just on her, keeping your eyes glued no matter who shows up, it counts.

(Especially if you make out in the parking lot.)

17

# The Dao of Dating

It's five o'clock Friday night and the kids are busy with friends. You call your wife. "Where do you want to go for dinner?"

"I dunno."

"Me neither."

"Um, what are you in the mood for?"

"Anything. What do you want?"

"I dunno."

"Okay, let's go to Denny's."

They're open. They have food. You're not cooking it. Done.

Who hasn't been lame in this department sometimes, but the so-called Denny's approach (could be anywhere) will really lay an egg on a Mommy Date. (Same is true for a Daddy Date.) Female people *love, love, love* us when we do one thing. (You know this already; it's just a reminder.) They get happy when we're the Man with a Plan. Women feel special when effort has been expended just for them. Daughters are just the same.

Don't get me wrong. There are times when the Denny's Grand Slam is perfect, like when you've raced to the outlet mall at 5:00 a.m. on December 26 and dropped off the girls for the after- Christmas sale and you're solo with the sports page, enjoying the eggs and bacon and getting endless java refills.

*(Note to self, though: being alone is not a date.)*

Let's face it, when it comes to betting on what will please a female, we're worried that we'll be standing in the loser line later. The good news is, I've been doing this Daddy Dates gig for a while now, and I think I have the basics down to a science. (Hey, it works at my address.)

The first couple of dates? No brainers. Dad's pumped and prepared. This is gonna be *great!* I'm *ready!* We're gonna *bond!* It's the eighth or ninth date that gets a little dicey. Maybe because we run out of ideas. Or steam. Usually it's because by every eighth or ninth date, guess what. She's *changed*.

The best advice I can give any man in a dating relationship with a human female of any age is to visualize what will be needed to succeed on the date, as you do with other priorities—like where you're going to park at the stadium or what you'll need at Home Depot to finish the deck. Know what you're doing ahead of time. Spontaneity is for later, after you get in a groove and you know more about the types of things both of you like to do.

Also, you both need to agree to park the cell during the date—no calling or texting, please.

Of course there will be flameouts and victories, no big deal, but if you've put some thought into it—and focus during it—I promise, you'll come out ahead.

After you finish this book, and you're ready to put Daddy

Dates into action, start slow and easy. If you've taken the quiz ahead of time, great. If you do it as an activity during your date, cool. It's just a basic guide to help you understand her needs and preferences and for her to understand you a bit better. Resist the temptation to stick your ideas about your daughter into any one "box" personality-wise. She's likely to be a more complicated mix, like all women.

Here are some basic insights and tips on how to communicate effectively with your girl during your time together, based on personality traits.

The Driver/Achievement kid (Lion) doesn't want long versions of your story. She is very impatient. Get the food *fast*. Get to the point quicker. She's okay when talking about herself and her achievements, but she might be checking the time on her mobile when the conversation is about you. By nature, she thinks in the short term and is a natural-born leader— which includes how she communicates with everyone, even Dad. Let her take charge and you ask the follow-up questions. If her more aggressive personality chafes when she's a teen, remember that this girl will excel at taking care of business (and maybe you) when she's a woman. Hooray!

The Expressive girl (Otter) talks, talks, talks. In circles, triangles, whatever. There may not be a point, except she loves to share. This could drive you completely nuts during dinner (even if you're an Otter too), but she needs to run out of steam before you jump in. Her biggest goal is to win you over to her point of view. The good news is, you can gently help her focus. Listen for what's going on in her life and for the opening to walk her through a problem or to check on progress on a project, since meeting deadlines is an issue for this personality type. But let her finish her thoughts—no matter how seemingly aimless—until there's a pause. Don't interrupt. Two key things about an Otter:

1. She will connect best with you when you are doing an activity together.
2. Most people need a single cone of appreciation. An Otter is definitely a triple scoop. So *after* you listen, pile on the praise and approval, Dad.

The Golden Retriever personality is very different. Family is a touchstone for the Amiables, who are wonderful girls who appreciate personal attention. She is also the "go along to get along" type who avoids risk, and she is private and protective by nature. She's the one with a mental filter for how any situation affects her, and change is hard because she likes stability so much. This daughter can be the touchiest one, though, which is a challenge because she has strong ideas that she may not share with you clearly. To get to what's in her heart, therefore, the less talking and more listening and questioning you do, the better. This will come naturally to you over time.

If you have an Analytical (Beaver) daughter, she is likely to be science-, tech-, or computer-oriented and will want to talk about something tricky like an avatar. (Not the movie. The one she created online.) She needs time to process information—and there's no such thing as too much data, so don't expect instant feedback if you expose her to a new idea or experience. Engage her by asking questions about what she's interested in. She will go on and on and *on* with details about whatever she's obsessed with, but try to look fascinated anyway—and awake. And whatever you do, avoid even a whiff of criticism in your speech or mannerisms. It's a big, wet blanket, and she'll clam up. The dad who is dismissive, judgmental, or makes her feel like a dummy is making a major mistake, because she'll just shut him out and stew in her own misery. It will be the longest and quietest date *ever*. (And when a parent shows disdain to an Analytical, it's a tattoo that doesn't fade anytime soon.)

○ ○ ○ ○

When I decided to write this book, my research buddy Karin Maake and I interviewed my kids to find out which dates they liked the best, a project that delivered more than a few surprises and some wonderful shared memories.

"There was my sixteenth birthday," Victoria told Karin. "My dad tricked me into thinking we were window-shopping to get ideas for a car. But he had gotten tickets to a Mark Shoals concert instead, and we got to go backstage and meet him! That was soooooo cool." I thought so too.

Then there's the school drop-in. Sometimes I'm traveling and swamped with work, and sometimes I have more flexibility than other fathers, so I've made it a habit to pop into the cafeteria at school to have lunch with a daughter. That counts as a mini-date. Younger girls think it's great until about the seventh grade, and then not so much. (You'll know when she looks more humiliated than joyful.)

I was surprised to learn that all four daughters say that one of their "best ever" dates was not one-on-one with dear old Dad. It was when I took them all out for a fancy evening on the town. Each one dressed to the nines and so did I. We hopped in a white stretch limo, the driver cruised around the city, and we ate at a swanky restaurant and had a blast—together.

What's funny about that is that I'm not exactly Daddy Warbucks, and this was a break from worrying about saving for college and paying for other necessities of life. (Most of the time we're Old Navy, not Nordstrom.) The group date was an unusual splurge because my seminar business had taken off and I thought, *What the heck, why not take all the junior lovelies out for one big special night?*

I didn't anticipate that this would be one of the best investments I've ever made. Apparently the Law of Unintended Consequences kicked in, and here it is years later, and they're each—separately—telling my research buddy Karin that it was not only their favorite date, it was the best evening of their lives. I did it on a whim and it's just dumb luck that it turned out to be a fantastic memory for all of us.

○ ○ ○ ○

Again, the trick is to exercise the muscle in your head when planning Daddy Dates. No woman appreciates being taken on a carbon-copy date, so I always make sure to personalize the Daddy Date according to each daughter's personality, since I have more than one girl to raise—and to understand. Trust me, you really don't want Daughter A telling Daughter B that she just had the most amazing time with you, only to have Daughter B say, "Hey, that's exactly what we did! [pause] *Daaadd!*" It doesn't matter if they are identical twins with identical tastes. The point is to treat them as separate and unique people since your relationship is just as special.

Besides, this is the stage of life where they need to sample the whole menu, not just the Super Bird. For dads who don't feel very imaginative in this department, there's a list of choices in the back of this book that was created to help you plan fulfilling and memorable dates to match the interests and personality of your girl. Exposing her—and you—to new ideas and enjoying these experiences together will open the floodgates of conversation and, more important strengthen your connection.

And here's the 100 percent money-back guarantee: in the end, going on Daddy Dates will be so worthwhile that you *definitely* won't need fries with that.

# 18

# Whatever Works

Although I'm a bit of a Texas redneck, I was actually born in Des Moines, Iowa, to a giant of a man and his tiny pretty bride. I was in the early double digits when we moved to the Lone Star state. My grandpa was a large Midwesterner, too, and he and my dad seemed bigger than life when I was a boy. Both men were farmer-ranchers who came here for construction and factory jobs. Sweat equity was their main currency, and they put in plenty of it every day of their lives.

The dichotomy between these two incredibly hard-working men shapes what I teach my girls about the role of work in our lives.

Dad is a real John Wayne character who jokes around with women, cowpokes, and kids. He's a big old goof, but when it comes to work, he always has his tough-guy game face on. As a boy I watched him make a respectable living working with his hands. We had a small ranch, but the cash he earned came from going into the city to work in a Firestone factory, making tires. After work he came home and took care of the livestock, fields, and such. He would put his full body into it and always be wiped out, with very little energy left for the family. Then he became a contractor, and now he's back ranching full time.

Whatever the task, John made sure his boys knew that a man's work was *serious*. You didn't joke, you didn't laugh. It is a mighty grim endeavor.

Then there was Grandpa. My mom's dad. He passed away recently, and, boy, do I miss that man. For good reason, I emulated my approach to work after him.

Grandpa was a driven guy, too, and worked just as hard as Dad. He also had a construction company. Same volume, the same amount of production, but the difference was, he would joke and play during that process. He was jovial and relaxed. I always wanted to be around him and learned that work could be enjoyable and isn't separate from who you are as a person.

I think that's what my girls have learned from Grandpa and me about work.

That's why the subject of "work dates" gets its own chapter. I think it's important for kids to see their folks in 3-D rather than just the woman who does the grocery shopping and yells "pick up your room!" or just the guy who's always behind the wheel or a grill. We're complete people with lots of roles to play. We have friends, colleagues, bosses, clients, customers. We have good days and bad days. We get raises and pay cuts, promotions and transfers, hired and fired. We have to learn to get along with all kinds of folks.

Some of the best examples of dimension and depth are found in a work scenario, where our children can see us function well—and, hopefully, happily—in that way. It gives them a real picture of life, not to mention a chance to meet the people who bought their Girl Scout cookies and ordered gift wrap to support the school band.

Let's say you're in customer service or sales and you bring your daughter to work. She sees you not governing but listening and dealing with people as a peer. It doesn't matter if you drive trucks or drive a point home in front of a jury; kids not only get a kick out of seeing Dad being liked and respected at work, it also gives them a model for how to act on the job when they get one. Every teenager is looking for something to shoot for.

My eldest daughter says that one of her favorite dates with me was tagging along on a business trip when she was fourteen. As we pulled into the pinkest parking lot on the planet, I looked over and saw her sitting up very straight and trying her best to look mature for the occasion. We went into the Mary Kay headquarters, where I introduced my daughter and joked with the ladies until it was time to give my speech in front of a pretty big group.

Afterward, I heard Tori tell friends that she felt really special that day—very grown up and proud to be with her dad.

Wow. And I thought I was the one busting my buttons.

# 19

# Princess Play-Doh

swear, listening to a chatty seven-year-old talk about her life is a bit like your fishing buddy telling the tale of *The One That Got Away*.

"Well I was with my friend _____ and she was_____! And then _____ and *then* _____ and she was so _____ and _____!"

Little girls. Cuter than kittens. They think you're Superman and they adore their mommy, and you think everything they do is adorable too. It took me a while to understand that a Daddy Date with a daughter under ten isn't babysitting and I needed to use her little tales to find out what is really going on in her world.

The younger she is, the more the date should be activity oriented. These little princesses are impulsive and energetic and can't sit still very long. Plus, it's just plain silly to attempt real conversation with most seven-year-olds without giving them the opportunity to let off some steam. And even then, it's like expecting a pony to be Mister Ed. You may want a quiet evening to talk, and that will be a good idea or a horrible idea depending on her maturity level. Often it's best to let her burn off as much energy as she needs before feeding her and attempting conversation.

In other words, you just may have to go to Chuck E. Cheese's.

Once she's worn out a little bit, she'll start talking, and even then it's most likely just an outpouring of chatter. Whatever it is, she's *really* excited to tell Daddy, and your job is to listen for things to ask questions about that are pertinent to her world. Like her favorite flavor or "bestest" friend.

Then you can chime in with some gentle insights to help her start to shape how she deals with people and interprets the world. It's kind of like letting a little girl stand on your feet while you dance, so she can know what it feels like to move to music with a partner.

Believe it or not, one of my most memorable Daddy Dates with a young one was to an art gallery. Yeah, I took a bullet for the home team and did something girly, because I noticed Madi loved colors. She uses the whole shebang in the sixty-four-count Crayola box—Apricot to Midnight. And I had a blast watching a fresh uninhibited reaction to an entirely new world for my baby Otter. That was one of our most memorable dates.

The number one piece of advice for any guy starting the dating process with any female is to leave your own bag of needs under a bush. This is especially true with daughters. It's natural for us to think that what we like is totally cool, so of course your girl is going to dig it too, right? Not necessarily. If you plan a date around your tastes, it's almost like going home during a college break to find your parents have planned out your entire weekend, including breakfast with Aunt Sally at eight o'clock.

The goal is not to have her orbit around what you like, because she'll be bored and you won't learn anything about her as an individual. It's to get to know a little girl well enough to be able to anticipate how she thinks and feels. Like, I dunno, a wax museum. Would that be scary? Or would she think that is the coolest thing in the world? If you know for sure for sure for *sure*, then you're cooking with gas. If you don't. Next.

Our daughters aren't waiting for Dad to say, "Hey, let's climb Kilimanjaro." Well, not on every date anyway. Not even rock climbing nearby (at least with most girls). Hanging with daddy somewhere without rocks and just connecting is where the real money is most of the time.

You can even do a home date with mini-kids. *Sometimes.* Make hot chocolate together and mold Play-Doh animals. Take a walk around the neighborhood with a flashlight after supper. One of the best home dates is to put up the card table in the living room and play restaurant. Tell her to go get dolled up in a party dress and you put on a jacket and tie (come on, it's not that bad) and have her meet you there. Play some background music and light a candle. Just sit and act like you're on a date and let her download anything that comes into her little mind while she munches grilled cheese and slurps lemonade. It takes talent to keep a four-year-old engaged and talking, but it's worth it.

Before you know it, she'll understand how it feels to be with somebody who cares enough to listen to baby Cinderella go on and on about Justin Bieber.

# 20

# Tweening

was a junior high stutterer. One of my biggest problems was beginning a sentence. I'd get hung up on syllable one and sound like a skipping record or like a Chihuahua had taken over my mouth. That first word just wouldn't come *out*. This, of course, was wildly entertaining to other kids. Immediately everybody would mimic me and start making that s-s-s-sound, and they'd all crack each other up. So, naturally, the laughing-stock became the class clown. And and worse, when somebody else messed up, I was the first to jump on the dog pile.

Eventually my mom got me into speech therapy and I was fine, and I guess in some weird way it's one of the reasons I chose to be a public speaker, although I never bring it up in adult company. My closest friends have no idea that I had that affliction, but as I write this I can feel a twinge of the old shame. I guess it's embarrassing for a guy to admit, even now.

But then I had an evening with my bright and inventive Madi, who has an auditory processing issue and sometimes the word in her mind comes out as some other word through the sound waves, which has a negative effect on her grades. (That girl is all Otter, and she is definitely Expressive.)

One night that's what I wanted to talk about on a Daddy Date, away from the family, and I opened the topic to see if she'd bite. And, oh boy, did she chow down. That's when I shared my own experience. I laid out the whole shooting match of frustration and alienation and what it was like for me to feel dumb as a box o' rocks. I was also able to tell her that it got much better over time and how one day—*poof!*—the stuttering was gone. I can't even remember how old I was when that happened, but I still wince remembering that earlier humiliation.

And guess what? She felt understood. She saw light at the end of the tunnel, because she started to believe that her therapy would work. Sometimes that's all you can offer as a parent.

But then she did something that blew me away, and I will remember that moment when I'm an old man. Madi reached across the table, touched my arm, and got that female "oh, you poor baby" look in her sweet eyes. "Oh, Daddy, I am really, really sorry the kids were so mean to you back then. That must have been awful."

Gulp. She was comforting *me.*

The tween years are an absolutely beautiful time in a girl's life. But there's one part of it that ain't so great for her father.

This is the stage when there's physical *evidence* that stuff is about to happen that's *way* out of your control.

I remember the first time I had to deal with seeing a daughter start to physically develop and realized that I was being pushed into a whole new realm against my will. Suddenly I just knew that those hormonal boys were going to be attracted to my child in the next few years, which had been just a vague, futuristic concept before that. I guess it was like labor was for my wife. Ouch. There's nothing you can do to prevent it, but then you get this beautiful person out of the deal.

The first time it happened I remember thinking, *Here we go, Greg. Get ready!*

Now I'm going through that a fourth time, and it is no picnic, let me tell you. All of a sudden Madi's developed little *curves.* And all I can think is, *She's got this walk, for the love of Mike, and some kid's gonna want some fries with that shake.* I want to scream, "Stop!" *Why is she walking like that? Cut it out. We need to get her ankles tested for agility! And what's with the skinny jeans?*

Really, I just have to fight back the nausea, then try and A) not focus on it and B) not make a big deal out of it, because when you dial it up, it causes the girl to be a lot more self-conscious unnecessarily.

I can have all this noise in my head, but I don't even joke about them changing because I don't want them to feel like it's even a topic or an issue. I feel like that whole thing called "developing" shouldn't even cross into dialogue with Dad *unless* and *until* she comes to me with questions about it.

And then I get off that topic ASAP. Their mom is more of an expert anyway. I think it's important for me to answer quickly and tell her that I am *way* more interested in how she's developing as a person on the inside than the outside. "You're going to change on the outside and gain the attention of boys. That's part of how nature works. You can be really pretty or homely on the outside, but if you're really cruddy on the inside, you're sunk. You can't fix that. So all I want to focus on is who you are as a person. I don't care if you're 902 pounds and have one eyeball in the middle of your forehead and long wiry hair coming out of your left nostril. Your behavior and how you think about yourself is what counts."

Usually once I get to the nostril, trust me, the subject has changed.

Yes, that's what they have to put up with from the old man. There's not a day—an hour—that goes by without major eye rolling and snickering from my peanut gallery. But no matter how silly they think I am, I know one thing for sure about the preteen years and my role in them: this is the stage where you will start to set her up to be a confident woman, and the stakes are high.

That means your job on Daddy Dates is to discover what is influencing her decisions. It's definitely not just you. You want to know who her best friends are and what they like, because just about now is when your opinion goes into a slump and a whole new team is on the bench. You want to know what their power plays, stolen bases, and sneaky pitches are all about. You want to know which celebrities they admire and which teachers they like. You want to know their favorite colors, TV shows, iPhone apps, and music. You want to know it all.

And you gotta ask, listen, and remember, Dad. Start that file *yesterday*.

○ ○ ○ ○

Somewhere between twelve and thirteen, while you're asleep, they go to DJ school and come back with a license to control the music, because as soon as they jump into the car, they take control of the sound system.

Your girl will say sweetly, "Let me help you, Dad," because you've been finger tapping to Barry Manilow on your commute and she wants to put on Black Eyed Peas. She's trying to educate you out of lamehood. So let her. Even though you're driving, you're in the passenger seat in the space pod to her planet, and this music is one peekaboo into her environment.

The whole point of a Daddy Date is not so she'll experience your world, but so you will experience hers. If she hates bowling, then don't take her any place with ten pins and bad chili. If she doesn't like wings, don't go to Pluckers. If she doesn't dig your music, then don't play it.

You can torture the family with all that stuff in a group.

I guess what I'm saying is that this isn't a real date for you; this is *work*. This is punching in and putting on your overalls and exploring the mine of your daughter's brain. And it's a real job, from getting in the car to putting the key in the door back home. No slacking off. No distractions. No vacay—until that wonderful day when you get your Daddy

Date groove on, and then it's as easy as sailing in Jamaica with Jimmy Buffet.

But get ready, thirteen is at the plate, and that's when the whole game changes, amigo.

# 21

# Lucky Number 13

One upon a time my wife and I lived in California and we had very irresponsible furniture. Here we were, two kids with two kids, and we still had a white love seat.

One day I came home and it was newly monogrammed with a big red W. Actually, it was indelibly scrawled with eleven cherry-colored dubyas.

"Whitney, honey, did you do this?" I said gently to the assumed culprit, who had been busy for weeks trying to write her big fat initial everywhere else.

"No, Daddy."

Now, no wasn't in the cards as an answer. I mean, what do you need for proof–*video*? Fingerprints? It's a W for heaven's sake.

Okay, she's scared, and she's *three*. How could I get her comfortable telling the truth?

"Whitney, Daddy loves you so much. I would beat up a hundred boogeymen for you. I really would. I just need you to tell me the *truth*."

"Okay, Daddy."

"Did you write on the couch?"

"No Daddy. I di-unt."

So I was thinking that maybe she wasn't my child. Yeah, that was it. Somewhere in the middle of the night she was swapped out for this look-alike, and I steeled myself to banish the mini monster in a kid suit.

"Honey, really, I mean it, if you don't tell Daddy the truth, I'm gonna have to punish you." (Back then I thought they were too little to understand any other kind of communication, and I wasn't experienced enough to have a better idea than a pop on the tush.)

Whitney looked up at me with the most pitiful face ever in the history of the planet, and the waterworks started. But I was strong, by golly. Dang it, I was going to teach her a lesson. I gave her a little pop on the tush and she wailed inconsolably, and I thought, *This stinks. Why do I have to be the bad guy? Just tell the truth, kid, please, so we can both get out of here.*

Then I left the room and saw my wife, who was as white as Uncle Ben's with no butter.

"Victoria did it," she told me. That little rascal had framed her sister, but when she saw I'd punished Whitney for it, she ran sobbing to her mom and 'fessed up because she couldn't stand it.

I offered Whitney ice cream every day for a whole year and still felt like a dirtball.

What does this have to do with anything? Well, things get topsy-turvy when "teen" is in your daughter's age description and the whole game changes, my friend. Sometimes you put two and two together and you come up with a conclusion that's foregone—and wrong.

And then, inexplicably, sometimes you're right-on.

The problem is when a girl morphs from child to teen, it's as if she's changed jobs but you don't have her new e-mail. Your behavioral cues bounce back and the relationship suddenly seems off-kilter. The solution is to get to know this young lady all over again, so you get clued in to what's real and that is far more likely to happen during a Daddy Date with just the two of you.

At twelve, they still like their mom and think you're the smartest guy in the world. They hug everybody a lot and will go to family events without griping and tell you stuff and sit next to you in PG movies and don't mind if their friends see them sharing popcorn with the folks.

But take my advice. Don't get too bunkered into that La-Z-Boy upstairs in your head. That sweet attitude of hers doesn't last, which can be hard on a parent who's accustomed to being comfortably adored. But you don't get a vote. Mother Nature gets the last laugh on parents. Teenagehood is messy but necessary, and you have to adjust the tempo in order to keep up.

When my eldest turned thirteen, I realized that I really needed to bring my A-game, because this is when daughters need Dad the *most*.

That's why the Thirteenth Birthday Daddy Date is a *really big deal* in the Wright household. It's the most emotional and meaningful one, by far, and critical to the success of our relationship. So for me, it's a must-do in the dress-up department. Austin's a laid back town, and I love that, but number thirteen deserves extra-special attention. She gets a new outfit; I spit shine my shoes.

This is definitely a special-restaurant date, and I am careful to choose one where we can really hear each other, because I want to talk to my brand-new teen about her life and what that will look like in the coming years.

Mostly, I use this occasion to make sure she knows that Dad is her go-to guy, and that she can count on me to come through, *no matter what.*

And as a token of that deep commitment, I give her a pretty ring to wear on her left hand so she will remember that I am giving her my heart (in a parental way), promising to be her guide in life, and will take care of her financially and emotionally until she's an independent woman or married to that special guy she finds later on.

I let her know years in advance that he will have to man up and ask for my permission for her hand in marriage. And *that's* when my ring comes off—when he puts his on and makes the same promises. It's what I call the "transition of care."

Does that sound old school, passé, or downright corny? Well, I hear story after story from friends about how their sons are relentlessly pursued by teen girls, and let's face it, now proms are all about the hotel after-party, where senior girls are expected—or planning—to have sex, right? I've been doing this Daddy Date thing for seven years now, and I'm more convinced than ever that taking one-on-one teen dating completely off the table as an option in high school is the *best* thing I could possibly do for my children.

First, there is *no* downside. Has anybody ever learned anything valuable about love in the backseat of a car? I want my daughters to value their bodies, sure, but also understand that their bodies do not define who they are. That's the plan, anyway. I am trying to teach them that sex—as fun and important as it is in life—will not deliver what they want, which is true love and real intimacy.

So pretty soon after The Ring, it's time for the Other Talk. This is the one that makes many parents squirm. But that's a different date, and it's not so much about sex as it is a romance talk that includes a real, honest, male point of view. For some families, this is part of Mom's job description only, but in my house I think it's important to have both perspectives. My talk is about how men and women experience love, what love is, and more important, what love *isn't*. (Actually, this conversation goes on for years.)

Who better to tell my daughters about man-brain than me? I'm the only testosterone-carrying human in the household—hopefully that gives me more than a small shred of credibility in this department. It's also an ongoing conversation about love that starts at thirteen and goes on for years.

Ask any adult woman: What's more important to you, sex or romance? For most, unless she's in the heady throes of a hot new relationship, it's always "show me the flowers." It's also "talk to me." Women want to share their feelings and to know what makes their guy tick too. So when I tell my girls about how little there is to check out from the neck up with boys (there's *really* not a lot of depth there), it's always news. I'm pretty straight about it. We are simple creatures wired to keep sex primary in the relationship, and women are more complicated emotionally and like to keep it secondary.

So I tell them that's why Daddy, a bonafide guy, believes in the concept of people waiting until after "I Do."

"Why, Daddy?"

"Because when you are that intimate with someone, you create a connection that you will never forget, and everything gets thrown out of balance. Especially in high school. You can't go feed the ducks without thinking about sex. You can't hold hands without him wanting to pull over. You can't have a cute outfit on without him doing a mental X-ray of exactly what's underneath, which means you'll start worrying about whether you're fat. (Which you're *not*.) You'll grill him about whether he thinks some girl is prettier, and you'll both start asking who's done what with whom in the past or might want to in the future. Insecurity and jealousy will jump into the mix, and pretty soon it's *all* about ownership, baby. And there's no upside to that.

"And when he dumps you or you dump him? One of you will think the world has come to an end, and you won't be able to think or enjoy anything. You'll cry buckets and everyone will get sick of you going on and on about this loser, and it will be a total waste of time. And if you stay together?

That's *worse*. You will make college and other choices based on your boyfriend, rather than what *you* really want."

In the next few years we talk about friendship as the real love act, not the sex. Young men don't get how to make their girl feel cherished, and heck, many older guys don't either. I try to show my daughters that love is not just words and compliments. Real love with a real man will be when he gets something for her when it's not her birthday. Or he swipes her keys and gets her car washed and brings it back to the same spot with a love note. A little effort and imagination goes a million miles more than just saying I love you.

Which brings me back to Daddy Dates. That's why they aren't cookie cutter activities. I show my girls that they are understood, valued, and cherished by the first guy who ever loved them *for who they are*.

I want the future Wright women to be good partners too. I share the insider's secret that the number one need of a male is not sex, anyway. It's up there, but it's not the top dog. A man wants to feel respected, important, and significant. (When a guy struts, brags, and chases women, it's always about wanting to feel important.) Any woman who understands how to communicate to her guy that he's appreciated has the key to a happy man.

That's why I'm the luckiest guy in Texas. Sure, things don't always run smoothly at my house, and nobody's saying, "Yessir, anything you say, Dad." But if there's one thing I get back, it's that I always feel loved, valued, and respected by four terrific girls. And if nothing else, that's what they will be prepared to give—and expect—in their relationships.

This is core to the Wright family values. In my way, I've marked them with an indelible W, too, but it can only be seen through the eyes of true love.

# 22

# The Apples Grow the Tree

M y ring days are over, and whew, the last one was a doozy.

Let's just say the caboose child changed the game. Madi is more like her mom, who didn't exactly respond as expected back when I did my original Magic Ring Moment.

I was just a kid when I proposed to my wife, working odd jobs and going to night school. I'd saved money so I could take her on a special date to pop the question. At the time I thought I was being very original, but in hindsight it was admittedly a little cheesy—I gave the modest sparkler to the waiter to present in a covered dish with a rose.

The other diners were in on it. I got down on one knee to pop the question. The room went silent. All eyes were on us.

"Will you marry me?"

"Um, I don't know, Greg."

Not exactly the scene I'd imagined.

A couple of days later, I noticed a pay phone while I was at the Laundromat matching socks. Suddenly, I got the idea to call her to make my case about why I wanted her to be my bride. I figured she didn't have enough information. Maybe she wanted to be in on the decision too! So I dropped in the quarter and punched the buttons with a shaky finger—and the others crossed—hoping she'd answer. When she did, I went on and on about how I felt and how wonderful she was and the qualities I had that would make a good husband. Then I thought, *What the heck, I'll give it another shot right* now.

I knelt down on one knee on the decrepit linoleum of the Laundromat, with the phone cord taut next to the folding table, not caring about the other customers looking at the nutcase on the floor.

"Will you please marry me?"

"Okay."

That's kind of how it ended up feeling with Madison, too, on my final thirteenth birthday event. The surprise was on me—a Daddy Date for the books. I took her to a special place and arranged for a secluded booth for the Talk. We ate, we joked, we had a wonderful time together while I was getting ready for the big emotional crescendo, fiddling with the ring in my pocket and not believing this was the last time I would have this moment with a daughter.

But wouldn't you know it, just when I was ready to start my spiel, the wait staff began pushing and shoving a long string of tables together right next to us, and about a hundred theatrical folks trooped in with a flourish and broke the spell. I'm pretty sure they were about to fire up the karaoke with "Fill Me Up Buttercup," when I choked down the crème brulee and hustled us outside and away from the racket.

I decided to make a play change and make the big

pronouncement on the wall under a tree. As we sat down, the music was playing softly. But I hadn't noticed one minor detail. We were sitting under the loudspeaker. And when the invisible DJ changed the tune, it felt like we were in the front row of a Metallica concert. "Honey, let's walk." I thought I was making good progress with my little talk, when my daughter complained, "Daddy, my feet hurt." Of course they did. She was wearing brand-new heels with her special outfit while I was strolling comfortably in my Florsheim's.

So we found another place to sit and I started launching—again—into my usual speech about boys and dating and friendship-not-ownership, when she piped up: "Oh, I want to talk about that too, Daddy! I think I should have a boyfriend because I will need the practice before college."

Hey, this is the Magic Ring Moment, not a debate! She's supposed to get all teary-eyed and say, "I agree, Daddy," like the other three. But I decided to roll with it and listened to my youngest. Finally, in a silly falsetto, I gently mimicked her fear about arriving on campus clueless. "Oh, I'd love to have a romantic embrace, Mr. Wonderful, but oh, my, *what* do I do with my arms? Oh no, where do my lips go for a kiss? Your armpit?"

She laughed. I laughed.

"I promise you, honey, when you get to college, you'll know what to do."

I then explained our relationship and exactly what I was offering, and I presented the ring as a choice, not a token of a foregone conclusion. "I'm offering this plan, and if you will accept it, I'm ready to commit, too, and I have something for you tonight to remind you of my promise. If you're not ready, that's okay, we'll wait."

It was a different gig with this one. The others went smoothly. The evening with Madison was more like an episode of *The Bachelor*. "Will you accept this rose?" Of course, there was going to be something completely wild and unexpected in the middle of a Madi Date, and I was going to have to find a new way to communicate with a female over the blaring din of real life.

I had to work for that yes. And it made me grow as a father too.

Honestly, when it comes to fatherhood, the girls are doing their best to raise me right. When I became a dad, I was just a sapling. The truth is, I wasn't much more than a wobbly stick in the ground when they arrived. Six thousand or so days later, they have not only rooted me, they make me stretch as a man all the time. I can't imagine how bland life would be without them.

Besides, they crack me up, laugh at my jokes, and wear rings that mean everything to me.

Yes, this dating thing was launched under an age-old pine, but it really started when I was lucky enough to be transported from Dude to Dad one night, by very special delivery.

# 23

# Almost a Woman

G et in a private plane, a Cessna, for example, and there are two sets of controls that move in sync. Either pilot can make it fly into the great beyond or nosedive into the turf, but the way a newbie learns to keep that thing up is by having her hands lightly on the yoke as the instructor works his or her controls, while they explain all of the other maneuvers to keep in mind.

If I were teaching the girls, at first it would sound like this: "This doohickey tells Daddy how high we are." Later I might say, "You take the controls for a minute, sister, and get a feel for it." And eventually it might be like this: "Hey, I'll pick you up when you finish your solo and we'll grab a bite"— after you know for sure they can land the thing safely.

That, my friend, is Daddy Dating with full-fledged teen-agers. (Or at least I think so, because frankly, the only thing I can make fly is a golf ball in an unintended direction.)

As each daughter matures at her own pace, Daddy Dates move correspondingly into the shared control direc-tion, which will happen on their actual dates in the future. Of course, the word *date* is really a euphemism for *decision*.

The endgame is for them to be able to take over, have good judgment, raise their expectations, and land on their feet if or when a real-life date's a jerk.

Now I have to play it cooler as they get older. I'm more of a mentor in some ways. My eldest, a Golden Retriever personality, has RBSS (responsible big sister syndrome) and is moving quickly toward independence. On dates she'll bring something up and I'll go through the pros and cons. "You have to decide for yourself about what you really want to do."

Of course, as the world makes its mark on them, the conversations get more complicated. From thirteen onward I really zero in on who they're hanging with, their struggles and interests, and what's impacting their thought processes. It pays to know all of the females in my daughters' spheres and where they're coming from, because when communicating with a teenager, you're never talking to that one cute human being in front of you. There's a whole chorus standing around whose points of view are coming in loud and clear on the special teen frequency—which Dad can't hear any better than a dog whistle.

Here's something I've learned the hard way. Females are inclusive by nature and can seem to change opinions on a dime after checking with other females. The problem is that it gives guys whiplash. A conversation becomes a whole new strange thing when another female enters into it. I will talk to Daughter A and she'll tell me what she thinks and feels, and I think, *Cool, I get it. Thanks for sharing.* Then a sister or a girlfriend waltzes in and they start talking about the exact same subject. Next, Female 2 chimes in with new shading on it, then Daughter A does a U-ey with me, and all of a sudden I'm confused. "*What* did you say? Did you just completely change your mind?" "No, Daddy, but—" and it makes no sense to her that I'm such a dunce I can't follow her logic. After all, I just heard the same thing Female 2 said, right? To me, it's suddenly going against traffic, but to her, it's just a little mental lane change and she assumed I saw the turn signal.

That's why I try to stay clued in to her siblings' and friends' opinions. By fifteen or sixteen, she's closing in on being a fully formed woman, and I have to remember that my influence is on the wane. When I forget that, life has a way of splashing ice water in my face in the form of the worst sentence in English language between men and women:

"How does this look on me?"

No question can shove a guy so radically from bunkered in his nice cushiony, carpeted room into a rocky minefield with snipers, stumbling around blindfolded. Men can get a brain freeze and think that it's a real question looking for an answer. Or that it's mathematical and solid—two plus two adds up to the fact of four, right?

Like, "Do these pants make me look fat?" And you want to say, "No, your behind is making itself look fat, but that's just the way you're built and I love you and I really don't care but, yeah, it's a fact that they're too tight in the hips, did the mirror break in the dressing room and really, sweetheart, can I *please* go now?"

In other words, there's not one good thing that can come

from going with the technical answer. Nor do I personally believe evading the question with something generic like "you look great in anything" is the wise choice either.

For one thing, especially with a spouse, it's not just your opinion she's seeking. What she's *really* asking is, "How does this make you feel when you look at me, and [*way* more importantly] will my girlfriends like it? I wish I were shopping with Janie and Jill but you'll have to do.

With five women in the house, I've had more than a little practice tiptoeing through this landscape on a lot of levels. The last thing I ever want to hear—now or in the future—is, "Why didn't you *tell* me?" No matter what the choice category, I think there's a way for a man to be authentic but also encourage her to move on, by saying, "It's okay, honey, but I've seen shorts that look better on you."

(For me, it's also preparation for the future, too, so when they ask, "Do you like him, Daddy?" I want to have some foundation for speaking truth when I say, "He's okay, sweetie, I don't really know the guy. I'm more interested in how you feel about yourself in this relationship.")

The question is so much trickier with daughters, because of that other factor that comes into play. I'd like to say that all of my motives are lofty, but come on. I can't just replace my guy glasses with dad glasses and call it a day. Recently, my wife and I took all the girls on a summer-clothes shopping trip to the mall. They each got a small allowance and were told that they could buy anything they wanted, with one little caveat: their purchases had to pass the Dad test.

"How does this look on me?" takes on a whole new perspective when a daughter says it, because I can't analyze that without my own mental circus kicking in, knowing how males will react to how they are dressed. With the mini-this and the plunging-that plastered all over the magazines and the store, I sometimes want to throw a blanket over the girls. But you can't do that.

Instead, I employ a different tactic: "What are you trying to say with that outfit?" I want to make sure they understand what they are broadcasting with their choice. "It's a little low in the front. Maybe a cami with that?"

"Oh, Daddy, it's *cute*. I think it looks pretty. Ashley has a top just like it."

"Let's think about that for a minute. Do you want everybody to look right *there*? Will you blame a guy and say he is creepy if he's only staring right *there*? I'm curious, because that's what will happen. I just want to make sure I understand what you are trying to say with that [tight/low/short] outfit."

Reality check. Let's say her friend Ashley just happens to haul in an armful of stuff to try on in that store at the exact same moment and sees my daughter and says, "Hey, that's cute." I'm toast. Yes, I've just had a completely logical interaction with my kid, and I'm the one who has the cash power—but when it comes to Dad versus girlfriend, what I have to say is paler than plain yogurt in comparison.

So that's how I came around to implementing my secret strategy: use Daddy Dates to keep tabs on their circles.

I try to be the dad who makes all of the friends laugh

and feel at home, because when the girls start to gripe, their friends will stick up for me.

The other given in our relationship is that my teens may not lie technically, but boy, they're the CIA about controlling information, and sometimes I make assumptions that can backfire. This is when the dating dance gets really interesting.

One time daughter number two wanted to go to a Switchfoot concert. She was fifteen. The night before the show, she set it up like this: "Switchfoot's in town. Some of my friends have an extra ticket, what do you think? Parents are taking us."

"Switchfoot, that's cool. If I were in town I would totally go with you. Have a good time." I was in a hurry and didn't ask enough questions.

Then a neighbor called me and asked, "What's this about so-and-so going to a concert on Sixth Street [the Bourbon Street of our town] without a chaperone and you approved it?"

My teen hadn't lied. She told me parents were taking them. She forgot to mention that the kids were getting *dropped off.* In this case my girl was crafty, but it's also human nature to edit stories. Everyone edits. They'll insert whole lines of what they thought somebody said, so most of the time I've learned to dig a little deeper in conversation to investigate what's really going on—and help my kids get real about their actions.

Let's say you're sitting with one of your daughters and she wants to gripe about something Mommy or a teacher or a girlfriend said, or something that a parent didn't let her do. Right or wrong, I always do this: I give them their time, every time, all the time. Unless there's some physical inconvenience and I can't sit and listen to them gripe right then, I let them say what's on their mind and get their frustration out. I don't cut them off or tell them they shouldn't even think that way.

I let them vent, and a lot of the time I don't voice an opinion. Ultimately, if it's a hiccup in a relationship with someone else—including their mom—it doesn't do anybody any favors if I chime in with, "Oh, honey, you're right, she's a big old meanie."

If it's something I'm confused about, or it sounds uncharacteristic that the person would say that, then there's a piece missing and I go for that. This is how to hold a mirror up to a kid so they can have a clear snapshot of reality too.

Right now three of my girls are at the age where their peers are involved in the boyfriend–girlfriend thing, and they spend a lot of time consoling friends in tears over breakups because the relationships start, heat up, and flame out in about the time it takes a kid to get over chicken pox.

It's a big theme on our dates now, but it only strengthens my case about dating too young. I'll listen, then make a very sincere observation like, "Do you see the depth of her pain? No fourteen-year-old should have to feel the hurt of being brokenhearted or jealous of seeing a boy parading a new girl around school. Man, that's like being an emotional prisoner. Do you think that's fair?"

In so many ways I'm taking my girls on imaginary flights over that rugged territory, and we're sharing the controls. On a Daddy Date it's just the two of us—no Greek chorus or outside influences—and if we hit an air pocket, we ride it out together. I'm hoping they will keep looking toward the horizon and land somewhere calmer and safer when they're old enough to go on the adventure of adult life, and someday—if they choose—with a steady copilot who loves them for just who they are.

Like I do.

# College Girl

My seventeen-year-old called me at nine o'clock one night when I was at the airport. She had a tough homework assignment. She was a junior in high school, not college, but it was the equivalent of inventing the cure for cancer. To me, anyway. It's so far past my pay grade that she might as well have asked me to build a space station for science class.

After all, she knows I'm a math dummy. She was not calling me about algebra; she needed encouragement to keep going so she could actually finish the problems.

"How many more do you have?"

"Nine." That's a lot when they're deep and each one takes twenty minutes. *Okay*, I thought, *first let's do a mental walk around the table.*

"You're stressed."

"Yep."

"You're worried that you're going to get too tired and you're not going to be able to stay up and finish this?"

"Uh-huh."

"Which means you're stressing about what that would

look like tomorrow when you walk in and your stuff's not done."

"Yes."

"Alright, so you really do have to finish this tonight so that you can feel better tomorrow morning, right?"

"Yes."

"And you're getting sleepy."

"Yeah."

"Got it. Here's the deal. Go take a shower. Not a hot one, but not chilly enough to give you a snotsicle. Nobody wants to see that."

Slight chuckle. Okay, a snort.

"Just cold enough to make you dance a little and wake up. Change your clothes, get something to drink, and then come back to it and hit it hard. I'll call you in forty-five minutes and we'll talk again. We'll see how you're doing."

We didn't have to play Marco Polo. I didn't have to dig around. She just needed Dad for a second, and we both acted as if I was just in the other room. I love it that my kids feel free to do that, but at the same time I walk the tightrope between being supportive and encouraging and doing too much for them.

An unattached, two-stepping friend told me a funny anecdote that reminded me of the difference. Last spring she drove way out to an old country dance hall—at least thirty miles from any real town—and when she was leaving, her heel caught, causing her to stumble into a railing and slice her finger open. She ran into the ladies room to stop the red gusher, and soon five good ole boys were crammed in the stall trying to help, all with the exact same handy dandy solution they grabbed from their F-250.

Within minutes she had a humongous black ball of electrical tape around her middle finger. All the men looked *very* satisfied with their work.

Of course, getting the sticky mess off later was another story, when she was home on her own. It seems to me that's what we do all the time with women. We're wired to rush to the rescue with answers and *solutions*, but sometimes it just makes the problem worse and often a young woman can figure it out on her own anyway. That's how she will learn to avoid stepping in the steaming cow pies of life later on.

I'm trying to be DIY Dad whenever possible, but it sure goes against the grain.

I don't know how I'll feel when Tori leaves for college in 2011. I would love to, so I could get my game face on, but unfortunately my crystal ball broke somewhere in the overhead bin over Iowa. As the girls go off to college, I won't be able to beam myself over to the dorm at Whatever U, but I will date them by remote. Hopefully. My plan is to set an exact window of time where we'll pretend we're on a Daddy Date and I will be mentally spiffed up and all attentive and focused and eager to share her experiences, when of course she'll be in sweats with a ponytail holder preferring to talk about the Other Guy (or *to* TOG) and will be lip-synching to her roommate, "Wait, wait, don't go yet, I'm almost off with my dad."

At that point (again, hopefully), I'll get the hint that I'm not the main man anymore, and I expect that will be a little weird at first. I'll try not to take that too personally because parenthood is one of the only jobs in the world where, if you're super-successful, you get demoted. And then fired. (Fortunately, I will probably get rehired later as Grandpa.) Still, I haven't navigated those shifting sands yet, but it's a-comin', so I guess I'll be giving myself the Man Up talk next year on a pretty regular basis.

But first, I think preparing for the college dating scene requires me to make sure each daughter gets an A in the mandatory core curriculum class, How to Be Rude 101, because women—and my girls are no exception—are taught to be nice and gracious and not hurt someone's feelings, and I want her to know how to say *no* effectively to a guy. So we'll role-play that potential scene until she can get her point across effectively without being downright mean. And she'll know when being downright mean is the nicest—and smartest—thing a woman can do for herself and those who love her.

The irony is that I also want to be careful not to lay too many "look out, kids" on them, but where do you draw the line? What I dig most about Forrest Gump is that he's so entirely clueless about the swirling world around him, yet comes out unscathed anyway. Children are like that. They don't know enough about the road ahead to be awed by someone or scared of something. What about coeds, though? I think my eldest has an extremely level head, but it's hard not to shove my big ole worry hat on it. I count on my wife to help me resist that temptation.

Maybe my girl will still call me for pep talks when she freaks out about exams. Maybe she'll remember that I'm good for that. If I'm really lucky my cell will ring at two o'clock a.m. and she'll feel better by two fifteen. And we'll both fall asleep knowing we were there for each other in the middle of the night.

I can't pretend that there won't be moments of anxiety as each girl moves into her adult role, but right now it's like Tori is my understudy and it will be natural at some point for me to bow out and let her take center stage.

And someday, in the future, I will be calling her for advice, but at a reasonable hour because she's wiped out from her day enjoying her wonderful life, which includes running after my grandkids.

I have no pearls of fatherly wisdom about being the dad of a woman. I guess the girls and I will just have to figure this one out together.

To be continued.

# Sliding into Love

On the way to the Alamo is another great Texas family pilgrimage. *Schlitterbahn.* I think it's German for "Gi-normous Slip 'n Slide."

Back in the olden days, in the eighties, it was just a big ole natural string of slippery rocks outside of New Braunfels, with chilly spring-fed water, puffy inner tubes, and a colossal parking lot. Now it's Disneyland submerged on a few dozen acres. That sucker has been there for thousands of years, but it took a bunch of entrepreneurial Bavarians to figure out how to make Mother Nature go *cha-ching* as loud as a factory whistle at quittin' time.

Anyway, if you're a Texan and it's stinkin' hot and you want to get the family off the griddle, you pile the kiddos in the car and head straight for the ultimate water park experience.

That's what I always do with the five Wright women as soon as school ends. We slather on the sunblock and away we go fifty miles south.

We all have a great time getting wet and crispy, but I've noticed that many of the other parents are shifting their feet in the endless curlicue lines, saying little or nothing to their kids. Or they'll be hanging out on Lazy River, while the teens are on the Master Blaster. That's inconceivable to me. Maybe this is the way many adults think about teenagers too. Every time we say things like, "I just don't get these kids today. I don't like their music. Their clothes are stupid. I hate the way they talk. And what's with all of this vampire business?" we're brushing off their world as impossible to understand—or respect. I call this the Lazy River way of being, because it doesn't require Dad to learn anything new. If we decide in advance that teens are unintelligible aliens, then it's okay to shut ourselves in a room while they disappear into iPodville and *voila*—unplugged.

If I am to be honest, though, sometimes I have to fight the temptation to just float along in shallow water, too, especially when work is demanding or there's a problem at home that keeps coming up. There are days when all I want to do is decompress, go into my man cave, and just chill or scroll through sports scores, but then I hear *Greg!* or *Daaaad!* from the other room, and I realize that they need me and I jump back in the deep end.

I have made so many boneheaded decisions in life regarding career, money, relationships, and the rest, that boy, if Achilles had one busted heel, I probably have two along with a couple of busted elbows. But the evidence is there that I'm doing one thing right. I bet on Daddy Dating and hit the Daughter Lotto, because my girls are super cool and we're tight, so the payoff's been huge. As the older two have become increasingly busy, I am stunned that they still want to shoehorn me in. Like the time they actually volunteered me to go to a youth event in Alabama (the organization needed more parents) instead of wanting a summer vacay from the folks. The leadership came to me and asked, "Greg, what are you doing to make your kids want to be around you so much? What's your secret?"

I didn't know what to say, because I didn't know that I was such an oddity.

There are so many great things about being the girls' dad, but then there's the flip side of parenting, which is the real challenge. You come into the parenting world innocent and courageous, then you become a father of a teen and suddenly it's Friday the Thirteenth. You toss your kid the keys, and by the time she catches them you've visualized her being pulled out of the inferno on the freeway by an axe murderer.

I guess that's why I am a chump for Gump.

Forrest Gump is the Einstein of love. There's nothing complicated about him. He lives totally in the moment and puts it all out there, with and without a Ping-Pong paddle. And most of all, he believes in Jenny.

Now that guy has guts. Forrest Gump goes the distance. Daddy Dating is totally wimpy compared to running across America for love, wearing a Happy Face shirt. If Forrest is naïve and dumb about the world, I want to be dumber. Forrest is brilliant in only one area. His universe is his mother, his son, and, of course, his Jenny. He keeps his heart and mind open to them for his entire life.

Somewhere between Forrest and Father Freakout Brain

there's balance, and that's what I want to show my kids. Unfortunately, while I have the usual list of Regular Joe qualities, when it comes to dealing with women, I do not have a poker face. In fact, I don't even have an Uno face. Or Go Fish. I'm just one big Etch A Sketch of emotion. This does not always serve me well as a dad when I want my teen to read "Don't worry, kid, everything's swell out there," while I'm really thinking, *Yikes, little girl, watch out!* and my mug shouts it like a yodeler in the Alps.

If someone were to ask me to list my goals in life, at the top of my list would be to have the courage of my convictions every day, to be in the game with my wife and kids every waking moment, and keep my heart valve wide open 24/7. But I ain't no saint. I'm like everybody else in that struggle. No doubt about it. Daddy Dating is the Master Blaster of love, and it takes everything I've got to raise four girls in a Lazy River culture that constantly whispers, "Grab a tube, dude. Relax. You may not really know your daughter, but not to worry, she'll be fine."

Seven years ago I decided that just wasn't going to cut it for me. The risk of not Daddy Dating was too great. At the end of the child-raising ride, I want to be able to say the same thing Forrest did to his sweetheart: "I'm not a smart man . . . but I know what love is."

And that's because I know who *you* are, little girl.

# Afterword

All women are daughters.

Just sayin'...

# Daddy Dates
# Pop Quiz

This quick and easy personality insight test takes less time to fill out than finding a good spot in a jammed parking lot on a Saturday afternoon. First, do one for yourself. Then fill out another based on your "best guess" about your daughter, without consulting her. Then ask her to take it for fun. Bring all three to a dinner date and compare your answers. Learn and enjoy!

## Step 1

Starting with the "L" box, circle every word—and the phrase beneath the words—that describes who you tend to be as a person. Go through all four boxes. Do not stop and think or second guess. There is no right or wrong, better or worse.

## **LOGB Strengths Assessment**® Dr. John Trent

| Takes charge | Bold |
|---|---|
| Detrmined | Purposeful |
| Assertive | Decision maker |
| Firm | Leader |
| Enterprising | Goal-driven |
| Competitive | Self-reliant |
| Enjoys challenges | Adventurous |

*"Let's do it now!"*

Double the number circled _____

| Takes risks | Fun-loving |
|---|---|
| Visionary | Likes variety |
| Motivator | Enjoys change |
| Energetic | Creative |
| Very verbal | Group-oriented |
| Promoter | Mixes easily |
| Avoids details | Optimistic |

*"Trust me! It'll work out!"*

Double the number circled _____

| Loyal | Adaptable |
|---|---|
| Nondemanding | Sympathetic |
| Even keel | Thoughtful |
| Avoids conflict | Nurturing |
| Enjoys routine | Patient |
| Dislikes change | Tolerant |
| Deep relationships | Good listener |

*"Let's keep things the way they are."*

Double the number circled _____

| Deliberate | Discerning |
|---|---|
| Controlled | Detailed |
| Reserved | Analytical |
| Predictable | Inquisitive |
| Practical | Precise |
| Orderly | Persistent |
| Factual | Scheduled |

*"How was it done in the past?"*

Double the number circled _____

### Strengths Assessment Chart

| | | | | |
|---|---|---|---|---|
| 30 | | | | |
| 15 | | | | |
| 0 | | | | |

## Step 2

Tally up the total in each box and DOUBLE the number. So, for example, in the "L" box, if you have seven words and the phrase circled—that's eight circles in the "L" box—and eight doubled would be sixteen. Write the number for each box in the space provided. Then you drop that total score on the graph below on the "L" line. Then do the same for the O, G, and B boxes, connect the four dots on the four lines, and you've got a graph that tells a story about your or loved one's strengths.

## Step 3

The box with the largest total equals your dominate personality type, the next highest is your secondary personality, etc. In other words, it is normal for people to have a mix of qualities, like being a lot of Otter (Expressive) and a bit of Lion (Driver).

"L" Box = Driver or Lion
"O" Box = Expressive or Otter
"G" Box = Amiable or Golden Retriever
"B" Box = Analytical or Beaver

Now this is why Dr. John Trent's test works for me: *Boom*, right off the bat you know and recognize the inherent qualities of each animal. It helps you appreciate what motivates you and others, and give you pointers on how to communicate with your girls successfully on a date—and beyond.

## Step 4

Take the same test for your girl, then give her one to fill out.
Compare notes.

## Step 5

Here's a quick snapshot of your personality and the apple of
your eye.

| | LION | OTTER | GOLDEN RETRIEVER | BEAVER |
|---|---|---|---|---|
| **Strengths** | Takes charge<br>Problem solver<br>Competitive<br>Enjoys change<br>Loves a challenge<br>Confrontational | Optimistic<br>Energetic<br>Motivates others<br>Engaging<br>Future-oriented | Warm<br>Relationship-oriented<br>Loves lists<br>Loyal<br>Enjoys routine<br>Peacemaker<br>Sensitive | Accurate<br>Precise<br>Cares about quality<br>Loves data<br>Discerning<br>Analytical |
| **The Flip Side** | Too direct<br>Impatient<br>Always busy<br>Cold-blooded<br>Impulsive<br>Suspicious<br>Risk taker<br>Insensitive | Unrealistic<br>Daydreamer<br>Impatient<br>Overbearing<br>Manipulative<br>Pushy<br>Avoids details<br>Lacks follow-through | Misses opportunities<br>Dislikes change<br>Stays in a rut<br>Sacrifice own feelings for harmony<br>Easily hurt<br>Holds a grudge | Too critical<br>Overly strict<br>Controlling<br>Skeptical about new opportunities<br>Loses perspective |
| **Communication Style** | Direct or blunt<br>One-way<br>Can be a poor listener | Can inspire others<br>Optimistic or enthusiastic<br>One-way<br>Weakness: high energy can manipulate others | Indirect<br>Two-way<br>Great listener<br>Uses too many words<br>Provides too much detail | Factual<br>Great listener about tasks<br>Desire for minute detail and precision can frustrate others |

(Chart is continued on next page)

|  | LION | OTTER | GOLDEN RETRIEVER | BEAVER |
|---|---|---|---|---|
| **Needs** | Personal attention<br><br>Recognition for achievements<br><br>Some authority<br><br>Opportunities to solve problems<br><br>Freedom to change<br><br>Challenging activities | Approval<br><br>Opportunity to verbalize<br><br>Visibility<br><br>Social recognition | Emotional security<br><br>Agreeable environment | Quality<br><br>Information<br><br>Exact expectations |
| **For Balance** | Add softness<br><br>Listen intently<br><br>Exercise patience<br><br>Show respect | Be attentive to other's needs<br><br>Let others talk<br><br>Be aware that too much optimism can be foolish | Learn to say no.<br><br>Establish boundaries<br><br>Learn to tell others when feelings are hurt | Accept that total support is not always possible<br><br>Learn that others may need less data and explanation<br><br>Socialize more |

You can find out more about this way of looking at personalities in a DVD series called the StrongFamilies Class 100 series (www.StrongFamilies.com), and there's even a powerful online instrument based on Dr. Trent's LOGB you can find at www.LeadingfromYourStrengths.com.

# Top 15 Daddy Dates

## The Dinner Date

Food + Focused Listening = Daddy Date 101

The only rule is that it has to be food *she* really likes, or would like to try, and you need to vary the setting so that she can both dress up and feel special, or hang with Dad in jeans. The core to any Daddy Date—connecting—is not the location or that the two of you are sitting across a table someone else cleans up. It's that she's safe exploring her range of emotions and options with you, and she *knows* you're paying attention.

Glee-k or on Team Underwood or prefers Panic at the Disco! A Daddy Date based around music rocks.

## The Coffee Date

Coffee + Listening = Daddy Date Lite

Every town has a java hut. Let your daughter order, settle in, and get the scoop on what's going on in her head.

## The Bookstore or Library Date

Books, magazines, music, and snacks.

What's not to like? Or learn. This is where you hang back and see where your daughter's imagination takes her. Does she prefer fashion, fiction, or football (one can hope, right?), *People* magazine or *Poetry Journal*? Maybe you can't tear her away from the travel or history section. After she cruises around and makes her selections, go for a beverage and let her talk about her interests, as well as her friends' tastes. Enjoy the joe, say things like, "That's interesting, I didn't know that about you," and nod your head a lot.

## The Fancy-Schmancy Date

Daddy and daughter dressing up and going to the theater, business gala, or special concert is the occasional treat that she will remember forever. If you can swing it, this is an investment that will pay off for the rest of your life.

## The Music Date

For most tweens and teens, music is their lifeline—an extension of their personality. Of course, your girl is probably downloading her music and she thinks CDs are unbelievably old school, but ask her to humor the old man anyway and go to the actual store with you. You can also look up a recording studio and see if they have tours or will let you sit in on a session. But remember, it's how she experiences music that's important, not your taste or ideas about it. It's a way to connect and see what's influencing her. And you never know. She might ask Dad a question too! It doesn't matter if she's a Glee-k or on Team Underwood or prefers Panic at the Disco! A Daddy Date based around music rocks.

## The Date with a View

There's something about sitting under the stars, watching waves crash on shore, seeing a vast vista from the top of a skyscraper, or just staring into a roaring campfire that opens up the mind—and conversation. Getting your teen out of the house, apartment, or other enclosed space is good for the soul and great for your relationship. (Chances are you did one or more of these things with her mother, and it worked. Time to brush the dust off that skill!)

## The Stroll Date

There was a time when you pushed your baby girl around in a stroller, but now is the time to let her take the lead. The great thing about good weather is that it brings an abundance of outdoor activities to share with your daughter, and what's even better is that they're often free. Walk around the boardwalk or trail, go to the farmer's market, attend the goofy festival, drive out to the flea market, or take in the free movie in the park. Look in the paper or online and see what's coming up. She might roll her eyes at the thought of being seen with Dad, but choose something you think she might enjoy on her own. If you really can't figure it out, show your girl the list and ask her to choose, then be a good sport and do it—even if it's not your thing. When you get there, let your daughter set the pace and share what she knows—or is simply curious about. Whether she's into vintage clothes, organic farming, or kung-fu flicks, this is one of the great ways to connect with a teen.

## The Dancing Date

Remember moving to music in the family room with the cute baby in your arms? If you have the slightest skill on the dance floor, ask that now-grown girl to go two-stepping (or whatever) with Dad. She'll love it, and it's the talking before, during, and afterward that's the right move anyway. (Caution: Make sure to take your wife out dancing first.)

## The Good Sport Date

Most girls would love to know how to rack up billiard balls, throw a dart, or putter around with a golf club—miniature or otherwise. Any or all of these simple man-friendly activities also allow for easy banter between daughter and Dad. Be sure to say, "This is fun," even if she's not very good at whatever you're playing. You score if you act like an admiring date and not a coach. Put aside the need to compete. The game you're "winning" is her heart.

## The Craft/Hobby Date

Some of the best times with my dad were when we made stuff together, like that goofy derby car. Shoving a ship in a bottle may not float your girl's boat, but you'll have a blast on a date working as a team creating something side-by-side. Try

Home Depot's Saturday morning kid-friendly workshops, visiting a Lakeshore Learning center, or going to a ceramics store to turn mud into a coffee mug for mom. For easy daddy/daughter project instructions like making "Our 1st Daddy Date" photo frame, as well as a complete list of workshop destinations, please go to www.daddydatesthebook.com.

## The Picnic

So where is that Thermos, anyway? Throw together the basics—something to sit on, something to eat, and something liquid—and find a beautiful spot to relax and visit with the child you're working so hard to raise. Bonus points for feeding the ducks, throwing a Frisbee, or playing a board game she likes. It's all fun in the fresh air.

## The Great-Outdoors Date

Young women worry and fret a lot, so getting outside and hiking, running, hunting, fishing, and so forth is a great way to let off some steam or lessen anxiety. It's a date if it's something she loves to do, you're totally paying attention to her, *and* you get a smoothie or yogurt afterward. (Or eating anything when you're camping. Out there even peanut butter is a treat.)

## The Learning Date

Does she watch *Top Chef*? Sign up for a cooking class. Does she love jewelry? Schedule a one-on-one time with a gemologist at the local college or store. Does she fantasize about being a doctor—or a spy? From art, history, and espionage to the human body, there are cool museum exhibits for everything under the sun. Starting out clueless and becoming more knowledgable on a subject together levels the playing field and will be an entertaining and highly memorable shared experience.

## The Volunteer Date

The perfect twofer: giving time to your daughter while giving back to the community is a good thing for everyone. Ask her to pick a local charity event to volunteer for that is meaningful to her, and pitch in together. Spend a day helping to build a house for Habitat for Humanity, hand out Gatorade at a fun run for charity, or clean up the environment and enjoy the team effort. Top it off with ice cream and that's a winner.

## The Water Date

Whether fresh or frozen, *agua* makes for a good time with a girl of any age. Tubing, waterskiing, swimming, snowboarding, pond skating, whatever, it's refreshing for your relationship. (Drifting down a river is great for taking a load off and sharing a laugh; more extreme sports offer an exhilarating experience to remember over cocoa.) Geronimo!

If you'd like more ideas for great Daddy Dates, check out www.daddydatesthebook.com, go to the Greg Wright fan page on Facebook, or follow Greg on Twitter @WrightAuthor.

# Acknowledgments

Thank you, God, for giving me all that I am and all that I have.

Thank you, Amber, for encouraging me to reach beyond myself.

Thank you, Victoria, Whitney, Hailee, and Madison. You are my heartbeat. Thank you for giving me the coolest job in the world . . . being your Daddy.

Thank you to my parents, for always believing in me; my grandparents, for always praying for me; and my brothers, Doug and Dustin, and my sister, Traci, for always loving me in spite of myself.

Thank you to my accountability team, Jeff, Garvin, Cordel, and Bob, for being strong when I am weak.

Thank you to the Collins for unlocking your door, turning off the alarm, and adding us to your family.

Thank you to the many people who said, "You need to write a book!"

(You know who you are.)

Thank you to my agent/friend David Hale Smith, who opened the door to the literary world (and shoved me through it), and to my wonderful Thomas Nelson editor, Kristen Parrish, who knew how to get *Daddy Dates* out in the world beyond mine.

And thank you to Dee Covey and Karin Maake. Without you, there would be no book.

Greg Wright
September 2, 2010

○ ○ ○ ○

When we met Greg Wright for coffee one day—seemingly "by accident" in business—little did we know that we'd need more than one paper product. Tissue. First, we laughed until we cried, then we cried because of how deeply we were touched by stories of life in the Wright household.

Here we are over a year later, and we still chuckle and choke up every single time we talk to this inspiring father of four *really* great girls. Greg has had a profound effect on our lives and relationships, and we loved being part of bringing the magic of *Daddy Dates* to parents everywhere.

Our deepest thanks go out to the *many* pivotal people

who helped make *Daddy Dates* a reality by generously lending moral and material support to Team Greg: Dima Tochilovsky, Jill Prentice, Yolanda and Roger Maake, Megan and Lawrence Gleason, Kathy and Lionel Sosa, Jim Long, Barbara Covey, Wendy Free, Nancy Covey, Lance Avery Morgan, Ashley Wittenberger, Shari Wynne, Rick Ressler, Deborah Nitzky, Eddie Valdez, Lillie Morgan, Brittany Johnson, Shauna Callaghan, photographer Dustin Finkelstein, and the good folks at the New York Public Library. You have our humble thanks, and now you have the result of your faith, love, and free WiFi.

Dee Covey and Karin Maake Tochilovsky

# About the Author

Greg Wright is the founder and president of the Wright Track Consulting Company, working with businesses nationwide as a motivational speaker, corporate sales coach, and business growth specialist. Most importantly, the dynamic self-described "music nut" is the forty-year-old father of four teenage girls. If Greg has any qualifications to write *Daddy Dates* ("Questionable, at best," he says), Victoria, Hailee, Whitney, and Madison are the highlights of his résumé. The family lives in the Live Music Capital of the World—Austin, Texas. *Daddy Dates* is his first book.

To book Greg for a Daddy Dates or Wright Track sales seminar, please visit www.thewrighttrack.com.
Or follow Greg on Twitter @WrightAuthor.

Shattered Vocations

# SHATTERED VOCATIONS

Mark Jensen

**BROADMAN PRESS**
Nashville, Tennessee

ISBN: 0-8054-5447-0
Dewey Decimal Classification: 254
Subject Headings: CHURCH // MINISTERS
Library of Congress Catalog Card Number: 89-37086
Printed in the United States of America

Unless otherwise indicated Scripture quotations are from the *Revised Standard Version of the Bible*, copyrighted 1946, 1952, © 1971, 1973 and are used by permission. Those marked (KJV) are from the King James Version of the Bible.

**Library of Congress Cataloging-in-Publication Data**

Jensen, Mark, 1956-
    Shattered vocations / Mark Jensen.
        p.      cm. — (The Bible and personal crisis)
    ISBN 0-8054-5447-0
    1. Vocation.   2. Vocational guidance.   I. Title.   II. Series.
BV4740.J46   1990
248.8'8—dc20                                                              89-37086
                                                                          CIP

*To*
*the patients, families, and staff*
*of the Oncology Unit*
*of Baptist Hospital, Louisville, Kentucky,*
*with whom I was privileged to serve and learn.*

# Introduction

The ideas for books are often born in questions that refuse to go away. When the writer gets taken with the question, he or she begins to hear echoes of it everywhere. So it is these questions which form the heart of this book. It seems to me that I hear many people struggling for an understanding of vocation that helps them make sense of their experience.

I hear the question in teenagers, wondering whether they will go to college or not. I hear it in college students wondering about their major or what to do after they complete their degree. I hear it in people who are retired or retiring, struggling with self-worth now that they are no longer "productive." I hear it in people faced with a terminal illness, wondering what their purpose is for the time they have left. I hear it in parents whose children are taking leave of them. I hear it and see it in the boredom and despair that underlie epidemics of alcohol and drug abuse

"Why did God put me here?"

"What should I do now?"

"It seems since my child died, I don't have any reason to get up in the morning."

"I feel so useless. What purpose could God possibly have for me now."

These are the sounds of persons struggling with vocation. They are persons struggling to respond to what they discern as the call of God in their lives.

We have too long limited the "call of God" to a select few. It is time to renew that ancient concept and let it bring life to our everyday pursuits. It is my conviction that vocation does not fall out of a fortune cookie onto our plates. It is more likely to be found in exploring the frontiers of our hearts where the way may not be so clearly marked and wrong turns are part of the experience of journeying.

As you journey through these pages, my hope is that you may be encouraged to think about your vocation in new ways. I have intended these pages not only for those confused about vocation, but for those who simply want to "ponder anew what the Almighty can do."

# Contents

1. Vocation: Lost and Found . . . . . . . . . . . . . . . . . . . . . . . . . . 11
2. The Pain of Lost Vocation . . . . . . . . . . . . . . . . . . . . . . . . . 28
3. Creation and Covenant . . . . . . . . . . . . . . . . . . . . . . . . . . . 62
4. A Face in the Darkness . . . . . . . . . . . . . . . . . . . . . . . . . . . 86
5. Jesus and Vocation . . . . . . . . . . . . . . . . . . . . . . . . . . . . . 114
6. Starting Over: Pain and Grace . . . . . . . . . . . . . . . . . . . . . 140

# 1

## Vocation: Lost and Found

He had not built the fire, but was glad to see it—the evening had turned out colder than he anticipated. He nodded his head at another man who had been drawn to the flames inside the circle of stones, but he did not speak. He held his hands closer to the fire and rubbed them together. That seemed to help the chill in his fingers, but not the chill in his heart. It only deepened, so he stared at the fire and tried to slow his racing mind.

Too much had happened too quickly. He was not sure who his friends were anymore. He had been so sure of himself and his friends, but not now. He had seen, heard, and felt some ominous signs for some weeks, but had tried to ignore them. They had been all too true. The worst possible thing had happened. All he had been living and working for now seemed gone. A deep disillusionment was beginning to settle in as dusk was gathering. He rubbed his hands together again, and someone asked him where he had come from. He lied, trying to ease the pain of a heart that was breaking. The lie made him feel worse, because he had never imagined turning from the way he had chosen. Of course, he had never thought it would come to this. He turned his head away from the light of the fire, and wept.

You know this man and his story, though I have not named him. You may have already recognized him. It is the story of Simon Peter, immediately after Jesus' arrest. It is usually told as a story of failure, and it is certainly that. But it is more than that. It is the story of a man who had lost his way. It is a man who had his most profound sense of purpose ripped from him in a matter of days and hours by events beyond his control.

Peter had already had his life changed profoundly. His life of fishing had been transformed by one who met him at his nets and gave fishing a deeper meaning. The months to follow had been full of life-changing experiences. As part of the inner circle of disciples, Peter came to a new sense of hope and purpose in the company of this carpenter from Nazareth. Now this carpenter was going to be executed, and Peter did not know what his purpose was anymore.

He would return to fishing, a trade he had never really left, and would be met at his nets once again by the risen Jesus. He would find not only forgiveness for his failure, but a yet deeper understanding of what it meant to follow Jesus. Peter would go on to be the foremost leader of the Jerusalem church, an apostle of great stature. The Scriptures tell a little more of Peter's story, including some misunderstandings, conflicts, and changes of heart about what it meant to follow in the Way. I suspect Peter never forgot the conversations around the fire on the night of Jesus' trial, when his purpose seemed most lost.

## Losing and Finding

This is a book about losing and finding. Peter is each of us—searching, thinking we have found our deepest purpose and calling, being confused, being heartsick, struggling to find hope again. All of us know about the dramas of losing and finding. The joy of finding something is sweeter against the memory of losing something important. The pain of losing hurts all the more when we recall the excitement of discovery.

This is also a book about vocation. *Vocation* is an old word with a number of meanings. In the modern world it means very different things to different people. Webster's dictionary gives this definition first: "A summons or strong inclination to a particular state or course of action." In this chapter, I will begin to spell out what I mean by that word, and why I think it is important for persons of faith to think again about vocation. I trust that the remaining chapters will continue to paint a picture of what Christian vocation can mean. The context of that discussion will be the experience of losing and finding. They are the valleys and peaks of the spiritual journey.

Of course, the experience of *being found* is the most profound joy of all. I will give you an important clue about where I am headed with that image. My conviction is that Christian vocation takes root in the experience of being found by the loving Father who is always seeking us. Even though we affirm that God is always seeking us, most of us know the experience of wandering in a lonely place. Hopefully, most of us also know something of the experience of being found, of finding companions on the journey. The rhythms of losing and finding, of being lost and being found, mark the spiritual journey for most of us.

## Vocation: A Perennial Issue

Twentieth-century persons who call themselves Christians are not the first person to think about vocation, although the conditions of the twentieth century demand that we must think about it anew. Apparently, first-century Christians also had some questions about vocation and may have addressed those questions to one of their leaders—Paul.

In Paul's correspondence to the Corinthian congregation he addressed a series of questions they had apparently written to him (1 Cor. 7:1ff.). He briefly addressed the question of whether the calling to be a Christian means some other changes must be made in the way these people ordered their lives. Paul's simple advice to them was to remain in the state in which they had been called, whether slave or free, circumcised or uncircumcised. Most of our questions about vocation have little to do with escaping from literal slavery or deciding about circumcision, but questions we have, and they are every bit as real. Slavery takes on new and more subtle forms, and we substitute new legalisms for the marks of circumcision.

I have been interested in the question of vocation for some time. Like other children, I heard the questions of curious adults asking me, "What are you going to be when you grow up?" I also heard preachers and teachers talk about something called "God's will." I saw people declare to our church and others that God had "called them to special service." I wondered what all of those things had to do with one another. Those questions were to become more personal as I, like others, had to decide about a college major and job directions.

Early impressions stay with us a long time. I remember as a grade school child hearing the sermons and lessons about this matter of calling. I recall hearing that we believe all persons are called. I learned early a phrase called "the priesthood of all believers" and was told that each of us could interpret

God's Word and will for our lives. Among the things that the priesthood of all believers meant was that no matter what a person's job, we are all "called." Just what is meant by that word *called* may be the heart of the questions: called to what? And called for how long? And how do we know? I think it is time to declare again that we are all called and explore what that means. I think it is time once again to talk about the relationships between calling, work, family, and the life of faith.

We must do more than simply declare things. We must struggle with the hard questions raised by our declarations. We must also translate those declarations into food for our daily lives. We must test those beliefs through the tests of hard decisions, of unclear situations, of less than perfect lives and choices. It is one thing to declare God's approval when we are strong and successful, when we are taking life in stride. It is another to declare that we know what vocation means for us when life has dealt us a blow that staggers us. It is quite another thing to declare that we understand all about vocation in the face of a conspicuous failure.

For some years I have been in hospital ministry of one sort or another. For six of those years I was chaplain to a cancer treatment unit in Louisville, Kentucky. It was there that I began to struggle more deeply with what it meant to have a Christian vocation. It was not that I struggled so much with my own sense of vocation, although that began to change. What began to seep into my mind and heart was what I was being taught by the persons whom I ministered to every day and who ministered to me.

Many of these persons had been living vigorous, productive lives in their chosen station or profession. Then they found that they had cancer. They did not stop living vigorous and productive lives, but some found themselves faced with new and severe limitations as a result of their disease and its treatment. Others found themselves facing death. Things change when you look death in the face. Suddenly good people found themselves struggling with what purposes God had for them. People who had known few limits found their energy greatly limited, their choices greatly reduced.

Some of these people found that they could no longer keep the job that had meant so much to them. Some wondered if they would live to see their children grown; others began to grieve at the thought of leaving grandchildren. In the face of this real pain, I began to ask again what Christian vocation meant to these persons. I began to see how limiting it is to define vocation in terms of a single job or role that is bound to change, that is bound to know limits. Put simply, does the person with weeks or months to live, who has lost the ability to work, have a Christian vocation? What does our affirmation that "we are all called" mean in circumstances like that?

What follows I owe in large measure to the rethinking I was forced to do in ministry with those persons. I will not tell many of their stories in these pages, but I have taken it as part of my vocation to remember what they have taught me. Part of my vocation is to practice gratitude with my eyes open. I think that I am continuing to discover the depth of what Christian vocation means, and it has less and less to do with the particular job I have, although that is a part of my expression of calling. Calling is deeper and wider than any job can contain.

## Contemporary Predicaments

If Paul addressed the question of calling and societal roles in the first century, what makes this a question that bears asking again? What makes it a fresh question that needs again the wisdom of biblical faith? Several things make this question take on new seriousness in the latter half of the twentieth century for American Christians.

While Webster reflects something of the root meaning of vocation in his first definition, the popular mind seems to equate vocation with job. That is unfortunate. Even if the central thrust of vocation had to do with work, life in the twentieth century presents some particular challenges to the idea that vocation means job.

Industrial society produces jobs that are not always noble and dignified. Societies of all ages have produced jobs that were neither noble nor dignified, but the possibility of depersonalization seems greater on this side of the Industrial Revolution. It is cruel to hold up a definition of Christian vocation that says God has a perfect and fulfilling job for every person. No job is perfect, and some jobs are the opposite of perfectly fulfilling. What does vocation mean for the person who has menial, undignified labor that fails to keep a family above the poverty level?

Other forces have been at work in our society, changing the way we think about vocation. One of those forces is the growth of individualism. Centuries ago, having a choice about the way one would make a living was unthinkable. One simply did what one's family did. Certainly parts of our world still know this kind of family or tribal identity. It it not true of the society in which we live. Our society thrives on individualism, on the emphasis that each person chooses for himself or herself—chooses a mate, a profession, values, a car, and so forth.

That kind of individualism is marvelous in its emphasis on freedom of choice. It does, however, put a certain pressure on the individual that may not be apparent at first glance. In other days and cultures, individuals knew what their station in life was simply by the family and culture into which they were born. No one in such a culture wondered about which school would prepare him for which job. Their calling had been determined for them by their birth. That is less likely to be true in America as we approach a new century. The children of farmers are less likely than ever to be farmers. Suburban professionals work to create unlimited opportunity for their children. Mobility has become the servant of individualism.

A culture of affluence has also changed the way we think about vocation. Material wealth has liberated us from any number of forces which oppress the human spirit. In many cases, though, it has brought with it some more subtle entrapments. Boredom and meaninglessness run high in many affluent communities. The children of very affluent parents feel an incredible pressure to choose a way of making a living that at least preserves the high standard of material wealth that their parents have attained. Such pressure limits freedom and distorts choices.

On the other hand, poverty still limits the choices and opportunities of too many persons in this land and across the world. One of the tests of any understanding of vocation is if it makes sense to the poorest of the poor in the United States or a Third World country. Can we with integrity interpret *calling* to the poor as God's choice of "profession" for them? What meaning does that have to persons who have been so severely limited in opportunity that they will never have the chance at education, training, and opportunity that you and I have had?

As industrialization changed the meaning of work, secularization has also contributed to the need to reconsider the contemporary meaning of vocation. We face the temptation to think of all of life simply in economic terms, devoid of the context of the presence or will of God in our individual and social decisions. The religious life is thought to have relevance only in very limited and very private settings: an hour or so during the week when we attend the church of our choice, and in whatever private thoughts and feelings we have about God. These private thoughts and brief times of religious behavior are not supposed to spill over into the way we think about or order our lives during the rest of the week. That kind of split in our thinking about ourselves leaves us empty and confused or vaguely guilty, because it limits and trivializes the place of faith in the ordering of our lives. A new look at vocation might help us begin to bridge the gap between compartments of our lives that feel unrelated to one another.

## What This Book Is Not

Given the confusion about what vocation means, it is important to mention briefly some things I am not intending to do in a book about Christian vocation. The first thing I am not attempting to do is to define vocation as something that only happens to persons who are ordained ministers making their living doing ministry. Vocation is not something that only preachers and missionaries have, while the rest of God's people are left to choose from among the available ways of life. Such a definition of vocation does harm to clergy and laity alike, and this book does not draw great distinctions between the two.

This is not a book designed only for persons who are trying to decide if they are being called to ministry, although I would hope those persons might find real help here, too. Certainly it has been the church's task since the foundations of the New Testament to call out leaders from among the faithful and discern and recognize gifts. I would hope to both recover and deepen the way we think about that in the modern church. The tasks of discernment are not simply matters of choosing pastors—discernment is what each of us are called to do as we journey in the life of faith. Limiting "vocation" to a simple yes-no question about professional ministry is an unfortunate limitation of what vocation can mean. Clergy and laity both struggle with the meaning of vocation for their lives, and their struggles are more alike than otherwise.

Another popular understanding of vocation is that it has simply to do with choosing a job, so that an entire area called "vocational guidance" has sprung up in the professional world. This is not a book intended to help you choose the job which is just right for you. That kind of counseling can be a helpful part of the work of discernment, but it is not a focus of this book. This book will resist defining vocation simply in terms of work. In defining vocation as not being the same thing as work, this book might make a contribution to putting work in proper perspective. The job one has might be an important part of one's sense of vocation. However, if one's job feels like the totality of Christian vocation, then the stage is set for great disappointment; and the danger of neglecting other dimensions of Christian vocation looms very near.

Some readers of this book may be in a time of changing or choosing jobs or professions. Others may be feeling dissatisfied with the work they now do. I hope this book will be helpful to them, but it is not a how-to book about changing or choosing jobs. It attempts to build some biblical foundations for living Christian vocation in a way that all of life can be seen whole and as a part of the vocation of being children of God.

## What This Book Is

This is a book about the vocation of every person. I want to revive the meaning of Christian vocation for ordinary persons leading ordinary lives. I am claiming from the outset that vocation is more than work. I am claiming from the outset that vocation has something to do with our commitment to a way of life that seeks to follow Jesus.

This book seeks to recover some of the truths that Martin Luther and others began to make plain at the time of the Protestant Reformation. They trumpeted the reading of Scripture, not only in worship, but by common persons in the common tongue. Putting the Scripture in the hands and the language of the people meant that the common person could think, pray, and interpret Scripture and the dictates of conscience for himself or herself. The seeds had been sown by the invention of the printing press, and Luther's translation of the Scripture into German made the foundation of these reforms more sure.

It is not surprising that Luther began to reinterpret what vocation meant for the common person. He began to declare that the monastic life was not the only way to holiness. He claimed that marriage and the common tasks of family and work had the smile of God as Christian vocation and was as noble as being priest or monk. More will be said about Luther's renewal of the vocation of every Christian in the pages to come. It is enough here to mention that the roots of the thinking found in this book find their inspiration from Luther and other Reformers, particularly the Anabaptists who were on the fringe of the Reformation.

## Vocation: A Definition

I have already suggested that much modern misunderstanding exists around what the word *vocation* means. It means job or profession in the modern secular world. I have also said that what I mean by vocation is *not* simply job or profession. The roots of the word suggest something I want to recover. The roots of the word suggest responding to a call, to something deep within. *Profession,* a word that has undergone similar secularization, suggests in its history that one must respond to this inner call by committing to the way that this calling demands.

What vocation means in this book is simply this: the ways in which we seek to align the ordering of our lives with the purposes of God. Vocation has to do with feeling that we are cooperating with God's purposes for the world and for us in the way we are living our lives. The discovery and actual living of vocation are lifelong journeys of deeper understanding of the purposes of God, both for His world and for us, His children. I do not believe that if one is not sure about a college major or has a hard time choosing between jobs that one has missed God's will or has forever forfeited one's Christian vocation.

Vocation is feeling like the story of one's life makes sense under God. Vocation is feeling like one's life story is not so disconnected or random that it has nothing to do with the story of the world as God intends it to be. Vocation is about redeeming even the painful chapters of one's life in the redemptive purposes of God.

I have already suggested that our culture's individualism has served to distort modern understandings of vocation. I want to recover the conviction that vocation is as much about having an identity as part of a community, a group, a family, as it is about some perfect plan for one's life that supposedly falls out of the sky, unrelated to one's history and relational covenants. Vocation is only properly understood when it is lived out in the network of relationships that sustain us and our vocation. We can neither arrive at an understanding of vocation, nor develop the virtue to live it out without a nurturing and sustaining community from which we can draw strength, forgiveness, and understanding.

## Looking for a Sign

Jesus chided those who came to Him demanding a sign, and in His chiding pointed them to the prophets. He might have said, "If you have not heeded the prophets, then why would a new sign make any difference?"

This time in your life may find you at a vocational crossroads. The chapters ahead will speak to the experience of loss that comes with confusion and hurt in a time of crisis. I trust you will find some things that you can use to sort through the pain and find some hope and encouragement. In the meantime, we often wish for some sign, something to make us sure about where we are going or erase doubts about where we have been. What we seek is certainty.

We are tempted to look in the present or near future for a sign—something to make us certain, something to reduce the pain and risk of change. I am sure that the Christian life cannot be lived without risk and pain. I want to suggest that the principal sign for vocation has already been given to those who have committed to the way of discipleship—the sign of baptism.

Many Christians believe that baptism is not something magical in itself—it is a sign of obedience. Our instincts in that emphasis are very good. They recognize several things that we want to preserve, including that salvation is a gift that comes from God, not something transmitted by or in a ritual. They understand that baptism recognizes that the essence of the life of discipleship is a decision to accept that gift and follow the One who has bestowed it.

If we have missed something in our understanding of baptism it is in limiting our understanding of it to a sign of that initial decision to follow Jesus. Baptism is certainly a sign and celebration of our spiritual beginnings, but it is more than that. It is also a sign of our *continuing* to follow in the Way. It is a sign of a new life, one that begins with the decision to accept God's grace. Too many people who put emphasis on conversion have at times equated baptism with conversion and not connected baptism with the promise to follow anew and more deeply every day.

Baptism is much like the wearing of a wedding ring. The giving and receiving of rings that we do in the wedding ceremony are not signs simply that we got married. They are signs that we *are married*. They are signs to the world and to ourselves that we are in a covenant relationship. Being in a covenant relationship means that the covenant requires living out daily and that it needs attention and renewal.

Baptism is a visible sign that we have chosen a vocation and that we have been chosen for a vocation—the vocation of following. The waters of baptism signify an entry into a life that is new and always being made new. We enter the waters that others through the centuries have entered in response to the grace received through Jesus. The vocation we enter is the same as the vocation of untold numbers of believers who have seen in the way of Jesus a way to a full and meaningful life. When we are feeling like we have lost vocation, we often look to the future for some sign of the way to go. We can also look behind us to the waters of baptism, because there is the deepest and surest sign of our vocation.

My experiences in worship in my church in Louisville, Kentucky, helped me to see more deeply the importance of the sign of baptism. The pastor, Dr. Stephen Shoemaker, made the service of baptism one in which the entire congregation participated, not merely as spectators. He invited us, whenever someone was being baptized, not only to pledge our prayerful support to them in the days ahead, but to renew our own baptismal vows and remember our own baptism as a sign of our continuing to walk in the way of discipleship.

Baptism is the ultimate sign of our finding and being found. When vocation feels lost, we can once again return to that most central experience of finding and being found. Hopefully, as we continue our journey, we will continue to have a sense of finding and of being found. There will be times, however, when we feel like we have lost our way, and in those moments we can return in our memory to the covenant into which we entered at baptism.

Whenever we are searching for vocation, it is my assumption that we are searching for the continuing meaning of our baptism. We are seeking to recover, renew, or understand more completely what those vows "to follow" meant. It is one thing to pledge in marriage vows to be present in sickness and health, and quite another to discover how to live that way. The life of maturing in faith is similar. It is one thing to enter the waters of baptism. It is another thing, often frightening, to be formed in the experience of loss, conflict, and failure. The purification that began with our immersion in the waters of baptism continues in the floods that can come with daily living.

I will return to this theme of baptism in the final chapter of the book. If you have never thought of baptism as a sign of vocation, simply let this early mention of it be planted as a thought worth pondering. It is one of the ways I invite you to stimulate your own imagination about what vocation is and about what vocation under God means to you. I will be making other suggestions about what vocation means.

## A Look Ahead

I hope that reading the following chapters deepens your vision of what Christian vocation is and what your vocation as a disciple is and can be. Vocation is not a job, for jobs come and go. Vocation is not some particular place or some particular part of our lives. Vocation is that which helps us hold together the forces in our lives that threaten to pull us apart. Vocation is that which gives unity to the many roles that we inhabit, that we pass through. Vocation is that for which we have been grasped, to use Paul's marvelous idea.

Chapter 2 will speak to the reality of loss, pain, and confusion that you and I may encounter in living out what we feel to be our vocation. Often our exploration of the deeper meanings in our lives come in experiences of our deepest distress. That is the place we begin. Chapter 3 will talk about some important Old Testament themes that are the foundation to a sense of vocation that we feel inside. Chapter 4 will take a look at experiences of grace which mark the way and that may give us moments of special clarity in our searching. Chapter 5 will look at some scenes in the life of Jesus for clues about how the One whom we follow discovered and lived out His vocation. Finally, chapter 6 will offer some encouragement, some suggestions, and some images for helping us renew our vocations as children of God.

Vocation is the living out of a deeply felt passion. All of our passions require renewal, reflection, and attention. My hope is that you may be renewed in hope and understanding about finding and being found in the search for your deepest home.

# 2

# The Pain of Lost Vocation

When do we even stop to think of this thing we have called vocation? In many ways, a sense of vocation is like health. We usually don't give it a thought, except the fleeting word of gratitude or praise when everything is rolling along fine in our world. We give it little thought when we are enjoying its good presence. It is its absence that makes us sit up and take notice. Who gives thought to vocation? Most typically, we are concerned with vocation when we are searching for something we feel we do not have, or for something we have lost. Perhaps you have been there or find yourself there now.

The experience of absence or loss is real and painful. It may have been what led you to pick up this book, or to keep reading after the first few pages. Like other dimensions of the spiritual journey, our searching to find something comes from an awareness that we have lost something or that we need something. Admitting the need and the pain are the first steps toward healing.

Chapter 1 introduced you to several persons, including biblical characters, whose sense of vocation came to a time of painful crisis. The crisis of loss or confusion, that sense of being on the wrong track, can come from any of several directions. In the remainder of this chapter we will look at several of the ways that we experience a crisis in vocation. You may find some echoes of your own story in one or more of these kinds of losses. That in itself may be helpful. It is important to know in the midst of painful crisis that others have felt similar pain. It is also helpful in the midst of any crisis to begin giving the crisis names. We experience power over things to which we can give names. Much of the spiritual life consists of learning to call things by their right names: sin, grace, pride, joy. Calling things by their right names is part of the work of discernment done in prayerful reflection both in solitude and in the caring community of faith.

The other thing being suggested in this chapter is that we can expect some periodic fluctuations, confusion, or even crisis in our sense of vocation, no matter how firm it may have felt at one time, and no matter how firm our faith. The difficulties of life, which include growth and change, demand that we periodically reassess our own sense of direction and purpose in relation to God's purpose. Being creatures who are on the way to holiness and not creatures who have fully attained it, we can expect that reassessment at times to be uncomfortable.

If you are consciously committed to Christian discipleship, then it might be more difficult for you to admit a sense of loss of direction. It might seem that to admit some uncertainty about vocation or the pain of loss might seem to be a sign of weak faith. I find little evidence to support that either psychologically or scripturally. We find in the Scriptures persons who are honest and struggling to follow the leadership of God in their lives. Chapter 5 will turn direct attention to the Jesus of the Gospels and some of the clues we find in the Gospels about vocation. One glimpse of what you will find in that chapter is the Gospels' clear portrayal of Jesus as someone who constantly sought and at times struggled with what it meant for Him to follow the will of God. We must have permission to struggle as a prelude to learning to name correctly the places in which we find ourselves.

Here, then, are some of the normal and "predictable" kinds of crises in vocation that you and I might encounter on the way to perfection.

## Losses from Interruption

If you have lived long enough to be able to read this book, you have learned that life brings interruptions into the clear sailing and smooth seas we have planned for ourselves. Some of those interruptions are welcomed and some are dreaded. They almost always force us to rethink, reevaluate, and re-dream who we are in relation to God's creation and redemptive purposes.

### *Losing a Job*

Chapter 1 stated clearly that vocation and job are not the same thing; nevertheless, the loss of a job is a crisis that can throw everything out of order. It threatens our financial security. If we have been told or we suspect that we have lost our job because our "performance" was not acceptable, then our sense of personal security in our abilities can be threatened as well. Our confidence takes a beating. When we start to question ourselves, our sense of identity and purpose starts to erode.

The loss of a job is particularly difficult if the job was meaningful to us. It may have been the position you had worked for and waited for many years. It may have felt like the job that was right for you. It may have even felt like the job was one God had particularly prepared you for and prepared for you. One of the most painful experiences, tragically repeated too many times, is the experience of a church requesting or forcing one of its ministers to leave. The minister and church often felt the leadership of God in the employment of the minister and in the minister's early work. Now, after time and conflict, the minister is out of a job, and the church is without a minister. The pain is deep and real. Often both minister and church feel betrayed and misunderstood.

Sometimes job losses come from seemingly far away, made by people who have never heard your name, seen your face, or known your work. The company simply changed hands, and the new owners wanted to make changes. You get a politely written notice that you no longer have a job. A new technology comes along that promises to do the job you have been doing well. Suddenly the company for which you work sees a way to make the same product more quickly and at a greater profit. Someone else's technological breakthrough becomes your heartbreak. You didn't lose your job because you weren't doing it well. You lost it because someone designed a technology that promises to replace you, never get sick, and never need vacations.

Someone in the corporate office looked at a balance sheet and decided the budget needed to be cut so that losses could be trimmed or profits enhanced. They told the senior managers to cut 10 percent from the personnel budget. The senior managers told the supervisors to cut the budget by 10 percent. Your supervisor comes to you, genuinely sorry, but following orders from the top. You are out of a job.

Few people can simply take that kind of loss in stride. You explain to yourself that it had nothing to do with you personally. Still, the house payment will come due next month, and you worry where it will come from. You see the plush office of the person who made the decision to "let you go," and the flash of anger comes. A friend tries to be reassuring and says the wrong thing. All of those things fertilize the seeds of fear and self-doubt that sprouted in the middle of the night. "What purpose, oh God? Where did I go wrong? Did I misunderstand, disobey, or somehow deserve this? Is there a future for me that fits both my heart and your purposes?"

Why is it that the loss of job can be so devastating? How is it that losing a job shakes the foundations of our beings so much? A number of things help make some sense of this. One of the most plain is simply the number of hours we spend at a job. If you are employed full time, you probably spend more waking hours traveling to and from your job and working there than you spend at home not sleeping. Even with the coming of overtime laws in this century, many of us spend enormous amounts of time working. We cannot suddenly lose our work as easily as one clips a fingernail or brushes lint off clothes. It is a serious interruption of routine and a loss that causes grief—real grief.

In addition to the sheer number of hours that we spend at work, we invest psychologically and emotionally in our work. Sections which follow address the issues of overinvestment and underinvestment in our work. At this point let it suffice to say that we often draw important feelings about ourselves and our purpose from our ability to work. Even if we are not overinvested in work, we feel the loss of work acutely. Whether we lose the opportunity for work, the capacity for work, or the confidence in our ability, we often feel that loss and that threat very deeply. It is a pain we cannot ignore.

### Loss of Health

John, a young father, went to his doctor after feeling very tired for several weeks. At first, he and his doctor thought it was a case of the flu that had been difficult for him to shake. When it had lingered even longer, John returned and the doctor did some more tests. What he discovered made him call John and ask him to return for a talk. John could tell by the shaken and grave expression on his doctor's face that something was seriously wrong. "John, I don't know of an easy way to tell you this. The blood tests indicate something wrong. We'll need to do some more tests to verify it, but I fear you have leukemia."

John and Sheri were devastated. He had received the promotion he had waited for only months before. Their youngest child was four, and they loved being parents. Both were active in the church and looked forward to rearing their children in the warm glow of faith and community. Now they were faced with a life-threatening illness. John had to face the fact that he might have only months to live. His sense of purpose in working at a job, making a contribution to his community, being a husband and a father, and being active in the community of faith, all were threatened by this disease. What of his firmly felt sense of vocation? What of his firmly felt sense that things were right in his heart and in his world? These suddenly seemed shaky. His world had changed overnight.

Ruth was on the way to a committee meeting at church and never saw the truck that hit her small sedan. When she regained consciousness she was in an intensive care unit. She learned over the next few days and weeks that she was paralyzed, unable to move her arms or legs. While physical therapy would restore some minimal movement, her most heartfelt lament was, "I can't even hold my grandchildren. What use am I now?"

George, retired but active in his community and church, first thought he simply needed a new prescription. His vision just wasn't the same. He had expected some loss of vision in his later years, but secretly he was a little frightened. When he went to his eye doctor, his fears were more than confirmed. He learned that he had an eye disease that would slowly take most of his central vision, leaving him with only peripheral sight. No longer would he be able to drive, read, or even help his wife with the cooking. "I've never been afraid of dying," he was to say to his pastor the next week, "but this seems worse than dying."

For six years I served as chaplain in a cancer unit in a large hospital. I learned to admire and love the people with whom I worked. One of the recurrent themes that I heard from those people who were living and dying with cancer was how they struggled to regain a sense of identity and purpose after their diagnosis. The future seemed uncertain. Many were facing death for the first time. Many others found death not so frightening as the prospect of continued living without the accustomed patterns of work, play, and social interaction. They had built a sense of purpose based on their abilities to contribute to their work, their families, their church, their community. When those things were threatened by a chronic and life-threatening illness, their sense of vocation felt shaky.

When good health is threatened or lost, the ripples spread internally to the deepest parts of our hearts. Our very deepest sense of who we are is tied to the fact that we are embodied creatures. These mortal bodies aren't perfect, and we are promised they will perish; but they are all we know, and we express who we are and who we hope to be through them. When we have expressed our sense of purpose through our bodies, and they begin to fail us for some reason or another, we come to a crisis in our sense of God's purpose for us. Only the loss of bodily functioning begins to show us how tied our sense of purpose is to the doing of our hands, our feet, and our minds.

It is right and good that we experience this world's goodness through our bodies and that we express our sense of calling, purpose, and participation in God's goodness through our bodies. I would not counsel a kind of dualism that has us pretend that our bodies are not important or a self-image that ignores caring for and celebrating our bodies as God's gifts. Neither would I counsel that we can avoid the kind of grief that comes when we lose, through accident or illness, the full functioning of our bodies that we have enjoyed through the years. The question that comes in the midst of that pain is whether we can build a foundation for a sense of vocation that gives us resources to cope with these kinds of losses. Are there biblical resources that we can tap to help us regain a sense of purpose when all that we can see and feel is loss, and the future seems to be bringing more loss with it? I believe those resources are available to us. They can help us through the pain of loss, but they cannot protect us from feeling the pain of loss.

### Losses of Role and Status

The divorce was the last thing that Jenny wanted, and almost the last thing she expected from her husband. As unwanted as it was, it was undeniably real and painful now. She had enjoyed married life and now was facing life as a single parent and as a single person. How would she cope with the children mostly by herself?

Also frightening was the prospect of starting over in the world of dating and searching for companionship. How would she be seen in her church? All of the church socials had been organized around couples, and her social network was almost all married people. Would she be welcomed in her Sunday School class?

Jenny had always dreamed of a happy home and had envisioned her place and purpose in the world as being a mother and a wife. Her dreams were coming apart. She was going to have to go to work and would have to get some help caring for the children. She had never seen any of this as God's purpose for her. She could admit that she had contributed in some ways to the breakdown of the marriage, but she was also angry that Phil had decided to get out. At one level she felt like a moral failure and wondered if she would ever feel different. That raised different questions for her sense of vocation. Now that she experienced the failure of a marriage, could she ever feel again like she was experiencing God's smile at her place in the world?

Phil was experiencing losses in the aftermath of the divorce as well. The dream house had been sold in the property settlement, and he was living in a small apartment without much furniture. He, too, felt like he could not return to the familiar "couples class." In fact he felt uncomfortable in church these days and had not looked very hard for a new church near the apartment. His budget was much tighter after the divorce, and he could not enjoy the same standard of living he had before. He hated to admit it, but he felt like he had lost some status. He was not a respected leader in his church any longer. He was living in the same apartments as college students and newlyweds and did not get the same social invitations he had months earlier. He, too, wondered if he could ever recapture the sense of living and moving in the purposes of God. He was not sure where he fit. He was not sure where he was welcome. Most troubling, he was not sure of God's daily welcome any longer.

Phil and Jenny experienced a divorce, but they were also feeling the uncertainty of roles that had suddenly shifted and the pain of status lost. They were learning that the status of divorced persons is often not the same as the status of married persons in the church. Jenny was going from homemaker to provider and simultaneously dreading the role of "dating." Phil was losing the status of settled and comfortable family man and adjusting to the role of parenting on weekends without help.

All of the losses experienced by these persons—job, health, role, status—came as the result of unwanted interruptions. They came unexpectedly and unbidden as a part of life. They brought grief with them, as well as anger and confusion. Even as these people began to deal with the losses, they found stirring at a deeper level the question of their larger purpose in this world. Each in their own ways had settled into a way of life, a set of patterns, and a cluster of roles that felt right and comfortable and good. And they *were* good. But crisis interrupted their lives, and they had to ask again the question of how they might ever feel like they were resting in God's approval of them and their place in the world. This is one shape of the crisis of lost vocation.

## Losses Induced By the Life Cycle

The losses that came by unwanted interruption were in some sense "normal," in that they came to good people as they walked along life's way. They weren't necessarily the result of a grave moral failure. In another light, they might not be considered normal, in that few of us expect to lose our job, divorce, or suddenly find ourselves diagnosed with a catastrophic illness.

Some things we *do expect* to happen as we travel life's journey. We expect to have children (most of us). We expect for those children to grow up and leave home. We expect that some day we and/or our spouse will retire from work. We expect that we will face death. These are changes that come to us as a result of the normal human life cycle. They can be reasonably expected to occur to anyone who lives out the "three score and ten" that most of us feel we have coming to us. Of course, whether or not such a life span is guaranteed to us is another question. But let us assume the normality of statistics for a moment. Let us assume that it is a reasonable expectation that we will live a normal human life span of seventy or more years.

That normal human life span will bring with it changes. Many of them will be looked forward to and met with great anticipation. However, changes they will be, and often change is hard. Changes bring challenges to our self-perception and our patterns of thinking and doing that we did not imagine.

These normal and expected changes also make us rethink how we understand our vocation under God. They give us the opportunity to examine the way we had thought of our Christian vocation and see how these changes in the life cycle enhance and change the way we understand ourselves cooperating with God's purposes. We are even forced to think of the life cycle itself in relation to God's purposes for us. If the changes of the normal human life cycle are part of God's graceful provision and purposes for us as God's children, how do we incorporate them into our sense of vocation as disciples?

One of the important shifts in Christian thought that came out of the Protestant Reformation was the insight that God's purposes included our roles as family members, community members, and workers. In other words, persons who were committed to celibate, ordained, or cloistered lives were not the only ones who were following the leadership of God in this world—so proclaimed Martin Luther in the sixteenth century. His insight brought dignity and purpose to man of the ordinary tasks and roles of daily living (which is the secret to making common things meaningful in any sphere—performing the practical tasks with dignity and purpose). Chapter 3 will talk at greater length about how our status as creatures of God brings the potential to give meaning to the daily tasks of living.

What is at issue in this chapter is that this normal human life cycle, full of potential for God's purposes, also brings with it some inevitable losses. Some of the changes we can expect from this life are losses, and these losses give us the chance to reassess how we understand God's purposes for us and how we will follow those purposes. In the meantime, the loses are real, and they hurt. Such are the rhythms of spiritual growth.

## Marriage

It may seem odd to mention marriage in a chapter and in a section that is speaking of losses. Marriage is not seen as a loss by any of us as we joyfully enter it. It is the addition of excitement, intimacy, companionship, and dreams dreamed together. It is all of those things, good things. However, those good things, the result of a sacred covenant with another person, mean some losses for the single person.

For the single young person who is marrying for the first time, marriage brings about a change in life-style that incudes some loses. The unrestricted freedom of the single life is no longer a possibility for married persons. Joining one's life with another means some promising to be with and to be responsible to another person. The freedom to go and do as whims and impulses occur to us is a luxury of the past. Some newly married persons are surprised by this undertow of sadness that goes along with the tide of exhilaration.

The commitment which is marriage also means that one's ambitions—social, economic, and professional—also require reconsideration in light of the promises made to be a covenant partner with one's spouse. One of the myths to be found in contemporary professional circles is that unlimited professional ambition is fashionable and requires no sacrifice in terms of one's marriage and family.

## Children

When children come, they are often anticipated with excitement and welcomed with great joy. That is as it should be. Their appearance, however, does represent some losses in other dimensions. The lost freedom of the single life which comes with the covenant of marriage is paralleled in the life of the couple who has their first child. Their freedom as a couple to go and do whenever and wherever they please is lost with the birth of children. Time alone, either by oneself or just the two of you, is not as plentiful or available as it once was. That kind of time now has to be carefully planned.

The economic responsibility for children also restricts the freedom of the married couple, as additional medical care, child care, and educational expenses enter the picture. Housing needs change, and families of four don't fit well in sports cars. Depending on how important these things are or have been (or the dreams that they are just around the corner), these might seem like no loss or no great loss.

Sometimes the experience of conceiving and bearing children entails losses of various kinds for the married couple. One of the painful experiences felt by many couples is the inability to conceive, for whatever reason. This is particularly difficult if the couple has seen themselves as parents and has felt that part of their vocation, individually and as a couple, is to be parents. Certainly some options exist for these couples. Adoption, though often difficult and in itself often painful, can allow some to be parents. The procedures for testing for infertility and for helping couples to conceive are often emotionally and financially difficult.

If couples decide not to adopt or not to have children for whatever reason, they can experience their friends' celebrations of childbirth as painfully isolating. They either feel reminded of their own loss or find that they have less and less in common with their friends who are now preoccupied with their new babies. Not only have they experienced the ongoing sorrow of not being able to have children, they now experience the loss of closeness in their own social circle.

It is not uncommon for couples to feel, in the midst of this ordeal of trying to conceive, as if something is inherently wrong with them. The disappointment, grief, confusion, exhaustion, and isolation can take their toll on persons who have felt a sense of participating in God's purposes by seeking to have and rear children. These persons need the support and care of the community of faith to express, grieve, or redirect their dreams of having their own children as participants in the Kingdom.

Another painful experience for the couple having children comes with children who are born with some disability or special need. The parenting vocation is significantly altered for the couple who has a child that is physically or mentally disabled or impaired. The special care required for the child, financial stress, and uncertainty can sorely test one's sense of God's purposes and provisions. These parents often find that institutions of health care, education, and child care do not have categories or services into which they conveniently fit. Some are able to transform and renew their vocation as parents to include this "special" child. Others find themselves weighed down with the real trials, discouragements, and burdens of disabled children.

Normal children bring their trials to one's sense of vocation as much as the absence of children or disabled children. Children have a way of being who they are, despite our most vigorous efforts to make them who we want them to be. Part of the difficulty and grace of journeying in the vocation of parenting is letting a child be a unique creation of God, entrusted to our care, to be nurtured in the community of faith in such a way that he or she will want to be a disciple. We have to learn from our children that they will insist on being themselves, will be as imperfect as we, and can be sources of grace and forgiveness in our lives. Learning to ask and receive forgiveness from our children is a difficult spiritual lesson for most of us to learn, but one full of grace.

At one level the birth of children represents a loss of control. Certainly my own experience of spiritual growth as a result of having children has contained this theme. But I think I hear it in the other parents whom I know, teach, and counsel. Children will refuse to be completely controlled by us, though it is surely our parental duty to discipline, guide, and nurture them. They will find ways to remind us that we are not fully in control of them. I often say to parents, as I am leading workshops or counseling with them, that it is important to pick some battles that you can lose. We simply don't have to be right every time, win in struggles with our children every time, or be always in perfect control. At some level it is all right to let our children see us as the human and imperfect persons that we are. The deeper threat that children often pose to us is that they remind us, through demonstrating that we don't completely control them, that we are often not completely in control of ourselves, either.

The deeper one loves one's children, the more one becomes aware that it is a fragile and sometimes dangerous world in which we live. The experience of the death of a child is among the most devastating losses persons can experience in the human life cycle. We so extend ourselves into our children that we experience the death of one of our children as a loss of self.

It represents a loss of future, of the transmission of values beyond our own life span. The temptation, if one allows oneself to feel this fragility and threat, is to clutch our children to ourselves in a smothering and overprotective way. The difficult balance to strike in the vocation of parenting is to protect children appropriately with the knowledge that none of us is guaranteed life without threat or loss.

Indeed, children are born to be "lost" to us as parents, as they enter into adulthood and go their own way. The day comes when they leave for college, take a job, leave home, or get married. Their continued growth in the life cycle means that their needs from us as parents will change as they grow. Their leaving, even when celebrated as a sign of their growth and maturity, is felt as a loss by most parents. This child, who began to change our schedules and priorities, in whom we have invested so much of ourselves and our resources, rather gleefully leaves the nest one day. Parents are often left feeling strangely bereft. The parent who has taken seriously the vocation of parenting will likely feel a sense of lostness. How does one redirect the life energies that have been poured into parenting? The loss is real because patterns and energies that have been flowing in one direction for numbers of years now must be redirected. That is not easy.

Sometimes children, as they grow and go their own way, choose values or life-styles which we do not approve. This can be felt as a rejection of who we are as parents and is felt as a painful loss. It is certainly felt as a loss of control, but it can be felt or can even extend into a loss of close or warm relationship. When our children exercise their freedom under God in ways that we don't approve, we often feel our values and our selves rejected. Few things are more painful for a parent. These feelings of loss can lead to a sense of failure, which is felt more acutely if one has felt a sense of God's purposes to be parents. All of us want to be "successful" parents. We are called to be faithful parents. Among the Bible's most poignant stories are stories of persons, heroes of the faith, who felt loss or rejection as parents. The story of David and Absalom is perhaps the most moving. David's terrible pain in the face of Absalom's rebellion is recorded in 2 Samuel. It is clear that David, even when moving to stop Absalom's rebellion, never stopped loving his son. It is also clear that Absalom's rebellion and loss were felt as the deepest pains by David. At the same time, David's "failure" as a parent did not rule out his being used by God. Both things were true. His relationship with Absalom came to a tragic end that was enormously painful, but David was still an important vessel of God's grace in our world.

## Mid-life and Mid-career Losses

The middle years of life bring about a number of changes in one's interior life, one's family, and often one's career. Any one by itself can be disturbing, but taken together, they often make the middle adult years an unsettling time, and a time when one reassesses one's sense of purpose and direction.

The middle years often combine the great changes and stresses of having adolescent children, along with the shifting roles and stresses of having aging parents. Family relationships are shifting at both ends of life, not providing us the luxury of resting on our laurels as either a child or a parent. We feel a higher sense of responsibility for all the generations and feel our resources are taxed and stretched. We are called on to be flexible in these shifting roles. At the same time, it is easy to drift apart from one's spouse, as energies are drained by the demands of parenting, job, and relating to aging parents. Marriage can begin to lose its luster, and the temptation to imagine love and excitement elsewhere can appear strongly during these years.

Personally, the middle years bring the signs of one's own mortality plainly into view. The body does not work as easily as it did in earlier years. It does not bounce back from use or abuse as it once did, and it lets us know more quickly and painfully when we have exceeded the limits of good sense in diet, exercise, or the lack of exercise. One realizes that in the realm of physical accomplishment, the years for "achieving" are past. One trip to a church basketball league will provide plenty of evidence of men who are having trouble coming to grips with these realities.

Career and job often begin to feel different in the middle years. Depending on the job or profession, the middle years often make plain that choices made earlier have indelibly marked one's options for the years ahead. Honest assessments of the number of promotions still available on the current track often come painfully into view during these years. It is not uncommon for men and women to seriously rethink where they are going in their jobs and switch careers. For women, sometimes the career switch is coupled with the children's leaving home and redirecting energies that were directed toward the children. Other men and women admit a long-simmering dissatisfaction with job or career and seek to find new challenge or meaning in a new career. Still others don't like what they see of the opportunities that lie ahead in the chosen path and feel the discouragement of dreams that won't be realized.

The heavy family and financial responsibilities, the signs of finitude and narrowing options, can combine to make the middle years a time of great ferment for one's sense of identity, direction, and purpose. It is not difficult to understand why discouragement and fantasies of escape are sometimes the companions of middle age.

These years can bring with them a chance to reexamine values and commitments made in earlier years. It is not unusual for persons in these years to see their earlier commitments with a new clarity and a new commitment to simplicity. The deeper yearnings, longings, dreams, and feelings of the inner emotional life also demand to be listened to with new energy. These years can be very creative for the spiritual life and one's sense of vocation, but the losses that accompany these years are part of the years of this creative ferment.

### Retirement: Gains and Losses

When retirement approached for George, his friends began to tease him in a good-natured way. "Well, it sure will be nice to sleep all morning and play golf all afternoon, won't it, old boy!" George smiled and laughed and joined in the fun. "Yeah," he said, "I'll think of you guys here sweating it out in the old salt mine every day. Poor working stiffs!" The day of retirement came and friends at the office gave him a fishing rod and a watch with the company emblem on the band. George was proud of his years with the company, but found himself a little sad as he drove home.

Several weeks later, he realized he really did miss the friends at the office with whom he had spent so much time over the years. A few others had retired as well, and they saw each other occasionally. Whenever they did, the conversation turned to old office stories, and the laughter among them seemed a little forced. George tried to make himself sleep late, but he had discarded the alarm clock years before—he always woke up at 5:30. The fishing rod lay in the garage. He had talked about fishing when he retired, but had never taken the time to go. Now it just didn't sound interesting to him. He didn't want to go by himself. Most of his friends were still at the office, and Sheila, his wife, had a full day already. If he tried to get involved with her daily routines, they ended up snapping at each other. She confided to her friends that George was "driving her crazy." "He's irritable, wanders around the house all day getting in my way."

George was able to say to his pastor some weeks later that he just didn't feel useful anymore. When honest with himself, he remembered how good it felt to solve problems at work. He remembered that his colleagues had looked to him as a leader, and he had been trusted and respected in the company. He missed that. He had been amused at the senior citizens' group at church and their bus trips. Now, he kept turning down invitations to join them.

Speaking of church, he had to admit that he was feeling left out there, as well. He had been on the deacon council for most of his adult years. He had rotated off the council now, and he did not know all of the deacons anymore. The church was making some important decisions about budget, building, and programs. Before he knew it, deacons and committees were bringing motions to the church for a vote. He knew his vote counted, but he was accustomed to being in on the action. The new pastor seemed not to know how much of a leader George had been over the years. Some of George's friends were talking about voting against the new building to show that pastor he "can't ram this thing down our throats."

George really had looked forward to retirement. He was tired of the long hours and demands of work. He had to admit that he did not miss those headaches he used to bring home with him at 6:30 p.m. after a long day. He did not miss having trouble going to sleep thinking about what he would have liked to say to the boss. He had seen many of his friends leave the company and new management come in. He really did want to spend time with the grandchildren, and though his children seemed too busy to visit, they did drop the grandchildren by to visit.

Retirement was supposed to be the "golden age" of leisure and enjoyment. George wondered if God had any use for him now. Why did things feel so sour? When George and his pastor talked, George began to admit that as much as he had felt like he was supposed to look forward to and enjoy retirement, he had indeed lost some things important to him in the transition.

George had lost an important social network, even though that network had undergone many changes in recent years. It was not until he retired that he began to realize how much even those earlier changes had hurt. He had also, like persons who lose a job involuntarily, lost the major way he structured his days and used his energy. George had never developed hobbies that claimed some of his interest and energy. In the early years of his life, work had been his passion. Later years had certainly seen some of that excitement and energy fade, but George had never really developed other interests to which he could give himself, his time, and his energy.

George had lost a sense of importance. He could tell that he got in Sheila's way at home. While he knew she loved him, being a nuisance to her contributed further to his feeling he did not have a place. As long as he had been working, he had not really noticed that he felt out of the mainstream at church, too.

All of these losses were normal and in some sense to be expected. Almost everyone who retires feels, along with whatever sense of relief and gladness they anticipate, some sadness at leaving a place, a job, a role, or a circle of colleagues they have known for years. That sadness is to be expected, and is part of the transition. All of these losses made the deeper spiritual question more difficult to avoid. How does someone in George's place find a sense of cooperating with God's purposes in this world? When George gets most honest with his pastor, he says that he simply can't figure out what purpose God has left for him in this world. What is George's vocation now that he has left his profession?

In some ways, George's case makes most clear that vocation and profession can never be identical. We would never say that God has no purpose for people who have lost or left their profession or job. It is the church's task to proclaim and embody the truth that George can have a lively sense of vocation and God does have purposes for him and others like him.

George's case also makes something else clear. It was the experience of *loss* that drove George to admit and begin talking about his shifting sense of purpose. It was the sense of loss that put George on the path of consciously searching for what God intends for him in these days. It was the experience of pain that led George to ask questions that he has assumed he had the answers to for years.

George's sense of loss, like others we have looked at in this section, came from normal and expected changes in the life cycle. These changes started in shifting external events and circumstances. After the external changes came, deeper feelings and questions emerged from the inside. The losses from interruption followed a similar course. Something happened externally to change the course of normal events. These changes were followed by the internal sense of loss, pain, and then questions about the presence and purposes of God.

At other times our sense of loss of vocation can come more directly from the inside.

## The Pain of Overinvestment: Subtle Idolatry

We have said that feelings of sadness, anger, and other elements of grief are natural and predictable reactions to loss. We have been talking about loss in this chapter. In no way will this chapter, or the ones to come, suggest that we can structure our lives on this earth in ways that prevent the possibility of grief. Even the most spiritually mature (perhaps especially the most spiritually mature) among us feel grief in the wake of loss. No one walks this earth without loss.

Sometimes as we comb through our feelings and thoughts in the wake of loss, we begin to examine exactly what we had hoped and invested in the things, relationships, or hopes that now feel lost to us. What we sometimes discover is that we invested energies in tasks, roles, or dreams that were never intended to carry all that emotional load. We find that we overinvested in something, so that the disappointment and loss we now feel was inevitable. That kind of overinvestment can happen in several ways. One of the ways it frequently happens, especially to men, is through overinvesting in work. (For an excellent treatment of men's over investment in work see James Dittes' *When Work Goes Sour*.)[1]

## Overinvestment in Work

Men are sometimes taught, directly or indirectly, that a career is worthy of any investment of energy. We live in a culture that sometimes holds up for highest praise men who have given all of their energy to their work. The Bible speaks of work as a good thing, but it certainly does not speak of work as the chief purpose of humankind, and the Bible counsels regular rest from work. If you give work lots of energy and find your work fulfilling and meaningful, then do not interpret these lines as criticism of you. These lines are only offered for those who have felt, or are beginning to feel, some disenchantment with work and all it once held or promised.

What some find, both men and women, is a growing disenchantment with their work or work situation. They find a seed of bitterness growing inside that begins to affect their entire work situation. Perhaps it started by feeling overlooked or misunderstood in the work setting. You have worked especially hard on this project, and it gets filed in the boss's office, never to be mentioned again. Maybe you make insightful suggestions for what ought to be done in the next year, and someone else has the boss's ear. Your suggestions fall on deaf ears. Someone else gets the promotion that you felt you were really in line to get. The bitterness grows.

Perceived failure is not the only source of disappointment or bitterness in work. At times the hoped-for promotion does not bring the hoped-for happiness. While the raise makes possible some rise in standard of living and social status, it simply does not bring the internal sense of fulfillment for which we have longed. The success of one's business brings the expectation of expansion and growth, so you expand and grow. As the business grows, along with the signs of success, so do the demands of the business. The simple joys of the business or craft have been lost in the drive to expand in the wake of success. One wonders where the joy went.

Sometimes the disappointment of work can come in comparison to other disappointments in one's life. The hardworking manager simply can't seem to "connect" with his teenage son. The harder he tries to schedule time or plan an outing with him, the farther his son seems to retreat. He "works" at being a parent the same way he works at troubleshooting on the job: let's define the problem and take immediate remedial action. As well-intentioned as this strategy is, it often just won't translate. Our children don't seem to respond to our analysis and quick-action approach to "problems."

In our culture men in particular are taught to give work the energy that might in other contexts be seen as the energy of a major love. Occasionally one hears the wife of a hard-driving worker say "he is married to his work." The phrase "workaholic" was coined by Wayne Oates to describe a relationship to work in which one could not "not work." Many of us know the grip of work addiction.

We men in particular tend to make lovers out of work. Some of us discover that work as a lover simply can't sustain the excitement, the promise, and the passion that we have given it. We feel the grief of unrequited love. We have given work our whole heart, only to discover that it has nothing comparable to give us back. That is a painful realization, but sometimes is the beginning of wisdom. We can then begin to give work its proper due, but quit looking to it to fill all of our deeper love needs. We must begin to direct our passion in ways that passion was meant to be directed—toward human and divine relationships. For those of us brought up on work, that is not an easy adjustment to make. Like other losses we have been discussing, we must begin by allowing and feeling the grief of our overinvestment. Work can be a demanding lover, but for many never delivers the deep fulfillment that it seemed to promise.

The man who has the mid-career heart attack is another who is in a place to reevaluate the place and meaning of work. Some research has poined to relentless styles of work without relaxation as one of the contributors to heart disease. Many of us trapped in that style of working and relating to the world need that kind of health crisis to get our attention and lead us to reexamine how we are spending our energies and passions.

## Overinvesting in Roles

A similar trap has seemed particularly adept at trapping women who love being parents. Like work, the Bible lauds parenting and the good thing it is. Like work, however, the Bible tends to define the wholeness of being human in more than a single role. Women who know nothing other than being a mother sometimes cannot see the train coming: the train that comes and takes their children away to lives of their own, leaving the mother bereft of meaning and purpose.

No evil exists in enjoying and investing in the task and role of parenting. No suspicion should surround one who thoroughly enjoys guiding, nurturing, and relating to their children. Would that more parents could see the vocation of parenting as part of their calling in the kingdom and invest time and energy in learning to be better parents. What I am talking about is not the person who recognizes values and enjoys the trials and joys of parenthood. What I am speaking of is the person who only knows himself or herself as father or mother. What constitutes overinvestment is the man or woman who knows no self-worth other than their role as parent.

Whereas for many, particularly men in our culture, the spiritual temptation is to treat work as a lover. Another temptation, particularly for women, is to begin to see parenting as one's only true purpose. When children begin to make noises about leaving, the mother or father who has no sense of self apart from their children feels threatened.

Persons overinvest in parenting roles for a variety of reasons. For some, the nurturing of their children is a way of providing what they experienced too little of themselves—a warm and loving parent who is attentive to their needs. Some of us have found our children awakening in us an emotional life we never found full permission to express before our children came along. That is good, right, and part of God's grace in our lives; but we err if we attach that lesson too literally to the children who awakened it in us. We err if we do not learn to make that lesson our own, rather than think it belongs only to the part of us that is a parent.

When one overinvests in being a parent, children get the message that somehow the parent's well-being is wrapped up in the child's remaining a child. Children receive the message that their being dependent on parents means so much that they cannot learn independence without threatening their self-esteem. Certainly this is not the message that we want or need to give to our children. As much as providing for and nurturing our children may have meant to us, we need to be able to celebrate their launching from us and seeking God's destiny for them in this world.

As much as parenting may be a part of God's calling for us

in this world, our role as active parents is not one that lasts a lifetime. Our posture of caring and availability in relationship to our children may last as long as we live, but it will only be meaningful if we reshape our relationship to our children when they become adults. Moreover, if we attach our sense of God's purpose for us exclusively to our nurturing dependent children, we are sure to feel empty when our blossoming off-spring announce (in one way or another) that they no longer need us as they once did.

And the good news that parents need to know is that God's purpose for them is not done when they have finished rearing their children. From the feelings of loss that most parents feel when their children launch out on their own, the seeds of a renewed and deepening sense of God's calling and purpose can take root and spring. The feelings of loss are inevitable and normal. They are more disabling for the parent who has attached all of his or her meaning and purpose to the role of parent. The end of one chapter can, though, signal the beginning of another.

Some of the biblical accounts of parents who felt a sense of God's calling to be parents give us some flavor of this tension. The words of Simeon to Mary in Luke 2:35 are often left out of our reading of the Christmas story: "and a sword will pierce through your own soul also." At other points in the Gospels' accounts of Jesus' life, death, and resurrection, we see the writers giving some account of Mary's internal and spiritual struggle to understand the events around her. Simeon gave her a prophecy that let her know that in order for Jesus to fulfill His vocation, Mary would feel the pains of that fulfill-ment in her own heart. So it is in some ways for all of us who are parents. Simeon comes to us and warns us that God has purposes for our children that are bigger than our dreams and go beyond our needs to be needed. Mary could become the model of faith that she became only as she could see Jesus as someone God was calling to His own destiny.

## Underinvestment: Chronic Loss

As we have seen, persons who know themselves as only a job title or as only a parent find themselves lost when the job goes sour or when parenting roles change. As painful as those losses are, there is another kind of pain which springs from making no commitments. As a dogged attachment to one aspect of life or one role in life can make vocation more tenuous, so can the inability to give oneself to anything or anyone. It is less the acute pain of sudden loss and more a constant ache from never giving oneself. It is the pain of one who has always been life's spectator, never a willing participant.

The persons who underinvest may suffer from an inability to trust, perhaps in part, because of major deprivation in their early years. They struggle through their adolescent and early adult years without ever finding a framework of faith that helps them interpret their world. They do not form or give themselves to intimate relationships. They have never been sure of themselves as selves and fear being swallowed in relationship. They have had difficulty choosing values and so change them like clothes that change with each fashion season.

It is not only the person who has had tragic or traumatic beginnings who may struggle with commitment. Life continually calls us to choose and to make commitments, and the temptation is ever present to refuse that choice and hold all options open by not choosing. The verbal image that I have chosen throughout this section is the image of *investing*. I have struggled with it, because it evokes pictures of Wall Street and social pressures that are calculated to think of all things in terms of their potential for profit. Even with these limits, I choose to keep the image of investment because I believe much of the call to discipleship involves the call to *spend* ourselves in the cause of the kingdom of God. Persons who cannot invest in life refuse to spend themselves for anything. It may not be the hoarding of material things that is their besetting sin, but rather the hoarding of personal energies, for fear of losing some other chance.

The manifestations of this kind of underinvestment are seen in numbers of ways. The wisdom of the ancient marriage vows recognized the folly of entering into the covenant with mental reservations or with anything less than a commitment to give oneself to the other. The person who enters the marriage covenant with this kind of reservation makes more possible the failure of the marriage as the winds of change and conflict blow. The New Testament witness clearly uses human marriage as one of the principal metaphors for describing the relationship of Christ and the church. The metaphor of marriage is to be a parable of the meaning of covenant.

As mistaken as it may be for women to overinvest in their roles as mothers so that they know no other self, it is far too common for fathers to be uninvolved at all with their children. Fatherhood surely can mean more than physical provision, as important as that may be. Many of us males were not given role models of how to interact with children and nurture infants, toddlers, and preschoolers. Many men feel lost trying to relate to their young children and perhaps even more lost trying to help them negotiate the storms of adolescence. The church can take the lead in encouraging and instructing fathers in the ways of parenting. Parenting certainly has its trials and bad days, but men who presume they are missing only the dirty work of diapers and feedings may also be missing the joy of relating meaningfully to small people who have a lot to give. One of the deepening parts of vocation in my own life has been discovering the sense of calling to be a nurturing presence in my children's lives. That commitment means some other demands in my life have to know limits, but it is a commitment in which I have found myself growing personally and spiritually.

Others who struggle with commitment may fear abandonment, rejection, or failure. If abandonment or rejection have been painful patterns of their lives, they may be protecting themselves both from old pain and from pain they fear lies ahead if they risk "spending themselves." The church can reach out to these persons and help them learn to give of themselves in contexts where abandonment will not be the repetitive end. Vocation requires a willingness to spend oneself for the kingdom, and one who refuses to spend any of oneself will struggle, not so much with a loss of a particular vocation, but with the aching void of having never known any sense of purpose.

If a sense of vocation involves, among other things, the "spending of oneself" in the cause of the kingdom of God, then the wisdom of discerning what things are worth spending oneself for is necessary. We have spoken of the pain that follows from investing all of oneself in roles or endeavors that are not worthy or capable of containing that much passion. We have spoken of the pain that comes from not giving oneself to anything. Clearly the tension between these two painful extremes is the goal. Seeking that goal takes prayerful discernment, the wisdom that comes from making mistakes, and the wisdom of the community of faith.

## Grief: The Common Thread

This chapter has been about loss. The sense of being lost in terms of one's direction under God can begin at any time in one's journey, and as we have seen, can take many shapes. If there is a common thread to the losses that we have narrated in the previous pages, it is not that they occurred to evil people who were not trying as best they could. No, the common thread in the losses above is that they hurt—they were the occasions of grief in the lives of the good people who found themselves searching for direction.

Admitting the pain of loss and grief is the starting point for reconstructing one's sense of vocation under God. Remember, this is not a book about the calling that some persons may feel to be "full-time ministers" or professional clergy. This is not a book about feeling a special calling to a specific job at age twelve and then never doubting or looking back. If you know persons who have had that experience, celebrate with them. But do not think that if your experience is different you have missed God's will or purpose for your life. On the contrary, the good and hopeful news is that many persons begin to explore more deeply, listen more carefully, and discover more joyfully a sense of God's smile and purpose after experiences of intense loss.

Denying or minimizing the felt loss does not help us discover a sense of purpose any more quickly. It may delay our rediscovering a sense of direction by the acts of self-deception and the forcing of our grief underground. If you have experienced some loss of vocation, then do not compound your pain by denying it. While you need not speak of your grief to all, at last speak it to yourself and trust some other person with it. Let the grief be the beginning point for a new openness of spirit. Like all grief, it will not go away overnight. It will come like waves that seem to have little rhyme or reason. But gradually, with care, the waves will be less forceful.

Losses in this life are inevitable. Often these losses either force us or allow us to examine once again how we understand our place in God's kingdom and in this world and what one has to do with the other. If the pain of loss is your point of entry into a deeper exploration of Christian vocation, take heart. And read on.

### Notes

1. James Dittes, *When Work Goes Sour* (Philadelphia: Westminster, 1987).

# 3

_____

# Creation and Covenant

"Look to the rock from which you were hewn, and to the quarry from which you were digged" (Isa. 51:1).

Life crises can shake us to the core so that we wonder how we can align ourselves again with God's purposes. I suggested in the last chapter that this kind of personal and faith crisis can be a normal and deepening event on the road of discipleship. I also suggested that the biblical witness provides us with some resources that are reliable balms in times of pain. In this chapter, we will begin looking at some of the biblical stories from which we draw identity. It is my conviction that in returning afresh to these central biblical images we can find some guidance for forging a lively sense of purpose.

Biblical truths have a life that is rich and textured. The stories we learned as children take on new depth when we approach them with the pain and questions of adulthood. As we are considering the issue of vocation, we can take it to these powerful texts to see what light they can bring into our lives. In particular, two of the central images of the Old Testament, creation and covenant, provide trustworthy material for the construction of a sense of vocation.

## A Question of Identity

Before we turn to the biblical images themselves, let us look again at the question of vocation. In a culture that is preoccupied with profession, role, and status, we are tempted to come at the issue of vocation the question: "What am I to do?" Now that is not an inappropriate question when one has lost a job or is in the midst of a painful personal crisis that leaves one feeling helpless and bereft. I want to suggest, however, that the question of "What am I to do?" is itself built on several other questions, deeper and more profound.

"What am I supposed to do?" If we leave the question of vocation at that level, we have missed the richer and more nourishing dimensions of vocation that I believe are available to us. The power of redemption under God through Jesus is not simply the assignment of a task. The tasks of our lives spring from our understandings of who we are. "What am I to do?" rests on the deeper question of "Who am I?"

For generations parents have been sending their children off to school, job, or new city with the admonition, "Remember who you are." At that moment, no parent can give instructions to cover all of the new and challenging situations in which their offspring may find themselves. What a parent must trust (or in the absence of trust, hope) is that this emerging young adult will be guided by an abiding sense of who they are. We hope that an internal set of values has shaped their character and identity in such a way that they will be equipped to make good decisions in difficult situations. Parenting is not about instructing in all of the right decisions. Parenting is about shaping identity and character so that decisions flow naturally from them.

In the same way, the questions of vocation are shallowly conceived if we think of them simply as decisions about what we are to do. Questions of vocation are most profoundly about who we are—about character and identity. In times of crisis, it is often helpful to return to a sense of who we are. One of the threats that we feel in the midst of crisis is some anxiety about who we are, especially if we have lost a role or job from which we have drawn an important sense of identity.

One of the roads to healing is to return to a sense of our deepest identity. In short, what does it mean to be children of God? Are there sources of nourishment, guidance, and hope in that most basic description of who we are? The prophet Isaiah said to Israel: "Look to the rock from which you were hewn, and to the quarry from which you were digged" (Isa. 51:1). Valuable resources are to be found in that quarry, which give a rooted sense of identity. Some are trustworthy guides for our character and reminders, even in the midst of crisis, about "who we are."

## The Identity of Being a Creature

Let us trust that some exploration of who we are will give us some clues about what we are to do. Can we look again at the earliest Bible stories we ever learned, bringing to them the pain and questions of adulthood? In the midst of the pain of uncertain feelings about vocation, we can return to the truths of our identity trumpeted in the opening chapters of Genesis. We are creatures of God. How does that help?

One of the most important things that the creation account suggests, it seems to me, is we find our chief identity in our origins as children of God. Genesis is clear that God created human beings for relationship and companionship with the divine and as stewards of God's creation. We often skip that beginning point when we reflect on vocation. Our chief purpose is to be in relationship with God.

### *Being and Relationship*

It is easy to skip over a sentence like the last one of the preceding paragraph. Here it is again: Our chief purpose is to be in relationship with God. It is like a lot of our "churchy" sentences in that we have learned to nod our head in approval to it because it sounds good and we want to be good. We can, in nodding our head, fail to hear the radical power contained in it. Two words in that sentence are key and challenge our modern emphases on job, profession, and role. They are the words *be* and *relationship*.

Our most basic vocation finds its foundation in the fact that we were *made*, we *are*, and we are to *be*. The foundation for vocation lies in the action of God in making, prior to any action or achievement on our parts. That kind of definition of vocation flies in the face of contemporary overinvestment in titles, jobs, positions of status, power, and authority. If purpose is a function of identity, then identity for disciples is built in the assurance that we are God's. We have purpose in that we *are*, and we exist because God made us.

The second key word in that radical sentence is *relationship*. Identity has something to do with relationship. Again, building identity in relationship with God corrects our tendency to build a sense of purpose based on titles and tasks.

Let me put that in personal terms. When asked who I am, I hopefully respond with my name, Mark. My anxious and inadequate ego seeks to add a comma and some titles or roles after my name. "I am Mark, minister, counselor, and author." Each of those is an expression of my vocation, hope-fully, but Genesis reminds me that my primary identity is as child of God. It is possible that any of those roles can obscure both the name and the identity as child of God. It is possible that I can from the needs of my own fragile ego get the order wrong. I can build my self-esteem and my sense of purpose on the roles of minister, or counselor, or author. If, then, I lose one of those, my sense of purpose can be badly shaken. I can lose sight of the fact that my identity is most deeply one of a person with a name, created by God and made for relation-ship with God.

How can we translate that into something that is more than an intellectual affirmation? How can it be for us something that brings some measure of quiet to an anxious heart? First, I think we must confess that resting our identity on being and relationship can add to our anxiety. Many of us have grown comfortable resting our sense of self and purpose on our ti-tles, roles, social, and professional status. We enjoy the rec-ognition we receive, and we are more able to hide the places in our inner self where we feel inadequate, afraid, or lonely. Thinking about resting our sense of identity elsewhere threat-ens the ego gratification we receive from the titles and honors we collect.

Resting my sense of purpose on a relationship certainly makes me nervous. I tend to be more comfortable doing something than being in a relationship. What if I have to build my sense of purpose on a relationship? Now I am doubly threatened. I feel the threat of my secure titles taken away from me, and I feel stripped of what I know well—doing my way through life.

Resting our sense of identity on our being in relationship with God leaves us exactly where God went in pursuit of

Adam and Eve. We are prone to hide, because we feel exposed and ashamed. God seeks most simply to walk with us in the garden in the cool of the day, and we are hiding. We are hiding because we have sought to "be like gods." We have reached after immortality and omnipotence, and we bear in our souls the guilty knowledge that we have lost our innocence.

The guilty knowledge that we have lost our innocence causes us to resist the good news that comes from Genesis. The good news comes in seeing again the *blessing* that is present in creation. The refrain that echoes throughout the first chapter is God's blessing upon creation—that we were created is *good*. Certainly we have continued the obscuring of that goodness and blessing as did Adam and Eve. We seek to receive the blessing through achievement. We fail to admit to ourselves that we secretly seek to turn the blessing into reward. When we receive reward, the deep hunger for blessing persists.

The good news comes in letting the blessing conferred upon us in Genesis become one of the building blocks of our sense of identity and purpose. One of the catechisms that has been influential on Christian theology asks the question: What is the chief purpose of human beings? The answer that this ancient profession of faith provides is: "to love God and enjoy Him forever." How many of us, when asked about our sense of vocation, our sense of calling, use the verbs *love* and *enjoy* somewhere in the first couple of sentences? Usually, with stern faces impressed by our own importance and indispensable place in God's work, we use verbs that connote all that we are doing for God. God has called us to learn to love and enjoy being in relationship with Him. That is task enough for a lifetime.

We do not often think that we need to learn how to "love God and enjoy Him forever." With our emphasis on salvation, we tend to get lulled into thinking that in accepting God's salvation through Jesus we have made a response of accepting God's love. We may tend to think that in accepting that gracious gift, we have learned all we need to know about loving God. The truth is we have only started, just as in declaring our love to our spouse in saying "I do." We have only begun the journey of love. Loving another deeply is a lifetime endeavor that is made more possible by our continuing to be transformed. It is gift as much or more than it is endeavor, because we must continue to be transformed in order to learn of love.

Our vocation is to love and be loved. It is that simple. It is that hard. We are clumsy in love. We are possessive in love. We are afraid to be loved, for we would rather be admired. Our deeper yearnings are for love, but it makes us too vulnerable.

Our vocation is to "enjoy God forever." What in the world does that mean? Is that vocation enough? Our Puritan heritage makes that have a suspicious ring in our ears. If it sounds curious to you, you are not alone. It is a radical thought, and disquieting to most of us. Somewhere inside of us a voice suggests that this is a notion that smacks of laziness and of a lack of seriousness and devotion to the work of God—not at all. Instead, it suggests that our working should rightly spring from our deepening experience of loving, being loved, and "enjoying God."

### Hiding: A Hard Habit to Break
Genesis teaches us that enjoying God does not come natu-

rally to us who live on this side of the Fall, even if it originally came naturally to Adam. When we accept a vocation as children of God we accept the beginning of transformation that begins with accepting God's salvation through Jesus. But our transformation is not complete when we accept that salvation. Genesis not only teaches us about the original blessing that came in creation, it teaches us that we are not naturally inclined to cooperate with that blessing. We resist it. Yes, we even resist the continuing transformation of salvation, much as we resisted the original transformation of accepting God's salvation. We still resist standing naked before God. Our hearts are full of drawers filled with fig leaves we use to cover ourselves.

Having accepted the justification of faith through grace, we are resistant to the sanctification that is our continuing vocation. We are resistant to the continuing work of the Spirit in our lives. The answer to our resistance does not come from gritting our teeth and working harder. Sometimes our working harder has only given us a false and hollow sense of vocation built on our own accomplishments. We can hide in working hard, much as we can hide by doing nothing. For those of us prone to hiding by working, less than that sounds like doing nothing. "Enjoying God" indeed sounds strange to our ears. It is a challenge to let our work arise from a different place within ourselves, that place of resting in God's creation of us.

## A Sense of Belonging

I have two small children. With the birth of each we have participated in services of dedication. These services are times when we renew our vocation as parents to bring our children up in the warm glory of the faith. We dedicate ourselves to do what is best by them. In these services the congregation also joins us in our dedication. They pledge themselves to love and cherish our children. This service reminds me how frightening and impossible is the task of rearing children. I take great hope and encouragement from the sight and support of my congregation pledging to support me and my children.

In the churches we have been privileged to be members of, the congregation's support of my parenting has been more than a ceremony of dedication. People have reached out to love my children, include them, celebrate them, and nurture them. One of the growing joys of my life is the sense of *belonging* that my oldest daughter experiences in the fellowship of the church. People know her name. She knows them and their smiles. She flourishes in the light of their love.

When our second daughter was born, we were concerned about the reaction of our oldest to this "intruder" in her world. To be sure, there have been some difficult moments. But we have also witnessed some graced moments. One night at church someone who knows the oldest came up to admire the new baby. With great sensitivity, she spoke to Anna, the oldest, with warmth and affection. She listened attentively to her three-year-old concerns. When time came for Anna, her mother, and her new little sister to leave, Anna asked this woman: "Would you like to carry me to my car?" Anna was letting another carry her, and the profound symbolism of that was not lost to her mother and me. Much of the transition of going from only child to oldest child has been made easier by the extended, caring family of West Hills Baptist Church. She knows she belongs, and she thrives in the care of that family.

Those experiences of being "carried" by the community of faith will make it easier for her to know that being created by God means that she "belongs" in this world. Without quoting Genesis, this community of faith is living out its message in a way that my daughter can understand. Those of us who are adults need a sense of belonging, too. Hopefully the community of faith provides that in concrete ways for us as well.

The message of the creation account is that being made in the image of God means that we have a place. Yes, we have a home in heaven, as our hymns and our Scriptures proclaim. Yet the message of the creation account reminds us that we also have a place here. This earth, created by God, is home for God's people. We belong. You belong. As we shall see in the exploration of the image of covenant, the theme of being pilgrims stands in creative tension with the theme of home and belonging. Our sense of belonging is not limited to one piece of ground, just as it is not limited to one role, job, or time. We belong because God has made us and has made this earth.

One of the things that makes my daughter feel a sense of belonging within our congregation is that people know her name. How comforting it is to us when people know us by name. How we long for that. The message of creation reminds us that the God who made us knows our name. The God who made us knows who we are. The very fact of our creation means that our name is known by the One who made us.

### Out of Nothing?

As we are exploring the creation account for foundations for identity and vocation, we hear the central message that *God made us.* I want to suggest that there is a source of com-

fort in realizing and accepting that. Yet, we must also admit
that having been made also presents to us a threat. Our culture
celebrates persons we declare as "self-made." Most of us
long for those kinds of accolades and that kind of praise. Most
of us strive to be "self-made." When we strive after that, we
can obscure the message that our existence is a gift from the
Creator, not some achievement we have carved out of stone
with our own hands. Our task is to be stewards of the gift of
creation, always recognizing the Source of that creation.

The opening lines of Genesis describe that the earth was
without form; it was void of order. It was chaos. Later theologians of the church declared that these lines taught the doctrine of *creation ex nihilo,* creation out of nothing. That
doctrine was important to separate the Jewish-Christian creation story from competing accounts of the origins of the
world and of humankind.

Of what consequence is that doctrine to a discussion of vocation? Put most simply, I think that most of us resist the
knowledge that we are made "out of nothing." Many of us
secretly believe that God is pretty lucky to have us on His
team. We are hesitant to feel that radically dependent on
someone other than ourselves. We hesitate to acknowledge
that we are made "out of nothing," because we fear the threat
of nothingness. If we acknowledge that Another is the source
of our being, then we might also have to admit that we are not
completely in charge of our destiny as well. That is a bitter
pill for most of us to swallow.

When we acknowledge that we are not completely in
charge of our lives, we feel the threat of being "out of control." The deeper spiritual truth is that we are always, ultimately, out of control We have choice and responsibility, but

Genesis teaches us that Another is responsible for the origins and the destiny of this world.

Surrendering to that One, in a continuing and deepening way, in addition to being frightening, is, of course, the heart of good news. It is the deepest source of our identity and our vocation.

## Yes and No in Creation

Some other dimensions of the creation story deserve our attention in discussing vocation. God gave clear instructions to Adam and Eve as He placed them in the garden. Some things they were to do, and they were forbidden from eating of the one tree. Being creatures of God meant that they enjoyed God's blessing. It meant that they received the gift of the image of God in their own being. And it also meant that they were to resist evil. Saying yes to the vocation of being children of God implies that we say yes to the gifts of creation and that we say no to evil. A lively sense of vocation will include the command to do good and to resist evil.

Resisting evil in the journey of vocation is not a simple task. On one level it means that certain roles, tasks, or jobs deemed acceptable by society may not be acceptable to the Christian disciple. Some ways of making one's living may involve one in the doing of evil. Some ways of making one's living may involve one in destroying God's creation in violation of the primary vocation of tending God's world. One of the tasks of the contemporary church is to engage in serious moral reflection about jobs, roles, and ways of carrying them out that the church deems in violation of the call to be God's people.

Recall, of course, that we are defining the issue of vocation as larger and deeper than the question of what job one is to take, what profession one engages in, or what role one assumes. We are defining vocation as most fundamentally a question of who one is called to be and what kind of character is required by the calling and gifts of discipleship. The forbidden fruit of the journey of vocation is the fruit which, if eaten, will subtly change one's central identity as a child of God and a follower of Jesus. The fruit of vocation that we must resist eating include some contemporary measures of "success," which come at the high price of sacrificing the calling to love God and serve one's neighbor.

One of the pressures on contemporary youth in suburban cultures is to maintain the affluence level of their peers, or even their parents. Look at the kind of pressure that puts on them as they come to a time to choose a way to make a living. Automatically, one of the chief criteria for their choosing becomes what level of affluence this particular job will bring them. They may have a secret longing or feel a deep calling to spend themselves in some pursuit which is not financially lucrative.

Some denominations have come a long way up the socio-economic ladder from their roots. They must reflect on the ways in which that economic success may now put pressures on them and their children that obscure their ability to hear the deeper callings of discipleship. Children are masters at discerning what we are really saying with our lives. They can tell when out deepest drive is to be "successful" in the terms of the world. When being successful becomes our most cherished value, our children see and learn to imitate.

One of the clear messages we need to give to ourselves and to our children is to differentiate between success as portrayed by acquisition and status and success as defined by the shaping of character and growth in virtue. What we and our children must learn to say no to in vocational searching are visions of success which conflict with the biblical vision of the purposes for which we were created. Vocational expressions which hinder our ability to "love God and enjoy Him forever" are the forbidden fruit. The way we remain clear about that is by faithful attention to the deeper vision of why God has created us.

The image of walking in the garden with God is among the most compelling dimensions of the Genesis account. It is the picture of loving God and enjoying God's presence. It is the image of humankind before the Fall. It was upon hearing God walking in the garden in the cool of the evening that Adam and Eve tried to hide. They hid because they knew of their participation in evil, which separated them from the kind of close relationship symbolized in walking together in the cool of the evening.

The prohibitions on vocation that spring from this account have to do with those things that have the ability to separate us from communion with God. It also tells us that we are separated from that kind of communion with the Creator. The drama of redemption through Jesus is the beginning of a journey that will finally restore us to that kind of communion. We are forgiven for the guilt of that separation, but we must still learn how to have that kind of communion. The Genesis account reminds us that that kind of communion is what we were created for and is the source of our deepest longings.

The vocation of Christian discipleship is a way back to that kind of communion and a deep vision of restored harmony between God, humankind, and this world. What we are called to say yes to is participation in that drama of reconciliation, both in our hearts and in our world. We say yes to ways of life that allow us to participate in the growth of the kingdom in our midst.

Saying yes to participation in the kingdom and no to the evil which seeks to block the kingdom are matters that have both internal and external dimensions. The principalities and powers that battle for our loyalty wage battles in our hearts and the social structures which comprise our world. The community of faith helps us to guard our hearts and to participate in the growth of the kingdom on this earth. Sometimes we must say no in the inner places in our hearts, and sometimes we must say no to social structures that make us less than we were created to be.

Saying yes daily to God's purposes for us is at the heart of vocation. Even when crisis surrounds us, we can return to the resources of these great themes of the creation account. We can be assured that we are known by the One who made us. We can know that our having been created implies that we belong. We can remember that we were created for relationship and for celebrative stewardship of the gifts of the earth.

## The Identity of Being Covenant Partners

The Scripture passage which begins this chapter is from Isaiah 51. The first verse of that chapter exhorts Israel (and us) to look to the rock from which we were hewn. We have returned to that story of creation and its foundational meaning for constructing a solid sense of vocation. The second verse lays another foundation stone on which we can build identity, and remember that identity is at the heart of vocation. Here is verse 2: "Look to Abraham your father and to Sara who bore you; for when he was but one I called him, and I blessed him and made him many." This verse reminds us of the origins of another major biblical theme—covenant.

The calling of Abraham begins in crisis with which we can identify and which some of the persons we have seen in the first two chapters have known from the inside. Abraham sets off, not as a youngster just out of college, but as a grown man with a family, for a place he doesn't know. He only knows that he has heard a calling to follow. "Go . . . to the land that I will show you" (Gen. 12:1). Abraham followed the God who called him, and God made a covenant with him and with his descendants—the people of Israel.

The theme of covenant runs throughout the rest of the Old Testament and finds its fulfillment in the person of Jesus. The grand theme of covenant is another trustworthy part of the foundation that has been laid for us in constructing or reconstructing a biblical understanding of vocation that can carry us through life's trials.

As we know, Abraham took the risk and set off on the journey to which God was calling him. God was faithful in His promise to Abraham, and the nation of Israel was born. The drama of the Old Testament follows the trials of this tiny nation as it struggled to understand and live out the meaning of the covenant to which God continually called it. The covenant was built on the law, renewed and energized in the prophets, and was for the purposes of continuing to bring God's redemption to the world God had created and the people God had created.

One of the benchmarks of that drama of covenant on the way to salvation is found in the Shema—those words in Deu-

teronomy 6 which became for Israel the highest confession of
faith:

> Hear, O Israel, the Lord our God is one Lord; and you shall
> love the Lord your God with all your heart, and with all your
> soul, and with all your might. And these which I command
> you this day shall be upon your heart; and you shall teach
> them diligently to your children, and shall talk of them when
> you sit in your house, and when you walk by the way, and
> when you lie down, and when you rise. And you shall bind
> them as a sign upon your hand, and they shall be as frontlets
> between your eyes. And you shall write them on the door-
> posts of your house and on your gates (vv. 4-9).

It was in the tradition of this covenant that Jesus understood
His own calling and ministry. When the first-century rabbis
put Jesus to the test, they asked Him to enter a dispute of the
time: Which was the greatest commandment of the law? Jesus
returned them to the Shema, as the story is recounted in Mark
12:28-34. Jesus told the scribe that the greatest commandment was this one from Deuteronomy, and the second was
like it—to love one's neighbor as oneself.

When we are struggling for guidance about our vocation,
we can safely return here. When we are searching for guidance about what we are supposed to do, we can return to these
ancient words, quoted by Jesus, about who we are supposed
to be. Like Israel was instructed to do, we can recite these
words, writing them on the doorposts of our hearts as signs
about who dwells therein.

Notice that the great commandment of the Shema is addressed to a group of people. Abraham, the pioneer, had followed God's challenge, and God was making from Abraham's
descendants a people whose purpose was salvation. Now

God's word to that people was intended to give them identity and purpose. These were words addressed to the people God was calling out for His purposes. Any individual purpose that an Israelite had was secondary to and flowed from this primary identity of the whole people.

That is where vocation begins for all of us who have accepted the calling to discipleship. Our individual vocations flow from the vocation that we have inherited as the people of God. We are first and foremost a group of people who have been given a mission of witnessing to the birth of the kingdom of God in our midst. When the scribe to which Jesus gave His answer in Mark 12 responded that these commandments which Jesus had spoken were greater than burnt offerings and sacrifices, Jesus responded by telling him that he was not far from the kingdom of God. Often the roles we take on are like the burnt offerings and sacrifices that we hope will be pleasing to God. When we are feeling lost and far from the kingdom, one of the roads back is to return to this calling to Israel and to us—the calling to love God and neighbor. Again, the wisdom of that old catechism returns to us in speaking our purpose—to love God and enjoy Him forever.

The covenant was, to Israel, a sign of God's grace in the world. It is still an example of God's gracious movement toward humanity with the promise of redemption. It is God reaching toward the humanity that had turned away from Him in the garden of Eden. The covenant calls God's people to accept and join the work of redemption in the world. The nation of Israel gathered around it. The covenant gave them identity. What did it call them to be and to do?

Like the theme of creation, it called them to be as much as to do—to be people who recognized the one God who had not only made them but called them out of the bondage in Egypt. Like the image of walking with God in the garden, the Shema calls Israel to love. The heart of the Shema is for the child of God to love God. This task of loving is assumed to be a task that requires all of one's energy. Loving is to be done with all of one's heart, soul, and strength. The further task is to teach about this one God and about this task of love and worship to one's children, and to put it as a sign on one's house so that all who enter can see one's identity and allegiance.

Jesus added the crowning piece of the commandment to love and to be—to show that love to neighbor as to God and self. Jesus' addition to the Shema takes the commandment and gives it its communal origin and aim. The task of being and loving finds its logical and proper context by including the neighbor in the loving and being.

It was Martin Luther who began to reshape ideas about calling that have shaped several denominations. Luther preached that all persons, regardless of station, had a calling before God. In fact, the "stations" in which people found themselves were, for Luther, the context of vocation. But the hallmark of vocation for Luther was the emphasis upon serving neighbor. This was the purpose of any vocation under God. It is trustworthy guidance still.

### The Yes and No of Covenant Partnership

Like the tree in the garden of Eden, the calling of God to Abraham, Sarah, and their descendants was one that was full of blessing. God promised to give the childless couple descendants more numerous than they could imagine. God led the Jewish slaves out of Egypt and promised to lead them to a land they could occupy with God's blessing. Yet the covenant also gave them guidance by delineating the limits of covenant behavior. When one violated the Commandments and conditions of the covenant, one placed oneself outside the covenant community in need of restoration.

No one was able to keep the law finally and fully, and it served to point the way to a covenant based on grace. But the law stood as a trustworthy guide that helped the devout Jews know who they were. Their community lived by the law given to Moses, and it gave them unique identity in all of their journeys. The heart of that unique identity lay in the opening words of the Shema: "Hear, O Israel; the Lord your God is one Lord." The participants in that covenant knew themselves to be the follower of the one God, Yahweh, even when surrounded by cultures that worshiped many gods. The laws that they followed were holy because they were the words of the one Lord who had revealed Himself to them.

The Shema stood as the center of the law because it gave them the heart of all of the other laws. The "shalt nots" of the law were intended to help the covenant people guard their hearts from idols not worthy of worship. In saying yes to the God of the covenant, the people of Israel were required to say no to the multiplicity of idols that surrounded them. The covenant was gracious initiative from God toward a world in need of salvation. The people chosen as vessels of this salvation received a magnificent gift. In saying yes to that gift, they were required to say no to things that threatened to enslave them. To a people who knew their God as the one who had led them out of slavery, they knew that the law was a guide to help them avoid slavery.

The gracious gift of covenant relationship with God frees us from bondages of all sorts. The yes of vocation as follower of the God who led a nation out of slavery involves saying no to things that threaten to enslave us again. The things that threaten to enslave us are not always political tyrants. We can also be enslaved to jobs, destructive relationships, addictions of body and mind, and status and power. We find identity as a covenant people when we say yes to the covenant and say no to the things that compete with the one God for allegiance.

## Maps Leading Home

What differences do the great images of creation and covenant make to persons who, as we saw in chapter 2, may be struggling to align themselves with God's purposes for being in this world?

Several things come to mind. First, these affirmations about God's purposes remain for us all, regardless of life station, work station, or personal station. The calling to be, to love, and to serve neighbor come to each of us and are the *cornerstones of vocation for us all.* The person who has recently divorced can affirm himself or herself as made in the image of God (good news that they may need to hear again). That person is still under the command to love God and serve neighbor. The man or woman who has retired still lives under the covenant which calls us to love God with all our heart, soul, and strength and to love our neighbor. The person for whom job or profession does not hold the same allure and for whom work has begun to taste bitter is called to "enlarge their tent stakes" to envision ways of loving, being, and serving that are not limited to a particular job.

These great truths of creation and covenant are signs that lead the way home. For the person who feels the grief of loss and the pain of doubt about vocation, they do not take the pain away. But grief and pain can be trustworthy signs along the way of healing. The reminders of creation and covenant can be a balm to the soul that is feeling loss and grief. For persons who doubt their "usefulness," these foundations of vocation are reminders that our primary calling is to love and recognize the Source of life and grace. For persons who have equated vocation with a particular job, role, or place, these words challenge them to hope for a vision of vocation that is larger than any job or role.

On the other hand, recognizing that God is the source of the created order makes even the most common tasks have sacred potential. This was the insight that Luther brought to the Middle Ages. In a feudal society, the good news he brought to peasants was that they could live out a holy calling as husband, wife, son, daughter, farmer, or laborer. He encouraged them to see that these "common" and unglorified roles could be vessels of grace and instruments for the growth of the kingdom. In a contemporary industrial society some of the same challenges face us. Some jobs simply do not have social or economic status. Some jobs do not lend great dignity to the persons who perform them. Luther's insights, essentially the recognition that God has created all of this earth, echoes still. God can make the common holy, because it has God's blessing.

Luther's weakness, easier to see from the distance of several centuries, was being uncritical of social structures that were unjust. By recognizing the sacred potential in the common things of life, we must take care not to baptize injustice. Some jobs and some roles embody societal injustice. The great truths of creation and covenant speak to them as well. The creation reminds us that, even in a job or role that would demean us, we have the assurance of God that we contain His image and our being in the world fits the desire of God to have relationship. The image of covenant reminds us that the covenant people were led out of injustice and slavery, and the God of the covenant took notice of their plight. Injustice will not be fully gone until the kingdom has fully come. Until then, we are called to work for justice, hope for justice, and find comfort in the God who sees the plight of His children.

The grief we feel in the face of losses is no less real, even when we hear again the stories of creation and covenant. These reminders can serve as signs of hope, proclaiming that we will know again the fulfillment of knowing God's purposes for us. These symbols can help us to know those purposes even more deeply. They can provide for us a place to rest in times when jobs are not fulfilling. They provide for us an identity that will keep us from being swallowed or defined by any job or role. They remind us that we find identity in being made and redeemed and called to be agents of reconciliation. They remind us to resist evil, even when it is clothed in the disguise of success. They give us identity that will deepen as we face the sorrows and losses we encounter on the way.

You may be reading these pages from the perspective of a present sense of loss or confusion. The loss and confusion can begin a journey that deepens identity and drives you to the deepest sources of strength and sustenance. We are met by God as often in dark and uncertain places as in confident and airy ones. Gregory of Nyssa, a fourth-century bishop, wrote a treatise on the spiritual life based on the life of Moses. His treatise captures the themes of loss, uncertainty, and the mysterious presence of the God of the covenant. Of Moses he said:

> The manifestation of God to the great Moses began with light; afterwards God spoke to him in the cloud; next when Moses became more exalted and perfect he saw God in the darkness.[1]

In the cloud and darkness of loss and uncertainty one hopes and trusts that we are being made more perfect, even by our lack of light. There may not be a star leading you on a journey to a particular place. The light given by these themes from the Old Testament can provide trustworthy aids for navigation. The deep wisdom of the Old Testament teaches us that we learn to be at home being on pilgrimage.

### Notes

1. *Gregory of Nyssa: The Life of Moses*. Trans., introduction, and notes by Abraham J. Malherbe, and Everett Ferguson. (New York: Paulist Press, 1978).

# 4

---

# A Face in the Darkness

"Did not our hearts burn within us while he talked to us on the road, while he opened to us the scriptures?" (Luke 24:32).

You remember the story of the disciples on the road to Emmaus. Those two were the embodiment of discouragement and hopelessness. The crucifixion had dashed their deepest hopes and taken away the One they loved, and the One in whom they hoped. Their sense of purpose was in question, and their understanding of God's purposes was shattered. Having heard only rumors of the resurrection, they dared not believe them. They wandered down a road of confusion, trying to sort out truth from rumor.

A stranger began walking with them, and they told Him of their heartbreak. They told Him how they had dared to hope and understood (and misunderstood) the mission of Jesus and their own purposes. Then they told the grim story of the crucifixion. Their leader had been executed as a criminal. They were walking away from Jerusalem on the familiar road to Emmaus but, in a very real way, these two did not know where they were going.

They did not recognize this Stranger who listened so well, even as He taught them from the Scriptures. Their hearts did quicken, though, as He taught them. Some flicker of hope and memory stirred within them as they continued to walk and listen. As the time came for supper, they begged the Stranger to stay with them. He consented, and as He broke the bread, they recognized Him. What a joyous recognition that must have been as they saw the risen Lord! Their heavy hearts found hope and purpose again in the face to face encounter with the One who had called them.

Luke tells us that, just as quickly as they recognized Jesus, He vanished out of their sight. Seldom do our sermons and lessons on this passage deal with Jesus vanishing from these two discouraged disciples with whom He had been walking down the road. These two disciples say little about it as well, except to reflect about how their hearts had "burned within them" while He had walked with them and opened the Scriptures to them.

It is not difficult to put yourself in this story, if you have ever known the pain of discouragement, broken dreams, and hopes gone sour. If you have walked down a road that led slowly away from the crucifixion of some great hope in your life, then you have walked with these two disciples. Perhaps you have found yourself recently walking down a path filled with discouragement and confusion, and like these two, ponder what the future could possibly hold. You thought you understood what you were supposed to do and who you were supposed to be, but this pain, this event, or this loss has you wondering.

What is it that we all long for in such a time of discouragement? What is it that makes our hearts beat again with hope and purpose? For most of us, what we long for is some face-to-face encounter with the One we have committed to follow. That face-to-face encounter and that sense of being accompanied and understood as we walk down a road of pain is what makes for healing and hope.

This chapter hopes to lay further solid foundation for the construction or reconstruction of a sense of vocation in our lives. What we will explore are those mysterious, gracious experiences of having been met by a face in the darkness. What I am talking about are those times of special clarity, those times when we are sure of the presence of God, and those times when we have known and been known more fully than other times. Like the two on the Emmaus road, they often come at the time of our greatest pain and discouragement. They come unbidden. Even though our deepest longing may be to be met in just such a way, these experiences are not something we command or control. They are simply moments of grace so real and powerful that they are nearly unspeakable. Since words are the best we have, we must resort to them, recognizing their inadequacy to capture the depth of our experience.

It is with some hesitation that I undertake this chapter. Some dangers lurk in these words. Let me name several of them to minimize misunderstanding. First, what I speak of in this chapter as the experiences of special grace and clarity are highly individual experiences. I am in no way suggesting that any or all of these experiences must or should happen to any one person. If your experience gives you little to identify with in these pages (except perhaps the longing), then simply recognize that your experience has been different, not deficient.

Another subtle danger that lurks in these pages is the temptation to begin seeking or collecting such experiences. I have already said that they come as gifts of the Spirit of God and are not a sign of special favor, achievement, or maturity. To set out to seek them is to spend energy that can better be used elsewhere on the spiritual journey.

On the other hand, my experience as a chaplain and pastoral counselor is that many persons have had experiences of great power in their journeys that have gone unexplored in their ongoing life. A certain wisdom abides in not telling everyone about these experiences because they are intimate, powerful, and open to misunderstanding. Discretion regarding whom one tells or what one says about these kind of experiences is in order. That discretion often turns into outright secrecy or denial in that persons tell no one and doubt the validity of these special gifts that may occur along the journey.

I intend these pages to speak to the yearnings that exist in all of us to have our personal longings met by a caring face. I hope that speaking of some of these experiences will make us open to explore the meaning of them. I hope the meanings for our discussion of vocation become clear. Like the themes of creation and covenant, our experiences of having glimpsed a caring face in the darkness give us a profound sense of affirmation, belonging, and purpose.

## The Confirming Presence

As I write, our youngest daughter is several months old. We are enjoying the development of an infant in our midst. One of the things that she learned to do in her second month of life was to smile in response to a face. In the weeks ahead that generalized response of a smile to a face will become more specific, meaning that she will begin to know her parents' faces in particular.

James Loder has written about the kinds of moments we are talking about in this chapter. In *The Transforming Moment: Understanding Convictional Experiences,* Loder calls these moments "transforming moments" or times of "convictional knowing."

It is nearly impossible for us to do as adults, but let us try to imagine our way into the world of an infant. Recall that we have no words with which to symbolize our experience and feelings. We are completely dependent on other people to feed us and care for us. Having no language, our experience is dominated by sensations—hunger, wet, warm, cold, dirty, sounds of voices, and being held or not held.

Now let us imagine the infant's experience of a common scene. It is the middle of the night. It is dark, or mostly dark. You awaken to the darkness, and the dominant sensations are these: cold, wet, dark, and the pain of hunger. Remember, now, that we have no words with which even to think to ourselves about these sensations. They are simply powerful sensations. In our coldness, wetness, darkness, and pain we cry out. A face appears and some more light. That face smiles, speaks soothingly to us, picks us up and cradles us, warms us, makes us dry, and feeds us.

That is a common scene, but a powerful one. It becomes more powerful when we are able, even in a partial way, to enter the infant's world. It is a powerful one when we realize the absolute helplessness that is the infant's. Recall that not only does this newborn not have language with which to symbolize his or her experience, he or she also does not have the capacity to hold objects in memory. When the rattle cannot be seen, it does not exist. When the face cannot be seen, it does not exist.

Out of this darkness, helplessness, and pain a face appears or fails to appear. It is not difficult to understand now why psychologists tell us that the foundations are laid in these early months for our ability to trust. What a powerful experience for that face to appear! What an overwhelming experience for no face to appear! If the face appears, it is on this foundation we can begin to trust, before we have words to express it, that the world is a place where our most personal and powerful needs can be met. If that face consistently does not appear or speaks words of condemnation instead of comfort, then the seeds of distrust are sown about whether our needs can ever be met.

The face that appears to us as infants, speaks to us, and cares for us confirms that we are and that we are loved. It confirms our existence by being the presence of a loving other. It is someone outside ourselves who has the power to help us and bless us. Before an infant has words, he or she can bathe in the light of a parent's smile or wither in the hail of a parent's curse. The absence of a face can be a crushing experience and sow the seeds of doubt, mistrust, and despair.

James Loder has suggested, and rightly I think, that the appearance of this face in the darkness is the human parallel of transforming spiritual experience. In those moments of conflict, need, and doubt, the divine face meets us with a compassionate smile. The personal God who seeks relationship with us comes to us in our darkness and need. The light of God's presence is for us that presence of someone outside us who confirms us, holds us, and blesses us.

My daughters provide another point of contact with this discussion. The oldest is sure of her place in this family. We trust that we have been available enough for her so that deep inside her, probably not in a way that she can put into words, she knows that she *belongs*. We also hope that in our youngest this sense of belonging is beginning to develop in these first months of her life. Why is that important? One of the reasons is that I hope these foundations of trust and belonging they experience in this family will make it easier for them to love and trust God. I hope these early experiences lay a foundation for spiritual experiences which will come later in their lives as they say yes to God.

And if they can say yes to God who is more capable of blessing than their parents, I trust they will receive from God a sense that they *belong* in this cosmos that God has created. I pray that they will come to know that they have a place not only in this family and the family of faith, but also ultimately that their creation is a purposeful and graceful act of God. I pray that they will sense that they belong in this created order of God, because the Lord of this creation has met them with a face full of grace.

When we speak of a longing for vocation, we must recognize that one of the dimensions of that longing is a longing for the confirming presence of God. We long to know that this presence has met us, confirmed our being, smiled on us, and assured us of the fact that we *belong*. Finally, that longing, and that sense of belonging is a longing for *personal* relationship. The issues about place, job, and role must finally rest on an assurance that our personhood is affirmed by the God who confers blessing, meets us, and is a confirming presence.

## Moments of Turning

One of the things a crisis in vocation may cause us to do is to take some review of our life until this date. That review may come from some doubt about a former decision, a need to remember times that were less painful, or some other need. Regardless of the motivation, taking time to do some life review at a time of crisis can be a source of comfort and fresh insight. A helpful dimension of such a review is to revisit those benchmark events or times in our lives that somehow stand out from the normal flow of time. They may have stood out at the moment they occurred or perhaps only after some time and reflection had passed. If we stand at an uncertain crossroad in our journey, it can be helpful to look at previous turning points.

What kind of turning points am I speaking of? As people have been honest with me in hospital rooms, living rooms, and counseling rooms, they have told me that the most transforming moments of their lives were as likely to have taken place in the backyard or in a hospital waiting room as in a sanctuary or Bible study classroom. Unfortunately, these moments of extraordinary meaning in ordinary places have often gone unattended, leaving spiritual ore unmined or unrefined.

Beginning with the Bible, Christian literature through the ages has left a record of such moments of turning. Neither Paul's conversion nor the powerful experience of the two on the road to Emmaus happened in the Temple. The call of Isaiah occurred in the Temple. Moses' burning-bush experience revealed to him new possibilities about the God who was calling him to lead God's people out of the slavery of Egypt. The testimonies of saints through the ages include testimonies of such moments of incredible turning.

Two of the holiest times I have ever known were witnessing the birth of my children. They were times when I felt a cleansing of vision, deeper bonding to the woman I love, and awe at the miracle of new life. A hospital delivery room is hardly a church, but those moments were holy.

It is easy to be simply sentimental about the birth of a baby, but I think these events contained more than sentiment. While the births of both of our children were relatively uncomplicated, they still contained moments of crisis for mother and child. In those moments of crisis, it was as if I saw myself, this world, and others more clearly. I have worked in hospitals long enough to know how close death is in such moments. Such an awareness of the possibility of death can serve to take the sentimentality out of any moment.

Somehow in those moments and hours of new life being born something else was being born in me. One of the ways I have found to speak of that is to understand how those moments showed me how deeply connected I am to the people I love. I was able to realize at a different level what grace is contained in those human relationships. The love I have received from them is in no way something I have earned. It is gift. For someone who has been tempted to invest too much energy in work and too much meaning in achievement, these moments were times that challenged my habitual ways of seeking security. They called me to reorder my internal and external priorities. They called me to a deeper realization of relationship with God, my family, and this world.

Other moments have been times of quiet turning for me, and perhaps for you. For some persons, still moments of reflection in natural surroundings have resulted in a new opening of spirit or resolution of troubling conflict. Other persons have, in the midst of grave crisis, found themselves in the middle of moments of great release, surrender, comfort, or peace. Times of private devotion or public worship have resulted in new insight, deeper freedom, or internal healing for some. Times of prayer or meditation have brought with them moments of turning for others.

These moments of turning can be one source of comfort and guidance in the search for a renewed sense of vocation. For some, these times have been key in their understanding of their purpose under God. In times of questioning and life review, remembering and reviewing these times of turning can be another way of finding hope for participating in God's good purposes for our lives.

I want to make it clear that I do not hold that everyone or anyone *must* have a dramatic experience of turning to discover their vocation under God. For many souls, their decision to become a Christian and their spiritual experience in general are marked by a gentle, quiet progression rather than dramatic shifts and turns. These persons are no less Christian and certainly no less able to know and participate in the purposes of God. I simply know that large numbers of people have had powerful and unforgettable experiences that stand as mileposts on their journey. Sometimes a careful glance back at these mileposts can help us find some navigation points from which to plot our journey into the unknown future.

## Conversion Experiences

Many of us have put an emphasis on the call of Jesus to all persons to repent and decide to follow Him in discipleship. Our theological heritage is that discipleship involves a moment of truth, a conscious decision to commit and follow in the Way. Likewise, our Christian heritage is that we are a people who have learned that faith is, among other things, a matter of the heart often involving strong feelings. These two pieces of our heritage have led to an appreciation for and an emphasis on "conversion experiences." Too often the norm has been that a decision to follow Jesus must be dramatic and highly emotional in order to be valid. That is a distortion of the truths at the heart of our history. Often conversion experiences are, like other elements of the spiritual journey, an experience of quiet reflection. Intense emotion may be a part of a conversion experience, but it is not the essence of conversion. The biblical essence of conversion is repentance and the decision to follow Jesus.

The meaning of repentance is, of course, to turn. Repentance involves the acknowledgement that we have endeavored to be the sole source of security, that we have tried to be gods unto ourselves, that we have worshiped gods not worthy of worship. Repentance is the acknowledgment that all those endeavors at self-sufficiency have failed. Christian conversion involves accepting that Jesus is the revelation of God. That is never merely nor centrally an intellectual agreement about Jesus. It involves a *surrender* of oneself to the way of Jesus, accepting the forgiveness and life available through Him. For some persons that surrender comes dramatically and in the midst of enormous inner struggle. For other persons, that surrender comes quietly after a season of reflection. The ways to conversion are as individual as are fingerprints. Their essence is surrender and a commitment to follow.

### Paul: The Embodiment of Vocation

Paul is perhaps the early Christian about whom we have the most information from biblical sources. How would we describe the vocation of Paul? Most of us think of him as the apostle to the Gentiles. That certainly could describe his vocation, but not all of it. He was also an author, whose writings continue to minister to us centuries later who seek to follow the same Lord that called him. He was a reconciler, one who could build a bridge between the community of original apostles and the new disciples. He built bridges between devout Jews who were beginning to see in Jesus the fulfillment of messianic hopes and Gentiles who had never followed Jewish law. He was one of the first and greatest of Christian theologians, who could now interpret the law in the light of the life of Jesus.

With all of these roles, he maintained a trade with which he could provide a living for himself. Paul was an organizer, reconciler, writer, preacher, teacher, and craftsman. Now, what was his vocation? He himself described it in various ways, but most often as *apostle*. In doing so, Paul was referring to that central experience of calling in which the Lord invited him to cease persecuting and start following.

*Apostle* was never a profession. Neither is *disciple*. They are a vocation. Recall that the experience of conversion was Paul's experience of calling. To be sure, he experienced the leading of God in different ways and in specific times after that conversion. Paul apparently had profoundly deep spiritual experiences which we would call mystical. They no doubt deepened the commitment and calling which he experienced in his Damascus Road experience, but that never changed the fact that his vocation rooted in his experience of profound change and commitment.

Paul's conversion experience is probably the most famous Christian conversion experience ever recorded. I think it important to note that in the instant of the Damascus road experience, Paul did not have all of the knowledge and understanding necessary to carry out his work. He did not even completely understand the meaning of the experience. The central element of the experience itself was that he was met by the risen Lord. It was a personal encounter in the form of a light. We are told that it shook Paul to the core. The immediate effect of the experience was not one of certainty and sight, but of uncertainty and blindness.

He had to go to the house of Judas, where he was later met by a disciple named Ananias. Ananias' being there was no small act of courage because he had heard of Paul's zeal in persecuting this new sect of believers. However, Ananias did go, and it was his ministry to Paul that helped Paul begin interpreting what had happened to him on the road. Ananias was a crucial person in helping Paul discern the meaning of his conversion. It was after Paul met with Ananias that his sight returned, and he was baptized. Later Barnabas met Paul and introduced him to other disciples who were also afraid of him.

Not everyone has an experience of conversion as dramatic as Paul's. Not everyone has a Damascus Road experience, especially those who have been nurtured in the faith. But even among those of us who have had a Damascus Road experience, Paul's experience can be instructive. Conversion experiences require time and the wisdom of the community of faith to effect their full work in us.

I am convinced that many a conversion experience has continued to be a half-baked cake for lack of a courageous and wise Judas and Ananias. Conversion experiences can be as blinding as they can be cleansing, and we need the wisdom and nurture of others to be able to sustain such a radical change in our vision. Too many times we have rushed ourselves and others to the waters of baptism without the benefit of wise counsel and instruction. Conversion begins a work in us that launches us on a journey of seeking, growing, and discovering the meaning of baptism for us.

### Conversion and Vocation

Why spend time talking about conversion in a book about vocation? For one thing, the conflict that issues in conversion for many persons is a quiet or not so quiet unrest about their life direction. It is a growing awareness that they are adrift and without direction and purpose. In other words, the impetus for conversion comes from an awareness that our life is not aligned with God's purposes for us.

The decision to follow Jesus is the key decision in the search for vocation. That cannot be emphasized strongly enough. If one has made the decision to follow, then one has made the key decision regarding vocation. In that respect, Christians all have the same vocation. Some of our unrest about vocation may come from the fact that we are not being challenged regularly enough and strongly enough about the ongoing implications and challenges of that decision to follow.

Conversion is rightly seen as involving decision and will. We hold in tension the paradox that we must decide, but that we contribute nothing toward our own redemption. That redemption comes from outside us. We must decide to commit and to follow, but we cannot do anything that makes us redeemed. What we do is accept the gift that we had no part in purchasing.

A profession of faith is, as someone has said, "a commitment of what we know of ourselves to what we know of God." As we continue journeying, we come to know dimensions of ourselves that we had not known before. Likewise, we come to different and deeper understandings of God. A crisis in vocation may be just such a crossroad. One way to view such a crisis is that we have the chance to continue the work of conversion begun in us whenever we decided to be a follower of Jesus. The current unrest does not invalidate the former decision to follow, nor does it imply that we somehow were not saved. It may simply mean that we have journeyed to a place where we can commit what we now know of ourselves to what we now know about God.

For some, the decision to follow Jesus involved a deep and dramatic change in some dimension of their lives. Perhaps they were struggling with a particular form of personal addiction or a life-style that was destructive to themselves and others. Their own efforts to stop had been unsuccessful, or even a sense that they needed to be released from that bondage had not come. Suddenly the awareness of oneself as someone in need of forgiveness and change emerged. Along with the acceptance of that forgiveness came a release from the heretofore dominant style of living. For some persons, conversion is dramatic and involves this kind of radical change. For others, an experience of conversion is no less powerful, but the changes may be less visible to the observer. Those changes may root in the profound experience of being accepted, loved, and forgiven.

As the creation account tells of God's blessing of our having been made and outlines for us the purposes for God's creation, so the drama of redemption captures for us the redemptive purposes of God in this world. One of the chief texts of vocation for me is 2 Corinthians 5:17-19:

Therefore, if any one is in Christ, he is a new creation; the

old has passed away, behold, the new has come. All this is
from God, who through Christ reconciled us to himself and
gave us the ministry of reconciliation; that is, in Christ God
was reconciling the world to himself, not counting their tres-
passes against them, and entrusting to us the message of reconciliation.

In the language of Genesis, we were created to be stewards of
God's creation and for relationship with God. In the language
of 2 Corinthians, we have been recreated to embody the message of reconciliation. All other decisions about what we do,
where we go, and what job we take rest upon this foundation.

When one feels vocationally adrift, one source of meaning,
comfort, and hope is to revisit one's acceptance of the gift of
reconciliation. Allow yourself to feel again the grace and
power of those moments. Feel again the acceptance, forgiveness, and love based simply on the fact that God has made you
and wants to continue remaking you in God's image. Know
that your chief purpose is to explore and embody this mystery
of reconciliation. A crisis in vocation is, to some degree, a
crisis in identity—we are unsure about who we are and where
we are going. A return in memory and imagination to an experience of conversion can connect us to a powerful source of
identity and direction. We can return in memory to the appearance of the loving Face in the darkness.

Some have reflected on their experience of conversion and
been troubled by a realization that they did not fully understand what they were doing. They have even wondered if their
current distress is a sign that their regeneration was somehow
not authentic. The fact is none of us understood fully what we
were doing when we accepted the grace of God through
Christ and followed Him in baptism. Baptism is a door that

opens to continual journey, and we cannot see the whole ter-
rain of that journey from the door. The current place in our
journey may give us a vantage point to more deeply understand the meaning of stepping through that door in trust and
hope.

For some persons, a conversion experience also contains
some strong sense of a particular place or direction to which
they are being led. In other words, their decision to follow
Jesus in the Way is paired with a sense about where God is
leading them. It may be in a particular professional or personal direction. For these persons, the disintegration of that
particular job, position, or direction can be very threatening,
especially since the decision to head that way was part of a
conversion experience. If a part of your conversion experience included a calling to a particular task, role, or station,
and now that task, role, or station is lost, do not feel that your
conversion was not valid or is in question. Instead, your conversion is still being worked out in you, as it is in all of us; and
you may be being called to journey into the next chapter of life
and spiritual maturity.

For other persons, their conversion experience may contain
guidance that can be revisited in this time of crisis. That conversion experience can serve to remind us of the sense of trust
and surrender that now seems so far away. That experience
can remind us of the assurance that our worth before God is
not determined by the role or task that we have. Certainly
conversion was not a time when we enlisted as an officer in
the Lord's army. On the contrary, our theological heritage reminds us that our worth in God's eyes is through the grace of
God in Christ. Even if we have attained some measure of virtue in the years since, that virtue gives us no special status and

is still not the basis for God's loving and valuing us. Returning to that benchmark in our lives can help clarify our vision.

Conversion, whether quiet and gradual or sudden and dramatic, provides the heart of vocation. If vocation has to do with identity, the decision to accept God's love is the center of Christian identity. Nothing is more central to our identity than the decision to follow Jesus as Lord. Our most important vocation is that of disciple. All else is secondary. Unfortunately, we have at times unduly elevated "ministers," those ordained and set apart by the church, as having a more important vocation than others. Those of us in the ministry enjoy that kind of distortion because it feeds our sense of importance, but it is not the heart of the gospel. We are all given the high calling of discipleship. That is the calling to which Paul summoned the Ephesians to be worthy, reminding that one Lord, one Spirit, one faith, and one baptism extended to them all.

## Holy Ground Experiences

Not all of the significant experiences of the Christian life occur at the moment of decision to be a disciple. Recall that conversion, as we commonly use it, is only a beginning, though certainly an important one. Conversion assures us of our *justification*—our having been declared right with God through Christ. The continuing work of regeneration is *sanctification*—the ongoing task of growing in virtue and being made holy. Persons on the road of discipleship also have important turning points after the moment of conversion. These are the ones that often go unspoken and unexplored.

Some of these kinds of moments that I have spoken of may be very quiet realizations, powerful senses of leading or calling, or times of great comfort in the midst of distress. Most of us can look back over our journey and mark such times of turning on this side of our conversion. The passage from Luke about the two on the road to Emmaus which began this chapter describes them as disciples. These two had already decided to follow Jesus, and this appearance of the risen Lord in their time of discouragement continued to reveal to them the meaning of their decisions to be disciples. Now the meaning of their discipleship was clearer.

I like to think of such times as our continuing to be converted. They come to us and give to us an unusual clarity about ourselves, God, and the world. That clarity is often painful, especially as regards to ourselves, in that the continuing work of conversion is to strip away all of the ways we seek to justify ourselves. We come to see ourselves as continuing to strive to justify ourselves, resist trust and surrender, and be afraid of love.

One of the contexts in which these moments of special clarity come to us is the experience of suffering. When we are threatened with death and when we have experienced loss, abandonment, or rejection, we instinctively turn again to our Source. When our mortality comes to us in ways that we can no longer deny, we come to a place where we can see things differently. It is not surprising that these kinds of moments are times both of tremendous personal upheaval and remarkable grace. It takes remarkable grace for most of us to look our own mortality in the eye.

In an earlier chapter I mentioned that I worked for some years in a cancer treatment unit. Several consistent themes emerged as I worked in that context. One of the first was that the reality of death was moving from the background, where we like to keep it, to the foreground. Whether or not an individual had a prognosis of impending death, the diagnosis of cancer brought into focus the reality of death, and the possibility that this disease could take one's life. Although it is less so in recent years, cancer is still a symbol of death in our culture.

For others, in addition to coming to grips with their own death, they were also dealing with a forced change in lifestyle. Either because of the rigors of treatment or limitations imposed by the disease itself, many persons were simply not able to carry on with life as they had before their diagnosis. In the midst of that they rightly found themselves struggling with what their purpose was in light of this new and unwanted force in their lives.

As I ministered in the midst of and was taught by these persons, it began to dawn on me that they were no different from me. I did not have a diagnosis of a possibly terminal disease, but I do live my life with the certainty of death. The horizon of death circumscribes all of our lives. Any sense of vocation we carry is lived within that horizon, nearer than most of us like to admit.

I was often invited into the holy ground of their struggling with life's meaning in the face of death. In the context of personal distress and great inner conflict, I found myself an invited guest as persons asked again what their purpose was and as they came to new and deeper realizations of their vocation under God. The lessons they taught me have shaped the way I have come to think about vocation. The lessons they learned were often passed on to me and others. They were lessons for the living, not simply for the dying.

One of the most profound changes that I saw in them was a new and deeper inwardness about their own spiritual life.

They took on a new seriousness, possibly imposed by the limitations of their disease, about their own need for prayer, spiritual nurture, and the Spirit of God deep within them. I am not talking simply about a "foxhole faith." Some of these persons began to listen more intently to their own experience, both past and present, as they took their own faith into the refiner's fire. Entering that refiner's fire they discovered that some of the outer trappings of their faith were not as essential as that intentional inwardness in which they sought the presence of God in their own hearts. We would do well to follow their example, allowing a realization of our vulnerability in this world to drive us to an inwardness that seeks the face of God.

Predictably, these persons also struggled with what their purpose was in the face of disability. Many were no longer able to live the kind of active life through which they had expressed themselves and their purpose in the world. They had to find another foundation on which to rest their sense of purpose under God. That meant a realignment of their purpose from exterior roles of doing to peaceful ways of being. It is impossible to identify one's vocation with some role or job when one simply can no longer physically do them. What some of these saints were discovering, after much struggle and grief, was that God's care and loving purposes did not end when they ceased to be preacher, teacher, or farmer.

One of the questions I frequently asked was whether or not there had been any moments of extraordinary clarity, comfort, presence, or insight for them. A number of them said yes and went on to describe these moments. Sometimes they described particularly vivid dreams that had helped them resolve some inner conflict. Other times they described a hymn that had become a source of strength and hope. Some described memories that came back with particular clarity and comfort, like the woman who described the stained-glass windows of her childhood church. In particular, she described the window in which Jesus was pictured holding a lamb.

One need not be encountering the crisis of death before the grace of holy-ground experiences come. Holy-ground experiences do not always come in the midst of crisis, but they do sometimes come in that context. On the one hand, we are not all struggling with a terminal disease; on the other hand, mortality is a terminal condition that means the horizon of death is one which is in view of us all.

Again, the kinds of moments I am talking about are not to be sought and cannot be "produced," but attended to with care and the wisdom of discernment. They are seldom visions as spectacular and detailed as those of Ezekiel or John. Sometimes they are as simple as the comment, prayer, sermon, or biblical passage that seems to flash in neon at just the right time. Sometimes these ordinary moments take on an extraordinary quality, as they strike some chords of openness and need within us.

If these moments bring us comfort, then we can quietly celebrate the grace of God present in pain. If they bring us some guidance, we must usually test our sense of that guidance with persons we trust and who care for us. We must test that guidance against our own experience, the wisdom of the Scriptures, and the wisdom of the community of faith.

## More Darkness or the Still, Small Voice

I have been clearly hinting that our formative spiritual experiences may contain rich resources for our exploration in discerning God's vocation for us. More importantly, I am suggesting that the very nature of those experiences reveals to us some of the central, foundational elements of Christian vocation. They give us identity by reminding us that we did not create ourselves, we were made for relationship, our lifelong task is to plummet the depths of God's love, and to begin to embody that love toward our neighbor. Paul's great pastoral prayer for the Ephesians does not simply encourage them to do more. His deepest prayer for them was:

> For this reason I bow my knees before the Father, from whom every family on heaven and on earth is named, that according to the riches of his glory he may grant you to be strengthened with might through his Spirit in the inner man, and that Christ may dwell in your hearts through faith; that you, being rooted and grounded in love, may have power to comprehend with all the saints what is the breadth and length and height and depth, and to know the love of Christ which surpasses knowledge, that you may be filled with all the fulness of God (Eph. 3:14-19).

Far too often those experiences, very personal and moving, which have revealed to us that almost inexpressible love "which surpasses knowledge," have neither been shared nor explored for their transformative power and fullest meaning.

The danger in what I have written thus far is the false impression that these experiences are the norm or goal of the Christian spiritual journey. They are gifts that some receive, neither rewards nor achievements. In fact, more than one saint has thought the gift a possession, built an altar of pride to it, and thus sabotaged its transformative potential. The danger of pride comes with the holy-ground experiences of the spiritual life.

I want to speak to another danger inherent in a discussion

of these kinds of experiences. That is the false expectation that everyone who seeks or longs for these kinds of experiences receives them. We do not. Theophanies (appearances of God) are not produced upon request. Neither are they the sign of God's special approval. They are simply gracious gifts, not given according to merit.

For some who seek, the experience is one of continuing darkness. For some, memories of holy-ground experiences are not easily forthcoming, nor do they readily appear in the midst of the crisis. That may be your experience. The danger is that my speaking of those experiences has only increased your pain in a time already filled with pain.

Please hear me clearly. As the gift of what some might call mystical experience is not a sign of worth or merit, neither is the absence of that experience a sign of God's disapproval. The present time may feel like a withdrawal of God's presence or clear leadership in your life. Even if a face has appeared in the darkness before, the present time may be a time of seemingly impenetrable darkness. Do not add to that pain by assuming you are being punished or deemed unworthy of God's presence or comfort.

It is almost always a mistake to tell God in what form leadership or comfort must come. The risk in seeking a certain kind of appearance is that we may fail to turn aside and see God in the small, seemingly ordinary events of our lives. We, like Elijah (1 Kings 19), may think that God only appears in dramatic earthquakes or great winds. In fact, what Elijah learned, only after a long journey in the wilderness, was that God's presence came as a still, small voice.

Some of the great saints of Christian history have encountered seasons in the spiritual life that were best characterized

as a time of darkness. Instead of frequent comfort, clear guidance, additional knowledge, and visible presence, the season
was one in which God felt absent. Desolation more nearly
described what that time in the spiritual journey felt like.
Such times are disorienting and discouraging, when our familiar forms of seeking and knowing God seem to leave us
with no clear word or with no tangible form of comfort.

The best wisdom of the ages counsels against assuming that
such times are a sign that one is particularly unclean in God's
sight. The heart of our theological heritage reminds us that
none of us can by ourselves be "clean enough" to merit God's
special attention. The heart of grace is that whenever God
comes to us it is an undeserved gift from One who loves us
more truly than we love ourselves.

The wisdom of the ages counsels us to let others sustain us
in these times of wilderness that come to us on the journey.
We cannot set our jaws and will God's appearance to us. To
do so is not only to misunderstand God's sovereignty and the
nature of the spiritual life, it is to close ourselves off from the
more subtle ways God may be speaking to us. If we have been
fortunate to have had a warm sense of God's presence and
leading, we may be able to learn of God's sustaining love in
less visible and reassuring forms.

The further wisdom of the ages is that such times of spiritual dryness or darkness ultimately work to make us more
sensitive and dependent upon God. We must truly learn to
trust when we cannot clearly see the way before us. Such
times ultimately work toward the growth in us of humility and
identification with others who know suffering. Such times
show us the limits of our will. The result can be a painful kind
of cleansing and wounding that makes us more compassionate
instruments of grace.

Flora Slosson Wuellner has written movingly of making our pain a matter for prayer and meditation. We often pray for others, for guidance in times of decision, and for the work of the kingdom. We seldom make our pain something we hold in our awareness in prayer, letting it be available for God to touch as God wills. Wuellner goes on to reflect on the wounds of the resurrected Jesus as reported in John 20. She observes that John reported that the resurrected body of the Lord contained wounds visible to the disciples. Why, she asks, would the marks of suffering still be visible in this transfigured body of the risen Lord? She goes on:

> Are we not also receiving the witness that our wounds are never wasted? Even after we are fully healed and released from suffering, whether in this life or the next, the signs of our wounds—the scars of our deep committed living—will not be swallowed up in glory. Rather, they will shine forth from within us, no longer as sources of suffering but as sources of radiant light and richer loving.[1]

The fact that we may be in a time of relative darkness may be a wound that makes us more fit for richer loving. That is the intention of the loving God, whether in holy-ground experiences or in times that feel like desert wandering.

## Being Met By a Face

A couple of years ago I made a trip to another state to be examined by a group of colleagues in a professional organization. I wanted very much to be approved by these peers, and I was extremely anxious. In some real ways, I felt like my professional future was riding on my performance. The more I attempted to control my anxiety, the less in control I felt. Finally, I opened my wallet to the place where I keep pictures of my family. There were the faces of my wife and little girl.

Seeing those faces made a difference. My anxiety did not go away, but the importance of that day began to find some perspective. In seeing their faces I was reminded of who I was. I was reminded of people who loved me. I was reminded that no matter what happened on this day the vocations of father and husband awaited me, and they had already been rich, rewarding, and full of grace. I realized that these people's love for me was not dependent on whether I succeeded or failed on this day.

The anxiety remained, but those faces helped me find a center on a day when I felt the center was giving way. The professional role that I so longed for was still important, but was not all or even the most important part of who I was. I promised myself I would remember that no matter what happened in the examination. I hoped I would remember that and let it help me set priorities in the future. Those of us who have as a part of our vocation the role of minister can be tempted to neglect the part of our vocation that is husband and father.

Those faces were powerful reminders that I did not journey alone. These persons have been with me and for me, as I have been with and for them. Of course, even these relationships exist within the horizon of death. I can be sure that these relationships will someday know the painful parting of death. On the one hand, that frightening realization can lead to the temptation to guard my heart and refuse to love because loving will encounter the pain of separation and death. On the other hand, the realization that these relationships are set within the boundaries of time and death makes them all the more precious. If my vocation is to love, I'd better get to it.

Those faces were also reminders of the even deeper longing I have to be met by the face of God. In important ways they mediate the presence of God to me on this journey, while they are not God. I can make idols even of those I have been given to love. The deeper human longing is for a face that will meet us in the final darkness of death and be a loving light. Before that darkness of death, I will be met with other intrusions of darkness into my world. I long to be met in those times by the face that reminds me who I am and confirms my existence and purpose in Him. In those times when I cannot see God's face, I pray for the grace to trust without seeing and continue to be changed even by those times.

In the person of Jesus we have had the clearest revelation of the face of God. What is conversion but the invitation to be a follower of the Nazarene? In the face of Jesus we see God. In following Him we discover our identity. Like Paul, our daily life may cover a variety of roles, but none of them are more definitive of who we are than our being met by the One who calls us to participate in the work of reconciliation. The work of reconciliation was most clearly embodied in the life of that Carpenter from Nazareth. In the next chapter we will turn more specifically to the life of Jesus for clues about vocation.

### Notes

1. Flora Slosson Weullner, "When Prayer Encounters Pain," *Weavings,* Vol. 4, pt. 3 (May/June 1989), p. 41.

# 5

# Jesus and Vocation

At several places in the previous chapters I have suggested that the foundation of vocation consists of the identity of disciple. The modern world, and to a great extent the modern church, has placed the emphasis and meaning of vocation in the wrong place, that being role or profession. The *role* that we assume for a time, or the way one makes a living, is one way of expressing a deeper identity. As soon as a particular role becomes all, or even the major part of our identity, we have ceased to see the heart of Christian vocation. If the role or job becomes our sole identity, then we lose freedom. We lose freedom because we have to clutch it too closely for fear of losing identity, if the role or job changes. So much emphasis is placed on profession that we risk losing a sense of self apart from the profession. If we can count on anything, we can count on the fact that roles and jobs change.

If the heart of vocation is being a disciple, what does that mean? In the last chapter, I suggested that attending sensitively to experiences in the spiritual life that have been crucial turning points was one resource for discovering, rediscovering, or deepening our vocation. Those experiences themselves are given to us in order to help us along the road of discipleship. Like those two on the road to Emmaus who found themselves walking with Jesus, His coming near to them helped them again find purpose and meaning from simply having been in His presence. Recall that in that passage (Luke 24) Jesus did not give them explicit instructions about where to go or what to do next. He simply talked with them, taught them from the Hebrew Scriptures, and broke bread with them.

Recall that Acts tells us that it was after the resurrection and after Pentecost that the term *Christian* was coined. We are so accustomed to it that we fail to hear how radical a word it is. Acts seems to imply that the term was not something that those early disciples chose, but something that was applied to them from others. Why? Of the ways they could have described this growing band of people, they chose to describe them by naming them after the person whose life and ministry had become central for them. They called them Christians.

Apparently that was the most descriptive term available for what they were doing. They were telling and retelling the story of the life and ministry of Jesus. They were talking about resurrection and how this One who had walked among them was the Messiah, the Son of God. They were seeking to be like Him by following after Him. They were beginning to believe that the kingdom Jesus had announced was indeed being established.

Soon they would begin to gather the writings that told the story of Jesus and instructed them in how to keep following Him. The Gospels and the Epistles were clear that the name that had been given to the group of believers at Antioch was appropriate. The unmistakable theme of those writings was that Jesus was the Son of God and that with His life, death, and resurrection God was fulfilling His gracious purposes for this world. They set out to understand how to keep following and spread the good news that He had been and shared with them. This seemed to be the thing that marked them, that gave them purpose.

## The Jesus Story: Biblical Wisdom for Vocation

If our vocational identity rests in following Jesus, then we might get some help from the biblical witness about what this following entails. How might we discern some truths about vocation from reading the stories of Jesus? On the one hand such a suggestion seems so obvious as to be trite. Of course we will read the Scriptures about Jesus. We always do. Surely we do. But how often do we read them looking for Jesus' own discovery and nurture of His vocation? In the remainder of this chapter, I want to look at some events and some themes in the life of Jesus to see what wisdom may be there for those of us seeking a renewed sense of vocation. If Jesus is the one that we follow, then we can find in Jesus a model for vocation. Jesus is the embodiment of vocation.

### *Jesus' Baptism*

The accounts of Jesus' baptism are among the most fascinating accounts in the New Testament witness to the life of Jesus. We have very little in the New Testament about Jesus' life before the beginning of His ministry. Matthew gives us His genealogy, stories of the birth of Jesus, and goes immediately to Jesus' baptism. Mark gives neither genealogy nor birth stories and tells the story of Jesus' baptism within the first chapter.

Luke is the Gospel that gives two stories about Jesus between His birth and His baptism. He tells the wonderful story

of Anna and Simeon greeting Mary, Joseph, and the baby
Jesus in the Temple. They serve to point out that Jesus' birth
fulfills the deepest hopes of Israel for liberation. The next
story Luke tells is about the boy Jesus in the Temple con-
founding the rabbis and His parents with His questions. His
seeming rebuke of His anxious parents (Luke 2:49) reveals
that already He understood His purpose as one of discerning
the things of His Heavenly Father. The One who was to be
known as Rabbi was already listening and asking questions of
the rabbis. John's Gospel, after the sweeping and poetic prologue, tells of encounters between Jesus and John the Baptist,
but leaves no account of Jesus' baptism itself. He highlights
John the Baptist's preparing the way and pointing to Jesus.

All three of the Synoptic Gospels recount the story of
Jesus' baptism. What are we to make of this? What does
Jesus' baptism mean? The Gospels make it clear that John was
preaching and practicing a baptism of repentance. Was this a
quaint public relations move by Jesus to attract a crowd? What
does it mean that Jesus requested and received the baptism of
John?

It is difficult to say with certainty, because we have no
words of Jesus interpreting the meaning of His baptism. Several things seem clear, even without Jesus interpreting His
baptism for His disciples or us. First is that this act by Jesus
marks the beginning of His public ministry. Until then, as
Luke's story of the boy Jesus in the Temple demonstrates, He
was, no doubt, a serious student of His Jewish heritage and
this new prophet who was preaching repentance. But His baptism marks a new chapter in His life as He entered into a
public ministry.

Here was a new stage in Jesus' understanding and His obe-

dience to what He discerned of God's purposes for Him.
Even John's Gospel, in addition to the Synoptics, speaks of
the descent of the Spirit on Jesus as the sign of God's approval
and blessing of Jesus as His Son. We miss the point if we get
distracted by an overemphasis on Jesus' sinlessness making
repentance unnecessary for Him. To emphasize sinlessness
tends to make the event of Jesus' baptism irrelevant or meaningless. Clearly it was not meaningless, as evidenced by this
act of obedience and blessing being recorded in all of the Gospels. The issue is not that Jesus' baptism is evidence of Him
having sin(s) for which He needed to repent. The issue is that
He was entering a new stage of His commitment to obedience
of God's will for Him.

As John recognized Jesus as the One to come after him, so
Jesus recognized John and identified with what John was doing in his ministry. Jesus' choice of John to baptize Him obvi-
ously signals Jesus' blessing of what John had been doing in
his ministry of preaching and baptizing. John stood in the tradition of the prophets calling Israel to repentance, and Jesus
identified John's ministry as in that great prophetic tradition.
Thus, Jesus clearly stood in the tradition of Jewish expectation of a prophet like Moses, which echoes throughout the
prophetic tradition and Israel's hopes.

Jesus signaled His obedience and symbolized that His ministry would be in the tradition that John was renewing. John's
place is clearly a paving of the way for Jesus, and John interpreted himself that way in the Gospels. What else do we know
of John, other than his unusual diet and clothing? Luke contains some summaries of John's preaching. It must have been
the part of the ministry of John that attracted Jesus and that
Jesus blessed by choosing John to baptize Him (Luke 3:1-20).

John, in addition to pointing to Jesus, was proclaiming a pro-phetic message of justice and compassion—the sharing of food and clothing with those who had none. He exhorted those who were in positions of power (soldiers and tax collec-tors) not to abuse their power for personal gain (3:12-14). This is the prophetic message with which Jesus identified His ministry to come.

Another important element of the Gospels' accounts of Jesus' baptism is of extreme importance for our exploration of vocation. That is the appearance of baptism and temptation as events that occur in succession. Matthew and Mark illustrate this most clearly. In both Matthew and Mark, we have ac-counts of the baptism followed immediately by accounts of Jesus' temptation. Luke interjects only Jesus' genealogy be-tween the accounts of temptation and baptism. At first read-ing, especially in Matthew and Mark, the movement from baptism to temptation appears as an abrupt shift. We move from the warm, stirring scene of the descent of the Spirit on Jesus to the stark, fearful scene of the wilderness.

We are tempted to teach, preach, and interpret these pas-sages as if they are separate and unrelated, as if there is some kind of break between them. We teach or preach on one scene at a time, either the scene of Jesus' baptism (which is not a text for very many sermons) or of the temptation. We inter-pret these passages as if there were unwritten stage directions saying that the descent of the Spirit is the end of act 1 and the temptation is act 2. What happens if we leave them sewn to-gether as we find them. What happens to our interpretation then?

As I am reading these scenes in the early chapters of the Synoptics, I have found myself resisting this abrupt shift. It is as if I want to linger for a while in the glow of Jesus' commitment to a new chapter in His ministry, in John's recognizing Jesus as the fulfillment of his own ministry, and in the declaration of God's blessing upon Jesus. Yet an honest reading of these passages won't allow us to linger long.

> And when Jesus was baptized, he went up immediately from the water, and behold, the heavens were opened, and he saw the Spirit of God descending like a dove, and alighting on him; and lo, a voice from heaven, saying, "This is my beloved Son, with whom I am well pleased." Then Jesus was led up by the Spirit into the wilderness to be tempted by the devil (Matt. 3:16 to 4:1).

> And when he came up out of the water, immediately he saw the heavens opened, and the Spirit descending upon him like a dove; and a voice came from heaven, "Thou art my beloved Son; with thee I am well pleased." The Spirit immediately drove him out into the wilderness (Mark 1:10-12).

In both of these passages there is no lingering. The action moves immediately from baptism to temptation. It seems natural to separate these events in our mind, as later handlers of Scripture did by placing a chapter break between Matthew 3:17 and 4:1. Even then, the impression remains that these events are connected. We have not told the whole story of Jesus' baptism unless we add the dimension of immediate temptation.

Somehow baptism and temptation are connected. It is as if baptism is for the immediate entry into temptation. A new level of understanding and obedience is accompanied by a new level of temptation. A new bestowal of God's blessing, presence, and giftedness is accompanied by new temptations to abuse that giftedness. The temptations that awaited Jesus also await us on this side of baptism: the temptation to an inflated sense of God's protection of us, because we are special; the temptation to substitute temporary (and real) appetites for the deeper hungers of our hearts; and the temptation to trade our deeper vocation for fame or power.

This connection between baptism and temptation underscores that Jesus' baptism was no meaningless show. The public sign of a new phase of His following the leadership of God, His receipt of God's blessing, and His identification with the tradition and direction of John, symbolized a powerful coming together of elements in Jesus' life. This was not a "media event," staged for the sake of reporters. The bestowal of grace and the entry into temptation went hand in hand.

The same connection between baptism and temptation is present for those of us who follow. Our baptism is a sign of a new level of obedience and a commitment made and acted out in front of the community of faith. Baptism does not immunize us from either sin or temptation. Indeed, the commitment to live in radical dependence upon God will often result in a new awareness of just how needy we are. A new sensitivity to God goes hand in hand with a deeper awareness of our lack of righteousness of our own making. If we indeed appropriate the deep symbolism of washing away and new birth, then we must recognize that even our accumulated righteousness was a sin that kept us from realizing how deeply we needed God. If we are symbolizing new birth, we must recognize the radical dependence of those newly born.

We are reborn not to be taken above human spiritual struggles, but to enter them. We are baptized not in order to be taken away from the front lines of human need, but in order to enter the struggle aware of our own neediness and on behalf of our neighbor. We enter that struggle not with fame, power, and strings with which we can manipulate God, but stripped of those things by which we used to seek security.

Baptism, as a sign of following in the Way, may indeed send us into a wilderness of temptation. There, like Jesus, we may be tempted to feel that the grace we have received makes us different and better than others of God's children. We may, like Jesus, be "among the wild beasts," and some of those beasts may be our own inner conflicts that threaten to devour us. Those temptations do not signal the ineffectiveness of our baptism. Rather, they are signs of our having received grace and symbols of the way that grace can be distorted and misused.

Jesus' baptism, entry into temptation, and emergence from it did not signal the end either of His seeking the guidance of His Father or the end of His struggles in His own vocation. If anything, these stories early in the Gospels set a pattern of Jesus' retreating into solitude to continue to discern the way God was leading Him.

### Jesus' Solitude

It is no new discovery of New Testament scholarship that the Gospels portray Jesus as one who consistently sought out times and places for solitude and prayer. The life of Jesus, at least what we know of His public ministry, consisted of a rhythm of engagement and withdrawal: engagement with crowds, needs, conflict, and demands and withdrawal from public and crowded places into deserted, solitary places for prayer. This rhythm of engagement and withdrawal seemed to be a way of life for Jesus. It is a rhythm that may have much to teach us as we seek to follow and seek to clarify and deepen our vocation.

It is unwise to presume to see into the mind of Jesus. We cannot know what Jesus was thinking and feeling beyond what the New Testament text tells us. We cannot presume to know exactly what drove Jesus to solitude or what all of those prayers were about when He did withdraw. We do know that those prayers included some personal agonizing about what the will of God was for Him, embodied most clearly in the drama of Gethsemane. We know that the temptation experience that followed immediately upon His baptism was a time of conflict, for conflict is the essence of temptation.

While it would be saying too much to imply that Jesus was confused about His vocation, it would not be saying too much to conclude that these times of withdrawal included times of struggle in which Jesus sought to discern more clearly where His vocation was leading Him. We have already seen that His act of public obedience in accepting John's baptism was followed by a time of intense temptation. We see later that, before engaging in a public preaching ministry, He withdrew again to pray (Mark 1:35ff.).

What a discipline it must have been to withdraw time and time again to seek the presence, nurture, and guidance of God. The pattern that seems to present itself in the Gospels is not that Jesus withdrew only when meeting opposition. We see clearly that He withdrew at times when surrounded by adoring throngs. He resisted the temptation of the inflated ego and returned to His source of strength.

The experience of success can be a source of temptation as great as the experiences of loss or failure. The accounts of the wilderness temptation experience of Jesus foreshadow what

Jesus must have continually experienced. As word spread of Jesus' healing and authority, He withdrew to the lonely place to seek the presence and guidance of God. He might have been swept away on a tide of popularity, thus giving in to the temptation to trade His proclamation of God's kingdom for an earthly one built on His fame.

Apparently this regular retreat into solitude and prayer did not go unnoticed by His disciples. Jesus certainly taught about prayer. Matthew placed the Lord's Prayer in the context of the Sermon on the Mount, in a section on true religion (Matt. 6:1-18). In the entire section Jesus contrasted genuine religion with the kind that is concerned with impressing peers. He counseled that prayer be a matter of going into the closet—the secret, solitary place. He instructed that prayer is not a matter of seeing how many words one can make. Instead, the Lord's Prayer is a model of the economy of words, a brief prayer seeking the kingdom, asking for daily needs and requesting the grace to forgive and receive forgiveness.

Jesus' teaching about prayer went beyond the verbal instructions He gave in the Sermon on the Mount. In Luke the Lord's Prayer is given in the context of the disciples' noticing and asking Jesus about prayer:

> He was praying in a certain place, and when he ceased, one of his disciples said to him, "Lord, teach us to pray, as John taught his disciples." And he said to them, "When you pray, say: Father, hallowed be thy name. Thy kingdom come. Give us each day our daily bread; and forgive us our sins, for we ourselves forgive every one who is indebted to us; and lead us not into temptation" (Luke 11:1-4).

They saw Jesus withdrawing from the crowds. They saw Him

seek solitude. They saw Him pray, and they realized that this solitude and prayer were somehow central to what He was doing. So they asked Him to teach them to pray. They realized that part of following this One who had called them was learning what He was up to in those times of solitary praying.

The Gospels give us two other accounts of the words of Jesus' prayers. One is the Synoptic accounts of the struggle in Gethsemane. The other is the account in John 17 of Jesus praying for His disciples. Both are instructive for our look at Jesus as a model for vocation and, in particular, His life of solitude and prayer.

The Gethsemane struggle is a glimpse of profound anguish. An honest reading of those passages cannot allow us to maintain a picture of a dispassionate Jesus removed from the struggles of life. These were not merely the everyday struggles of life. These were struggles springing directly from following the way of God. These were the struggles of following the vocation God was leading Him to fulfill.

Jesus did not whistle His way to the cross. Matthew's account says that Jesus was "sorrowful and troubled" (26:37). Mark's account says He was "greatly distressed and troubled" (14:33). Some manuscripts of Luke include these words: "And being in agony he prayed more earnestly; and his sweat became like great drops of blood falling down upon the ground" (textual note to Luke 22:44). While not found in the most reliable manuscripts, these words correspond to the feeling tone communicated in Matthew and Mark in a most graphic image of internal struggle.

Any notions we have that our vocation is always made clear, filled with happiness, and marked by "success" surely come apart with an honest reading of these texts. If Jesus is the model of vocation in openness and service to God, then we can only conclude that such openness will include struggle. What Jesus modeled clearly for us is that His relationship with God was so honest that He did not need to deny His struggle; rather, He brought it freely to His Father as a matter of prayer.

Internal conflict is not a sign that one has not discerned God's leadership or that one has left the path of true vocation under God. Actually, following the leadership of God may lead one directly into conflict, internal and external. At times a troubled heart may be the sign of sensitivity, not of wandering or desertion. By now, Jesus' pattern of withdrawal into solitude and prayer was such that this deepest troubling of His spirit was a matter for honest struggle with God.

It is tempting for us to interpret Jesus' rhythm of engagement and withdrawal as simply the way He stayed focused on His vocation. That is no doubt part of the truth. We do know from the accounts of Gethsemane that Jesus sought direction from God about the cross He feared was in front of Him. He sought, in that time of agonizing prayer, to clarify God's will for Him in the hours ahead. The other part of the truth that I think we often miss is that the rhythm of engagement and withdrawal was not merely a way of clarifying vocation, it was vocation itself. Solitude, reflection, and prayer are not the only ways to clarify and deepen our vocation. They are part of the vocation of discipleship, modeled by Jesus throughout the Gospels. Prayer is not only a means to vocation; it is vocation.

Like the disciples, prayer is not something that comes naturally to us. Simply agreeing to follow Jesus did not mean that they knew how to pray. Part of the following itself included watching their leader and asking Him to teach them to pray. In other words, part of learning how to be a disciple was learning how to pray. So it is for us.

One other feature about Jesus' pattern of praying and teaching about praying that we see in the Gospels deserves mention here. That is the emphasis on privacy and solitude, at times even secrecy. A return to the first chapter of Mark underscores the point. Verse 35 says that Jesus withdrew to "a lonely place." The words translated *lonely* is from the same root that is translated in verses 12 and 13 as "wilderness." The ministry of John the Baptist had taken place in the wilderness, recalling the themes of wilderness in the Exodus. Immediately after Jesus' baptism, He was driven into the wilderness, a place of forsakenness and danger. After the calling of some disciples, we see Jesus now returning to "a lonely place" for prayer.

It is clear that at times the discipline of prayer and solitude will take us to a lonely place. Honest searching for the purposes of God in our lives will at times be a lonely undertaking, full of struggle. In the last chapter we spoke of experiences of God that were full of light, warmth, perhaps even ecstasy. These are important resources for the Christian life. At times, however, it is clear that prayer will not be marked by ecstasy but by loneliness and struggle, such are the rhythms of the journey.

### *Transfiguration: Seeing Ahead*

The Synoptics contain another central event in the life of Jesus that looks backward and forward: the account of His transfiguration. In all three Synoptics, the account of Jesus' transfiguration finds its context in the sayings of Jesus about the cost of discipleship. Jesus had talked about the cost of following and predicted that some standing there with Him would not die before they saw the kingdom in its splendor. Immediately the event of transfiguration is narrated, and Peter, James, and John witness the fulfillment of that prediction.

Like Jesus' baptism, this is one of those events of Jesus' life that does not get a lot of exposure in sermons. One of the questions for interpreting it must be: how did it function for that inner circle of disciples? The context of the prediction mentioned above gives one of the main clues. It was that glimpse of the kingdom promised to the "some standing here" (Mark 9:1). (I will be following Mark's telling of the story. For parallels see Matt. 17:1-8 and Luke 9:28-36.)

The setting for this glimpse of the kingdom was a "high mountain." Throughout the passage the scene of wilderness will be recalled. The high mountain recalls the wilderness scene of Sinai where Moses received the law from God (Ex. 24:12-18). Suddenly Jesus was transfigured in their presence, and they saw also Moses and Elijah. Jesus, who began His ministry in the wilderness of Judea, being baptized by John, took the disciples to a wilderness place, where they were met by the great prophets of the desert.

What was occurring before the disciples' eyes is much like the Old Testament appearance of the majesty and splendor of God. This was a holy place, a high moment, and important things were being revealed. Jesus'clothing itself became as a light, "glistening" (Mark 9:3). Jesus talked with these great desert prophets whose missions He was fulfilling with His own and whose promises he embodied. This moment lifted them out of the ordinary flow of events with an exclamation point.

It was such a high point that Peter misunderstood. And who would not? Peter, glimpsed the kingdom, saw Jesus glorified, recognized Moses and Elijah (we're not told how), and asked Jesus if they could build booths here. That time and that place was so marvelous that Peter wanted to mark it with a tabernacle, a monument. Mark added the telling comment when he explained Peter's suggestion: "For he did not know what to say, for they were exceedingly afraid" (Mark 9:6). How often have we expressed our confusion and fear by saying something distracting, when silence would have been the better part of wisdom?

Peter's wanting to build booths has been the one part of this passage that has most consistently been the subject of sermons. In the moments when we understand most clearly who Jesus is and when we see Jesus revealed to us most clearly among the temptations that we have is to build a tabernacle in that place. It is the temptation to never leave the mountain of holy experiences. It is the temptation to remain in the high and remote places where we have seen God most fully.

What happened next recalls both Sinai and Jesus' baptism. The mountain was covered with a cloud, and they heard a voice coming out of the cloud: "This is my beloved Son; listen to him" (v. 7). Moses ascended Mount Sinai to receive the law and was covered by a cloud, out of which God spoke to him. The disciples went up the mountain with Jesus, where they saw Moses and Elijah along with Jesus. A voice spoke to them out of the cloud as well, but what was revealed was not the law, but the glory of the transfigured Jesus. The words that are spoken to them recall the words of the baptism, declaring blessing on Jesus.

As the voice at Jesus' baptism confirmed His obedience, so

does this voice confirm it again. In the context of Mark's Gospel, it particularly confirmed what Jesus had said about the conditions for discipleship and His prediction of His passion. Jesus had begun to teach them about His passion beginning in Mark 8:31, and it was Peter who failed to understand again. Peter began to rebuke Jesus and was himself rebuked. Immediately after this scene, Jesus told the disciples and others that any who would be His disciple should understand that the way of discipleship is modeled on this sacrificial love. Finally, He made the prediction that some who stood with Him would see the kingdom of God revealed, and the scene shifted to the transfiguration.

What has any of this to do with our look at vocation? Some summary observations are in order. First, it is too easy to look at the actions of Peter in the eighth and ninth chapters of Mark and wonder at his stupidity. We secretly, or not so secretly, marvel at how anyone could miss the point so repeatedly. If that is our attitude, then we have missed the point. The Gospel of Mark, more than any other, models for us what it is to be a disciple. Repeatedly in Mark, disciples missed the point, misunderstood, or only partially understood. It is a portrait of me and you.

Who of us has not known the temptation to build a booth marking the spot of our clearest understanding of God. In the moment when Jesus' promise was being fulfilled that they would "see . . . the kingdom," Peter could not imagine anything greater, anything on the other side of this high moment. And as soon as he sought to build the booth, the cloud came which obscured their vision.

That is often our story, too. Our lives contain times or events or relationships in which we understand God more clearly than ever. They are powerful and important stations on the road of discipleship. Our temptation is to resist moving from such a place, feeling surely that God would have us build a tabernacle there.

One of the temptations for us is to build a booth to our career or job. If we have never felt more fulfilled than we did in that job or if we have never felt more useful than when our children needed us more, then it may be difficult for us to move off that mountain to another place. It may be that some storm has knocked us off the mountain, and we are trying to decide whether to ascend the same slope or move on down the road. While I would not presume to answer that question for anyone, I can speak of the temptation to believe that God's presence is limited to the mountaintop where we last saw the kingdom.

It is clear that the journey includes times when a cloud covers the mountain, and seemingly the valley below. It is clear that the journey includes moments or seasons when we are afraid. If the Gospels are correct, discipleship will contain as many times when we misunderstand or partially understand as times when we understand perfectly. No less a disciple than Peter, the "rock" of the early church, repeatedly did not grasp the whole meaning of Jesus' words and actions. Witnessing the transfiguration did not put a stop to Peter's or the disciples' tendency to misunderstand where Jesus was leading them.

They were particularly resistant to understanding what Jesus was saying in teaching them about His passion and way of suffering love. Particularly at those times they would (and we) prefer visions of Moses and Elijah to a road that leads along a way of suffering.

## *Gethsemane: A Way of Suffering*

It seems that Jesus, too, struggled with a vocation that was leading Him to make the ultimate sacrifice, when "success" was ready to greet Him at every turn. The scene of His praying in the garden recalls much of what we have sketched about Jesus to this point. It was a time of withdrawal for solitude and prayer. It no doubt was another entry into a wilderness in which He sought to discover more fully the meaning of His baptism. The temptations which confronted Him in that first wilderness experience were no doubt present in this final struggle as well.

Even in Jesus' final hours His disciples had failed to clearly understand that His mission was not to establish a political kingdom. Surely there was popular sentiment that might have supported such an undertaking. The temptation could have been there to seek fame instead of His deeper vocation. Surely the tempter's words returned: He had only to put God to the test, and He would be rescued by a legion of angels. What an excruciating hour this must have been.

To make matters worse, the disciples, who spent these years with Him, who saw Him transfigured in the company of Moses and Elijah, and who saw His ministry, deserted Him in this hour. They slumbered nearby, unaware of the agony of Jesus' spirit. Hours later, they would physically abandon Him as well. He knew not only the inner suffering of His tortured spirit, He knew the suffering of betrayal and abandonment.

Mark described Jesus as "greatly distressed and troubled" (14:33). Jesus told the disciples, "My soul is very sorrowful, even unto death" (v. 34). It is clear from the biblical evidence that He did not want the suffering of that moment or the suffering He no doubt saw in the hours ahead. It is clear that He did not seek it. Rather, in the hour it came to Him, He sought again to discern the will of God concerning the vocation He had been given.

It is not ours to seek suffering either. We have all known persons who see every inconvenience as the persecution of their sainthood by unbelievers or weak believers. We have all known persons who know how to get nurture and support by rehearsing how they have suffered for righteousness' sake. All of these persons go looking for suffering in a distorted manner of drawing attention to themselves. That was not what the cross was about. The cross was not a model for seeking out suffering. It is a model for seriously seeking to discern the will of God.

Few of us are called to the kind of cross which Jesus suffered. Yet the model of Gethsemane shows the very humanity of Jesus, agonizing about what it meant to still "be about my Father's business" (Luke 2:49, KJV). That is the agony that many know who feel themselves searching for God's purposes for them. The agony you may feel is not a sign of failure. It is merely a sign of your taking the struggle seriously, as did Jesus.

If Jesus is a model for us, then we can be assured that there will be times of struggle. The One called to be Son of God did not walk whistling through the pages of the Gospels. He modeled for us a faithfulness to enter the struggle, seek the face of God in the midst of it, and resist the temptations to forsake the calling for which we have been grasped.

### *Discipleship: Needing a Second Touch*

Throughout much of this chapter focusing on Jesus, I have relied heavily on Mark's Gospel. The primary reason for that is the way Mark's Gospel treats the disciples. The shortest of Gospels, Mark may also be "hardest" on the disciples. At almost every turn, they came away looking like they simply did not understand. They misinterpreted, failed to see, and rebuked Jesus for following the course that led to His way of suffering love.

A theme of abandonment runs throughout Mark's Gospel. With characteristic terseness Mark reports: "And they all forsook him and fled" (14:50). The disciples lead the way in abandoning Jesus in the final hours, but finally Jesus declared that He had been abandoned by God (15:34). Mark minces no words about the difficulty the disciples had in trying to follow and in the struggle Jesus had in continuing to be faithful to His mission. Neither Jesus nor the disciples fulfilled their callings without struggle and, in the case of the disciples, misunderstanding and failure.

Why choose to highlight a Gospel that puts the disciples in such a bad light? One of the reasons is that, if you are struggling with a sense of vocation, you may feel like a disciple who is struggling and perhaps failing. That struggling and failing is made worse for any of us when we compare ourselves to some ideal. Ideal images of who we want to be or ought to be can be helpful, but they can also be harsh sources of self-criticism. That is seldom helpful when we already know ourselves to be struggling.

Put simply, I think the Gospels have two main functions. They tell us who Jesus is, and they tell us what it is like to be a disciple. The Gospels' descriptions of being a disciple include times when we will fail to see and encourage Jesus to take a way other than the way of suffering love. We will struggle with concerns over who is the greatest. We will be tempted to build booths at the time and place when we see Jesus and the kingdom most clearly. We are likely, at times, to simply run away or drowse into sleep when we have been asked to stay awake.

Yes, these slow-hearted people were the disciples. They went on to be the leaders of the early church, being responsible for spreading good news and shepherding the flock of first-century believers. Tradition has it that some followed Jesus in a martyr's death. We do neither them nor ourselves a service to project onto them some ideal of discipleship that excludes their struggling or ours.

The vocation of discipleship is the vocation of following this One who is at the center of the Gospels and of all of the New Testament. Following, it would appear, was at times hard work, and the disciples did not do it perfectly. They kept learning about this Man who had called them, deepening their understanding. That is our story, too. Part of our vocation will be to realize that we are continuing to discover who this One is whose story we find in the New Testament. Even when we have transfiguring experiences, we still misunderstand, we still fail to follow, and we are still restored again to the journey.

What following means to pilgrims removed thousands of miles and years from the dusty roads of Palestine is the task of a lifetime. We do not have that printed plainly for us the instant we become a Christian. We must seek our own rhythm of engagement and withdrawal and be open to seeing Jesus anew, understanding anew what the journey of following means for us.

Mark is the only Gospel that contains a story that, for me, speaks some of what it is to be a disciple. That is the story of the blind man of Bethsaida found in Mark 8:22-26. It is a brief story, taking only four verses to tell. It follows immediately one of the passages in Mark in which Jesus had chided the disciples (again) for not understanding. He rehearsed for them some of the wonders they had beheld while following Him and challenged them to see the deeper meaning of those events. Jesus even said to them: "Having eyes do you not see, and having ears do you not hear?" (v. 18).

Immediately following that passage we find this story about a man whose vision needed healing. Jesus spat upon his eyes and laid His hands upon the man. When He asked him what he saw, the man replied quite honestly that he could see better, but not perfectly: "I see men; but they look like trees, walking" (v. 24). Without a word, Jesus laid His hands on him again, and his sight was restored fully. Coming where it does, I see this story as a parable of discipleship among other things. In the context of the disciples not seeing, Mark includes a story about vision that needed more than one touch of the Master to be restored. That is me. Discipleship is the constant healing and training of my vision that I might see the world as it is more clearly, myself as I am, and Jesus as He is. The training of my vision is vocation for a lifetime.

## Jesus' Vocation and Human Vocation

It may run against the grain a bit for you to consider Jesus as a model for vocation. Is that not a strange notion to us, given our emphasis on the uniqueness of Jesus? Does our recognition of Jesus as unique disqualify Him as a model for vocation? I think not. Schillebeeckx says in *Jesus: An Experiment in Christology* that in Jesus we have a transforming model of what it is to be human. Jesus not only reveals God to us; He reveals to us the vocation of humanity under God, deepening the meaning of what it is to be truly human. Surely we have in the Gospels a witness to Jesus' vocation as Son of God. If John's Gospel is right, Jesus' vocation makes those of us who follow Him children of God, and that is the vocation that we also see modeled in the Gospels.

Our emphasis on the uniqueness of Jesus rightly preserves His status as the Savior, the Messiah, the "only begotten of the Father." We are not called to be Messiah, Savior, and Lord of Creation. But that does not exclude Jesus as a model for vocation. One of the things that we have looked to the Gospels for is *how* Jesus went about seeking relationship with God so that He could follow the vocation He was called to assume. In the *how* of Jesus' relationship to God and neighbor, He modeled the fulfillment of what it is to be human.

What is our vocation? It is to be human. We were created to be human. Here is the link between that great catechism and the redemptive purposes of God. The life of Jesus reveals to us the how of that purpose of "loving God and enjoying Him forever." Here is the fulfillment of the Shema, the mandate to love God with the whole self, deepened by Jesus' command to extend that love to the neighbor. That is our deepest human vocation, worth a lifetime of struggling.

What have we meant when we have spoken of Jesus' humanity? When we affirm in our statements of faith that Jesus was wholly human and wholly divine, what have we meant on the human side? Too often we have said that Jesus' humanity consisted only in His being subject to human bodily needs, aches, pains, and temptations. We have interpreted "humanity" in a way that sees it as a collection of inconveniences and the temptation to do things not good for us. Our interpretation

of His humanity has been colored by our experience of fallenness. In other words, we have defined humanity as sinfulness
and limitation. If we are to continue to affirm Jesus' humanity
and leave any meaning to that statement, it must mean more.
It must mean that somehow Jesus fulfilled what it is to be fully
human, not only that He resisted temptation. Jesus' perfection
consisted not only in His *refraining* from doing certain things
but also consisted in His doing human things well.

Jesus' humanity consisted in His fulfilling the purposes for
which God created humans. Jesus continued to experience the
kind of relationship with God for which we were created. By
so doing, He made possible our restoration to the possibilities
of that kind of relationship. Jesus' vocation was to be Son of
God, and among the things that Son of God means is that He
lived fully His life as a human.

One of the things that life as a disciple means is that we can
be delivered from a vocation that is too narrowly conceived.
Among the things that Jesus learned at the knee of Joseph was
a trade. Would we describe the vocation of Jesus as carpenter?
Surely not. Only those who misunderstood Him reduced Him
to that role. Jesus is referred to (in disbelief and derision) as a
carpenter (Mark 6:3) and a carpenter's son (Matt. 13:55) by
those who failed to see His vocation.

The continuing work of conversion means that we can be
freed from a preoccupation with our role and freed to carry a
growing self into the many roles that might be ours. In seeing
Jesus as a model for human vocation, we can begin to let go of
the fear that we are missing a particular purpose or role. We
can grow into the assurance that we have purpose, no matter
what the job, role, or task. We have the purpose of living fully

the life we have been given, resting in the grace that comes our way.

Jesus' interactions with people time and time again freed them from the constraints of a role. In Jesus' company, fishermen became fishers of men, tax collectors became gift givers, and women became disciples and preachers of the resurrection. A thief joined the ranks of the redeemed, and a soldier present at the resurrection saw in the suffering of Jesus the identity of the Son of God. In being followers they found an identity that was larger than their trade, their social status, and their moral past. It is to that cloud of witnesses we have been joined.

# 6

## Starting Over: Pain and Grace

One of the concerns that has run throughout this book is that you may have some questions about what vocation means for you. You may be in a time of transition in your life that is disorienting: a move, a loss, a change you did or did not ask for. You may simply be someone who is curious about the meaning of vocation. In this concluding chapter, I want to focus on how to carry on from here, assuming "here" is a place of questioning, loss, or pain. I will name some specific things that you can do as you build or rebuild and discover or rediscover what your vocation under God is. At the same time, I want to paint some pictures of vocation that rest on the foundations of earlier chapters.

### Vocation as Vision

Depending on whether an acute sense of loss or a mild curiosity has led you to read this far, you may be reading with some deeply felt pain about losing something or not finding something. Regardless of whether that pain is small or great, vocation has to do with how the world looks and feels to us. In the previous chapter, I suggested that discipleship was a vocation that had to do with training us to see the world anew and continuing to sharpen and deepen our vision of the world and of the kingdom.

## *Chastened Vision*[1]

When we move through a painful time in our life, we often are given to lament in one form or another. That is right and good. One of the forms of the psalms in Scripture is that of lament. A common way of expressing our lament over painful chapters in our lives is saying that the world just doesn't look the same to us anymore. One of the things we feel is "disillusioned." What does it mean to be disillusioned? Quite literally, it means "to free or deprive from illusion," as Webster's dictionary defines it. In the middle of disillusionment, it always feels a lot more like deprived than freed.

None of us like to think that what we hold or cherish are illusions. We all think we see the world as it is. The truth is, as we continue to grow, we are continually revising the way we see the world. We find that the way we saw things was a little distorted. We find that with the best of intentions we thought the world was one way, and it is not. The way we saw things may have been intimately connected to our faith, and so the "disillusionment" is even more troubling, because it strikes so close to something important to us. None of us like to think of our faith as in any way "illusion." Indeed, we may feel deprived, not only of a particular view, but a whole way of seeing the world that was important to us.

Recall our discussion in chapter 5 of the blind man at Bethsaida (Mark 8:22-26). His vision was not completely restored by the first healing touch of Jesus. Mark's narration of that story does not in any way imply that there was anything wrong either with this man or with Jesus that required this

continued healing. It is simply told in a straightforward manner and in the same chapter as the disciples being chastened
for their failure to see.

What happens to us in a painful time of loss and "disillusionment" is that our vision of the world is chastened. That
hurts and often feels like something very important is being
taken away from us. We feel deprived, but we do not like to
think of what we are being deprived of as illusion. Perhaps it
was not, but it was at least vision not completely healed.

Webster's definition has in it a certain implicit wisdom.
What at first feels like deprivation has at least the potential to
become freedom. If healing continues, we can at times begin
to realize that what felt like the only possible way to see ourselves and the world actually constricted our vision. If our
grief heals, then our vision is often sharper. We have been
freed to see the world more as it really is.

### Several Dimensions of Vision

There are several dimensions to this thing I am calling vision so intimately related to vocation. At the heart is the way
we see ourselves. What continues to cloud our vision is our
tendency to self-deception. That tendency never leaves us this
side of perfection, and perfection never comes to us in this
life. Thus, the stripping away of layers of self-deception is at
the heart of growth in the Christian life. We continue, often
with great resistance, to see ourselves more honestly. We are
able to put down, in the security of God's love, the illusions
about ourselves to which we grow so attached.

Another dimension of our vision that continues to grow is
how we see others. One of Jesus' parables (Luke 20) speaks to
the workers that were hired at different times during the day,

all for the same wage. At the end of the day, those workers who had been hired early in the day grumbled about being paid the same wage as those who had come late in the day. They thought they were intrinsically better and worth more than those who had come later. Like the elder brother in Luke 15, they resented the redemption offered to someone whose sins were "greater" than theirs. One of the illusions most of us take great care to nurture is our private perception of ourselves as greater than others. The New Testament subverts that self-perception at every turn.

Another distortion of the way we see ourselves has to do with the limits we have placed on ourselves. We may have "always seen ourselves" doing the thing we have just lost. In other words, we had never imagined ourselves doing anything other than what we were doing. It may be that we never saw ourselves as capable of doing anything else, or we may have taken as gospel someone else's description of who we were and what we could do. A crisis in vocation invites us to imagine ourselves experiencing joy and fulfillment in circumstances we had never before imagined. A crisis in vocation invites us to hope in directions we had never before hoped. We are challenged to see ourselves anew and dream a new dream about who we are and where God may be leading us.

Finally, our vision includes the way we see God. As we saw in the last chapter, the disciples continued to see Jesus in new ways throughout the Gospels. They responded to His call to follow. As important as that response was, it did not mean that they understood completely who it was they were following. Our following the Nazarene continues to reveal to us who God is. The New Testament witness is that those first disciples underwent a process of continuing to understand what it meant to follow Jesus. As they followed, they understood more deeply what it meant to follow. Their deeper understanding of Jesus meant that they had also a deeper vision of God. Our understanding, picture, and experience of God change as we grow.

Seldom in the midst of a painful event do we understand the changes occurring in the way we see. Only in living through the events, including the pain, do we come to a gradual understanding of what is happening to us. *Disillusionment* means that we can never see the world in the same way again. It does not mean we cannot see, just that we will see differently. What we see differently may include ourselves, others, and God. We can expect that as our vision changes, however painful that may be at times, our understanding of the life of faith changes. Our understanding of our vocation may change as well. As frightening as that may be, it may also be the sign of growth and the work of sanctification in us.

### *Through a Mirror Dimly*

Another biblical image is applicable in this discussion of vocation and vision. That is Paul's marvelous reminder to us about the limitations of our vision. It is an image of both comfort and hope: "For now we see in a mirror dimly, but then face to face. Now I know in part; then I shall understand fully, even as I have been fully understood" (1 Cor. 13:12). Paul's poetry reminds us that as our vision is being healed, it is never perfect. That comes as comfort to those of us who are hard on ourselves when we realize we do not fully understand. Understanding is partial from our side.

Paul went on to sing the comforting assurance that he is fully understood. In the midst of a crisis of any sort, that is a healing source of comfort. Paul rested in the assurance that he was fully understood, even though at the moment he did not fully understand. Perfect understanding of the ways of God is not attainable in this lifetime. However, Paul's marvelous writing expresses the hope that understanding will grow.

Notice the image on which Paul rested his hope of future understanding. It is the image of seeing "face to face." While confessing and perhaps lamenting his lack of understanding, Paul rested his hope on the appearance of the face of God. He longed to be met by the face that called him, stopped him on the Damascus Road, and appeared to him as a blinding light.

Vocation is never a perfect understanding and never some perfect attainment of some perfect plan. It is resting in the assurance that we are fully understood. It is being comforted by the memory of God's appearances to us and the hope of seeing face to face. Our understanding of the ways of God, including our vocation, is "through a mirror dimly." We are called to acknowledge that and live boldly and joyously, knowing that grace and forgiveness are with us. We press on knowing that our vision will be partial and our understanding never complete in this life, but resting in the assurance that we are fully understood by the One who created us.

## Listening to One's Own Story

I do not think we press on in absolute blindness, although at times it may feel that way. As we find ourselves in the middle of a crossroads in vocation, one of the things we can do is look back and see again where we have been. I believe that vocation for all of us is related to our unique stories of grace.

Consider Paul again. At several points in his journeys, he was faced with some person or group who, out of curiosity or hostility, wanted to know more. One of the things Paul did was, quite simply, tell them his story of encountering grace. In Acts the story of his conversion is found three times. Paul explored his own history and utilized it in the service of the One who met him and called him.

Certainly what Paul was up to at the time of his conversion was despicable. He was persecuting those new followers of the Way. But Paul's history contained more than that. It included years of study in the Jewish law. It included having learned a trade with which he could support himself. It included a personal determination and apparent forcefulness that would serve him well as Christianity's most famous missionary.

What happened at Paul's conversion was not that his history got erased. Instead, his history found redemption and a new direction. He discovered that grace was such that he could use his history in the service of the One who had stopped him and called him. There were portions of Paul's history that he was proud of and that he was not proud of, but his story found a wholeness in his new calling to be a disciple.

At times vocation may feel like a whole new story, a change in direction, purpose, and even role or job. At another level, though, vocation does not represent so much a new story as a growing wholeness to the story that is uniquely ours. Vocation is a sense of identity that helps the seemingly unrelated aspects of our own story stay together. We are not asked to ignore or throw away our own story. Rather, we are asked to make that story available for deeper understanding.

Christians have embraced a doctrine called Providence for centuries. When we say we believe in Providence, we are affirming that, without violating our ability to choose, God is constantly at work in our lives, often without our awareness. We affirm that events that at the time seemed random and meaningless have contained the mysterious grace of God. It is the doctrine of looking back. It is the doctrine that with surprise and wonder sees the grace of God in times and events that otherwise seemed common and meaningless.

Providence links the doctrines of creation and redemption. Creation affirms that there is grace present in the world and in our having been made. Redemption affirms that our fallenness is redeemed in Christ. Providence affirms that the grace of creation and redemption are linked in the events of this world in ways not immediately visible. Providence affirms not only that in the "fullness of time" did the Messiah come, but that time itself is full of the creative and redemptive purposes of God.

Vocation affirms that what we believe about Providence on the plane of world history we also believe about our own stories. Examining again our own stories may provide us with a new look at a thread of continuity we had not seen before. Looking again may provide us with a depth of understanding about who we are in light of where we have been.

Often we are hesitant to look again at our own stories because we have seen very little grace in them. We are aware only of their pain. Persons come to my office every day who want to forget as much as they can of painful pasts. I do not pat them on the head and tell them to look on the bright side. That is not what I mean by examining our own stories of grace. Indeed, looking to our own stories may involve facing some pain that we have sought to escape. My conviction is that God's grace can contain and touch that pain, perhaps through the sensitive listening of someone trained to help us sort through that kind of pain. Old pain can hold us in bondage. Looking again at our story can release us from the bondage of old wounds and free us to see in those wounds a way of finding grace that we can offer in the service of God.

## The Well-Lived Life: A Vocation of Virtue

One of the lost dimensions of the meaning of vocation that I want to argue for is the pursuit of virtue. If the continuing work of redemption is sanctification, then we are each called to see the pursuit of virtue as our continuing vocation.

Often I ask persons in a teaching context to identify those who have been most influential in their lives. Most people can do that with little reflection. I usually go on and ask them to try and name some of the reasons that person was such a model for them. The answers are different, of course, but some common themes emerge. Among those themes is the response that people who have been influential have done so as much by how they lived as what they did. Most of us have some key persons after whom we have more or less consciously patterned our lives. Often we see in those persons the embodiment of particular virtues.

I am influenced by persons who live their lives well—persons in whom virtue has taken root and flowered. Often it does not matter what these persons do for a living that leaves its mark on my life. Rather, it is how they do whatever is theirs to do. I have been most impressed by persons who lives were filled by a quiet and deep rootedness that did not need lots of explanation or defense. Certainly I have been influenced by persons in ministry along the way. Those who have been most influential did it through the quality of their personal living, not simply in the way they went about the tasks of ministry.

All of us are deeply influenced by our parents or the persons who reared us. That influence can be negative as well as positive. I am fortunate in that I find myself continuing to be positively influenced by the model my parents have given me. I do not make my living the way either of them have. I do find myself admiring the way they have chosen values and quietly and consistently lived them out. I was fortunate to witness an agreement between what they believed and how they lived. I witnessed some virtues that I neither fully appreciated at the time, nor realized how uncommon they were.

Regardless of how they made their living, my parents' vocation as parents has profoundly shaped me. How would someone have described their vocation twenty years ago, when they were both employed and their children were living at home? While I cannot answer that question, I can witness to the fact that it included being a parent. I can also witness to the fact that their children were watching and learning. We did not learn a lot about what they did to make a living, though we certainly knew about that. We were learning deeper lessons.

One of the things I have admired about my parents is that they have never spent any energy pretending to be anything other than what they were. I mention that because a danger lurks in my lifting up a life of virtue as one of the central components of Christian vocation. That danger is the temptation to live out virtues that we do not possess or try and pretend that we are better than we are. The paradox of growth in virtue is that it is only possible through a thorough honesty about oneself, including one's need for grace. Growth in virtue finally comes only through grace, and the beginning of

growth in grace is admitting our need for it. Denial is not a
virtue in any rendering of the Christian virtues.

If you are reading this book from the experience of crisis or
loss, then hear this. The life of virtue through grace is available to all of us, regardless of station, rank, job, or role. Virtue is not achieved by denying the present pain you feel, nor
making light of the loss you have experienced. On the contrary, it means making that pain available to yourself, caring
others, and God's transforming grace.

How do any of us learn virtue? Certainly prayer and study
are important avenues for growth. I believe, however, that
most of us learn virtue through seeing it in the lives of other
people. We learn virtue through seeing it and imitating it. We
have made too much of "successful" careers and too little of
*well-lived lives* in our churches.

At times the well-lived life may even need the courage to
say no to the temptations of "success." Our vocation as disciples will include a multiplicity of roles related to our families
and our communities of faith in addition to our jobs. At times
we may need to say no to the demands or temptations of work
and the recognition that it brings. We say no in order to be
more fully who we have been called to be as husband, wife,
father, or mother. At times the price of further success may be
one that involves pretending we are something we are not.

Hear again the subtle temptation present in pretending we
have virtue. Hear the temptation to spend enormous energy
trying to make others believe we have our spiritual, emotional, or interpersonal lives in perfect order. None of us does,
and most of our attempts to make others think we do only
ends in disappointment for us and them.

Stanley Hauerwas, who has influenced my thinking about

the place of virtue, describes Christian living as patience and hope in the face of being out of control. We simply do not and cannot secure our future through our own efforts. The ability to live in hope, patience, and trust in the light of elements of our existence that are out of our control is at the heart of Christian virtue, according to Hauerwas. We must resist the temptation to build personal or communal Towers of Babel to secure our future.

## Render to Caesar

At several points in this book I have mentioned the possible conflict between discipleship and the ways we make a living. I have suggested that in our tradition there lies a clear prohibition from "unrighteous" ways of making a living. Those have traditionally been defined as ways of making a living related to personal vices and individual sins, such as gambling. While that is one application of that principle, the deeper meaning goes beyond not making one's living from gambling or other vices.

The gospel may also be calling us to look again at industries or ways of making a living that create social injustice in addition to personal vice. Some have called for serious conversation about Christians involved in industries that make war more likely, that profit from the weapons of war, and that seriously damage the creation with which we have been entrusted. It is not as simple as listing jobs or companies that are "off limits" to Christians, and surely there will be differences among persons of good faith. But that kind of conversation would lend a new seriousness to our concerns about vocation and a new level of engagement around important moral questions among the people of God.

Of course, no job is free from temptations to carry it out in less than ethical ways. We are required to carry dignity, honor, and ethical standards into any job that we have. It is in the marketplace that many of us have tremendous opportunity to be persons of virtue and the example for the well-lived life that makes discipleship evident and attractive. It is also in the marketplace that we find the most subtle of pressures and temptations, as well as ethical dilemmas that call upon our deepest virtue and our best thinking.

Some denominations have their roots in the wing of the Protestant Reformation that emphasized the separateness of the church from the ways of the world. For better and for worse, that emphasis has been largely lost and trivialized in recent times. This is not the place to develop a whole argument about recovering the best of separatism, but the rendering of vocation developed here moves in that direction. The definition of vocation which I want us to recover makes our primary identification come from our identification with the people of God.

On the other hand, we cannot make a living without some engagement with "the world." I do not think that we are commanded to have no commerce with the world. We each have to determine the application of Jesus' wisdom to render to Caesar the things that are his and to God the things that are God's. When pressed to see if He would advocate the overthrow of the Roman rule, Jesus wisely sidestepped the question without giving unlimited authority to the government. He said that the government is due a limited loyalty and God is due ultimate loyalty. We will find no job that will not require us to render something to Caesar. Jesus reminds us to do that, but also to recall what the Shema calls us to do: to love God with the whole self.

## Utilizing the Inner Circle

In times of crisis, we need the love and support of those around us. A crisis in vocation is no exception. We need to let persons whom we trust care for us. One of the distortions of religious decision making that we have fallen prey to is a distorted individualism. There is a certain hallowed individualism that some cherish as having to do with soul competence and the freedom of the individual conscience. I am not suggesting that we do away with that good emphasis.

I am suggesting that one way to find some help in a struggle with difficult decisions about vocation is to share some of our dilemma with persons who know us well. We cannot give them responsibility for our decisions or simply get them to tell us what to do. But we can convene some of our trusted inner circle and let them know how we are struggling. Quakers have such a tradition in making difficult life decisions. Individuals gather an inner circle of persons whom they are convinced are for them, and this group asks "clarifying" questions of the person seeking help. They do not tell the person what to do. They instead seek to quietly gather, listen, and aid someone seeking to discern the will of God.

Often we do not even have an inner circle. Each of us should cultivate that kind of network of support. While a prayer list or request for prayer in "unspoken requests" are good, they may not provide us with the kind of in-depth understanding of our struggles which is potentially available in the community of faith. If you do not have a circle of friends with whom you can deeply share, you might begin by simply cultivating one relationship with a trusted friend. This friend should be a person whom you know has your best interests at heart, is a good listener, and with whom you can share some of your struggle. There is far too much quiet pain in the pews of any church that is multiplied by loneliness.

Remember Paul's images of being fully understood and of seeing face to face. He is talking about the understanding of God and of being met by the understanding face of God. One of the ways of making that hope real is for the people of God to learn to understand and let themselves be understood by others in times of struggle. To provide that kind of deep understanding for one another is to incarnate the kind of understanding Paul affirmed was present in God. For those of us who may have trouble feeling God's understanding, experiencing the understanding of fellow pilgrims can be a powerful parable for God's love. We are the continuation of the incarnation to one another and to the world.

## The People of God: Corporate Vocation

Individual vocation finds its nourishing roots in a sense of corporate vocation. Individual identity finds its bearings by having a history and being part of a group. The group from which we draw primary identity is the people of God. Part of the way of grace in a time of individual crisis is to renew our sense of identity as part of the larger people of God. We can draw identity and direction from our being a part of a purpose and a group, visible and invisible, which transcends our individualism.

### *Baptism: The Sign of Vocation*
When we become believers we indicate that decision by confessing it to a group. We make a public commitment to follow the One who has called us and is redeeming us. The most dramatic sign of that public confession and commitment

is baptism. When struggling for vocation, we can turn again to this public sign of grace and commitment. What does it mean?

Churches have individual traditions, but baptism has been an event that is both public and private. It is observed in the presence of those who are committed to the Way and who have likewise decided to follow Jesus. It is public in that we cannot baptize ourselves. It is public in that we deepen the significance of the commitment we make by acting in the presence of a group of caring and committed believers. It is a private event in that it signifies the decision of an individual who is responding to the gracious call of God. It is private in that it takes place in the presence of a group of persons similarly committed, not in the marketplace of the secular arena.

Baptism is a sign and a vow. It is a sign of our accepting the grace, forgiveness, purpose, and identity offered to us in the person and life of Jesus. It is a sign of being washed, cleansed, and born anew. We signify that we have received something when we accept the ordinance of baptism. In believer's baptism we are also making a commitment and taking a vow. Like receiving the ring and saying vows at our marriage, we are not only celebrating the love we have received, but also declaring our love and our commitment to nurture that love. We are declaring our commitment to the One who has invited us to follow.

In baptism we are declaring our solidarity with those believers through the ages who have stood in rivers, creeks, lakes, and church baptistries and participated in the same ordinance. Many churches through the centuries have included in the observance of baptism the wearing of a robe, often a white robe. The symbolism of having our garments washed is a powerful biblical image of forgiveness and salvation. When we come to the waters of baptism, we are enacting that symbol of being washed and putting on the garments of grace made personal. We are receiving an identity that does not destroy us as individuals, but joins us to the cloud of witnesses, visible and invisible, who have likewise received the good news of the kingdom of God. We are joined to the others who have been washed, who have received dazzling new garments.

One of the signs of various professions in our world is the uniform. Doctors wear one thing and nurses another. Police officers have one uniform and stockbrokers another. Farmers have overalls and giveaway caps, and astronauts have space suits and helmets. In hospitals and other organizations, different departments wear different colored uniforms, and rules dictate the bounds of acceptable dress. You can tell who a person is by the uniform he or she wears.

The baptismal robe is the principal uniform of Christian vocation. It identifies who we are most deeply. No matter what other uniforms, secular or religious, one might put on, the robe of baptism into the community of believers is the one most determinative of identity. Likewise, if you have lost a uniform that you once wore proudly whether an apron or a business suit, the garments given you when you accepted the grace that washes clean are garments that can never be taken away. If you are searching for a uniform that you will never outgrow, that will give you purpose, identity, and meaning, then you have one in that robe. You have adopted, or more properly, been adopted, into a vocation that countless others have known through the ages.

Baptism not only connects us to the entire cloud of witnesses in Christian history; it connects us to the visible group of believers who are gathered in whatever local congregation we have chosen to participate. Our corporate identity extends backwards to Antioch and Ephesus. It extends globally to believers in the USSR whose names and faces we have never seen. But it also grounds us in the here and now with names we know and faces we recognize. We declare our intention to join hands with those people for mutual support, nurture and instruction, and joyful ministry. We declare our intention to join with these persons to welcome and nurture the kingdom of God in our community.

## *Vocation: Church Universal, Church Local*

On the one hand the mission of each congregation is the same. It is to celebrate the good news of grace in Jesus Christ and proclaim that grace in word and deed. That is the mission that all churches share. On the other hand, the mission of an individual congregation should be locally shaped and refined, according to the particular challenges which confront that congregation. The underlying mission of a new, suburban church will be the same as an older, inner-city congregation. The particular shapes of the ministries and emphases of those two congregations might look very different. That marvelous diversity is what makes up the beauty and mystery of the body of Christ. Just as my individual story may give shape to my expression of Christian vocation, so a congregation's particular history may give shape to its individual mission.

I fear that local congregations often do not have a self-conscious sense of mission. Often we have not given time and serious thought to a consideration of just how this particular group of believers is being called to shape its mission in this place and at this time. Church conflicts erupt when one group holds to a sense of mission forged years ago and another group feels a different mission. Rather than letting that conflict be a creative opportunity for dialogue and deepening of mission, we accuse one another of being less than holy and retreat into self-righteous criticism.

One of the ways that we can rejuvenate our sense of Christian vocation is to have a clear sense of what in the world this local congregation has been called to do in this place and this time. When we feel a part of a group with a mission we put less pressure on our other roles and jobs to carry all of our meaning and purpose in this world. In fact, a sense of mission that has roots in and feels connected to a group with a strong sense of mission gives energy and new creativity to all of our other roles. Churches ought to be asking themselves what their mission is and how it relates to their individual history and the current challenges before them and their community.

### *Vocation and Social Justice*

Part of a renewed sense of vocation for any of us includes resisting unjust definitions of vocation imposed on us by a society whose mission is not the church's. The church too often unquestioningly adopts the system of values and status of the culture that surrounds it. So it is that we import definitions of "success" into our congregations that have nothing to do with the norms of discipleship as we see them in the gospels. So it is that we continue social systems that strip some persons of dignity and opportunity. So it is that we redefine the well-lived life into the well-heeled life, pretending that affluence and virtue are identical.

The identification of affluence with virtue does not only

oppress those who are not affluent, but it also oppresses the affluent as well. They must pretend that their wealth has made them happy and virtuous, when in their heart of hearts they long to be fully known and cease pretending. The church must not make it more difficult for anyone to cease pretending. The church denies the meaning of Christian vocation if we fail to work for the dignity of all.

A passage from Luke's Gospel speaks to this dimension of Christian vocation. It comes when Jesus was beginning His ministry. Recall that it was Luke who told the story of the boy Jesus being found in the Temple going "about [his] Father's business." After baptism and temptation, Jesus was found in the Nazareth synagogue announcing His understanding of the business to which His Father was calling Him. He opened the scroll to Isaiah and read:

> "The Spirit of the Lord is upon me,
> because he has anointed me to preach
> good news to the poor.
> He has sent me to proclaim release to
> the captives
> and recovering of sight to the blind,
> to set at liberty those who are oppressed,
> to proclaim the acceptable year of the
> Lord" (Luke 4:18-19).

The passage goes on to report that Jesus declared this prophecy had been fulfilled in their presence. Jesus was announcing His identification with the prophetic words of justice written by Isaiah.

If we are called to follow Jesus, we are called to identify ourselves similarly with His call for justice in our world. Our

Christian vocation includes working to make all work dignified work and give all workers justice and fairness. We have
been looking at the question of vocation and work throughout
this book. I have argued that it is a mistake to equate vocation
with work. Indeed, vocation transforms work from something
that holds us in bondage to an avenue of service to God and
neighbor.

Some of us are in bondage to our work because we can find
no worth outside of our job. On the other hand, some work
can hold persons in bondage because it offers no dignity inside the job. Christians must speak to social systems that ex-
ploit laborers in order to make a profit. Profit is never worth
the price of exploitation. Moses took that charge to Pharaoh
and led the people out of Egypt to escape the bondage of slave
labor.

We have a sinful history in our nation related to slavery. As
I write, our denomination has renewed the call to repent of
racism and work against vestiges of racism is our society.
Racism was systematic in our land from its founding, and its
social and spiritual ugliness are still with us. The central insti-
tution of that racism was the exploitation of a whole race of
people for labor that robbed them of dignity and the fruits of
their labor. Racism was and is bigger than the issue of labor,
but we must be vigilant in our duty to protect the dignity of
labor.

In the days since the abolition of slavery, we have continued
to push against systems of labor that have exploited men,
women, and children, depriving them of rest, dignity, and a
fair wage. Our calling is to continue to transform work from
something that demeans to something that ennobles and from

something that enslaves to something that liberates. Regardless of your job, you can exercise your rights as a Christian citizen to work for this kind of justice. If you are starting over, you can resist being enslaved by work.

## Foundation and Furniture

If you have looked to this book for some simple "how-to's" on finding the perfect job, you must be disappointed by now. If you have persisted to this point, no matter what you expected, you have discovered that I have been traveling a different path. Much of the direction of that path has been my conviction that we have been seduced by modern notions of vocation that have little basis in biblical faith. I have, in some ways, turned the notion of vocation on its head.

I would go so far to suggest that in some ways, it does not matter what you do. Certainly that statement is not absolute, given that I have already developed sections on the mooring of vocation in the norms of the community of faith. But the statement "it does not matter what you do" at least serves to shock us into realizing our preoccupation with the perfect job. While you will find many biblical texts concerning listening to the will of God, you will be hard pressed to find a biblical theme that has persons fret over what job they will have. Compare that to the pressure we place on our youth to choose a job or profession.

What I have been concerned to try and develop here is a discussion of the deep meaning of Christian vocation. Much of this book has been an attempt to develop the *foundations* for Christian vocation. If we build our sense of vocation and identity completely around the job we have or the role we now occupy, we are building a house upon shifting sands. The deep meaning of Christian vocation finds a more solid foundation than job or role. The foundations of Christian vocation find their foundation in the calling to be a follower of Jesus, and join with a community of believers in welcoming the good news of the kingdom of God in Jesus Christ.

To extend the metaphor, the role or job that we occupy at a given time is the *furniture* that we place upon the foundation of vocation. It is the chair we sit in, but it rests on a foundation that supports the whole house. Certainly some chairs are more comfortable than others. Some mean a lot to us because they have been passed on to us from another generation. Some suit our tastes better than others or fit with the rest of the furniture in the house. Some we might have built ourselves. But it is still furniture.

Furniture can be moved. From time to time we might decide to rearrange a living room. That does not change the fact that it is a living room, nor does it change the foundation on which the house rests. Few of us nail our furniture to the floor or anchor it in a concrete foundation. We rest comfortably in it because we feel secure resting on a foundation that is secure.

From time to time we might even decide to get new furniture. Sometimes even favorite chairs and sofas wear out and need to be recovered or discarded. It may be hard for us to do because we liked the old furniture, but it simply was not useful any longer. So it is time we begin to break in a new favorite chair. It may take a while to feel like it fits us like the old one.

Jobs and roles are the furniture that rest upon the foundation of Christian vocation. From time to time the furniture may change. When the chair wears out or breaks, we do not burn the house. We seek a new chair that we think will fit us.

## Finding Hope Again

If these pages have found you seeking, then take heart. A genuine seeking is the beginning place for blessing, according to the Beatitudes. It is often the case that a genuine seeking begins with an awareness of loss, lack, or restlessness. That is almost always uncomfortable. Often it feels like a pain that dominates your world. Seeking and longing have something of pain in them.

The first step toward discovering or rediscovering hope in the search for vocation is to be honest with ourselves about that pain. It is difficult for us to move to a different place, if we are not willing to honestly admit to ourselves the name of the place where we find ourselves. Hopefully, we will also find the courage to allow ourselves to be honest with a person who cares for us. Pain held in isolation grows because of its secrecy. The pain of loneliness adds to the weight of any burden.

Be gentle with yourself in the process of admitting your pain. Your pain is a sign of your humanness, not simply a sign of failure. There will be time to admit failure, but you need not compound it with self-loathing and condemnation that denies grace to yourself. Part of being gentle with yourself is not to expect that your pain is a sign of weakness or that it will or should go away overnight. A crisis in identity shakes us to the foundations. That is not an experience from which we simply get up and shake off a little dust. That is an experience which requires some reflection, some sharing, some waiting, and some time.

If you have lost a job that meant a lot to you or if you are no longer fulfilling a role that fulfilled you, then you have lost something important. It may feel like you have lost a part of yourself. It may feel like you have lost not simply a favorite chair, but that the foundation itself is cracking. If so, then do not try to patch the foundation by placing a new chair directly over the crack. Give some attention to the foundation.

It may be time to hope in the midst of your grief for a renewal of your imagination. What does that mean? It means that you may have thought of yourself or your vocation in ways that were too limited or too small. It may be that a renewal of vocation for you includes expanding your horizons concerning yourself, God, and the world. Appropriate grieving will eventually allow you to exercise your imagination in the service of hope. It may be a liberating, although at first frightening, experience to allow yourself to see yourself fulfilled in a different role.

If your crisis is one of "uselessness" after a career of being extraordinarily busy and useful, then I invite you to slowly shift the ground of your self-esteem to God's gracious love in creating and redeeming you. I invite you to think of a vocation which includes learning to "love God and enjoy Him forever." I invite you to project new ways of service to God and neighbor, even if that service may be one of prayer and contemplation. Our Catholic brothers and sisters have for centuries blessed some in their midst who have felt a call to a life of prayer. We have traditionally held that we are all called to a life of prayer. So be it, but few of us are content to see that as a major piece of our vocation. We are too activistic for that. We are too busy earning our sense of worth through doing, and we resist seeing our vocation as a calling to *be*.

For the church to once again renew the biblical meaning of

calling, we must resist identifying it with outward roles such as a profession. We must rid ourselves of the pressure that one job, one task, or one role is our only and true vocation on this earth. Instead, we must rediscover that vocation is identity grounded in God that gives a center to all of our roles and helps us hold the several pieces of our lives together. We can come to realize that we have several vocations. I am father, husband, minister, and writer, but, most of all, disciple. The identity of disciple helps give order and purpose to all of the other roles.

My oldest daughter is getting her first acquaintance with the notion of death, a concept all but impossible for three year olds to accept. Interestingly, what sparked her curiosity was a Bible story about the children of Israel dying from serpents outside their tents. As I walked in the door from work, she greeted me, and said: "Daddy, when are you going to die?" I put her on my lap, we talked about it a bit, and she moved on to play other things and ask other questions. One of the things her question stirred in me was that this vocation of father is transient and changing. I will always be her father, but that vocation will call upon me to learn to let her go. The simple and joyful tasks of being father to two young children will not last forever. That realization brings a certain sadness, but is also a reminder that I am more than father. The identity of disciple puts even that role in perspective. God calls me to journey in that role, through that role, and ultimately beyond that role.

The same thing is true for the other roles in my life. What I can count on is that they will change. What I am called to admit is that my control over my future is not absolute. I could lose my job. Illness might come and change everything.

I will be vulnerable to those changes. If and when they happen they will be painful. I will need the support of others around me who care for me. I pray for the grace to see myself in some other collection of roles loving God and serving neighbor in response to the good news of the kingdom. I finally pray for a vocation that transcends role and rests in the identity of having been created, redeemed, and called to participate in the vocation of following.

The difficult issue of choosing still confronts the sensitive person who seeks to be a faithful disciple. While having options feels better than having no options, it can still be a frightening, even paralyzing prospect. From all of these choices, which of these help me express the unique vocation to which God is calling me? I have no perfect formula for that. I can even guarantee that you will probably make some wrong choices along the way. I do believe that sometimes our mistakes do more to transform our vision of ourselves, the world, and God than anything else. They are sometimes a painful avenue for growth that we might not have experienced otherwise. Such is the mystery of Providence.

But choose we must. To my mind, the advice of Thomas Kelly, devoted Quaker, continues to shine in its simplicity and wisdom. In *A Testament of Devotion,* Kelly writes about the inner life and is concerned about where the inner life of the Christian intersects the outer world. Kelly argues for our simplifying our lives, mostly inwardly. He also recognizes that we must choose among the multitude of worthy possibilities for investing our energies. His advice is that we wait for the "outward calling" to be met by the "inward rising." We must wait, he says, for an inward rising to move us toward the engagements with the world that are possible, but from which we must choose. What Kelly is arguing for is an inner life that transforms the outer dramas in which we daily engage, to give them a center, an identity in God which orders them so that they do not order us in ways that fragment us.

Vocation is finally more about journey than destination. That is why, I think, that the most important verb the Gospels give us for being a Christian is the simple verb *follow*. It is not that we are being led to a single destination about which we must always be anxious. It is that the discipline, mystery, pain, joy, and suffering of *following* are themselves the vocation to which we have been called.

### Notes

1. I am indebted to the writings of Stanley Hauerwas for deepening my appreciation for the importance of vision and virtue in understanding faith.